AVA

A V A
My Story

AVA GARDNER

BANTAM PRESS

LONDON · NEW YORK · TORONTO · SYDNEY · AUCKLAND

TRANSWORLD PUBLISHERS LTD
61-63 Uxbridge Road, London W5 5SA

TRANSWORLD PUBLISHERS (AUSTRALIA) PTY LTD
15-23 Helles Avenue, Moorebank, NSW 2170

TRANSWORLD PUBLISHERS (NZ) LTD
Cnr Moselle and Waipareira Aves,
Henderson, Auckland

Cover photo courtesy of The Kobal Collection

Grateful acknowledgement is made to William Graves, the
Robert Graves estate, and St. John's College, Oxford, for permission
to use the poem 'Not to Sleep', which Robert Graves dedicated to
Ava Gardner, and for the four lines taken from 'The Portrait', by
Robert Graves, Collected Poems, © 1955 Doubleday & Co.,
Garden City, New York

'Someone to Watch Over Me'
(George Gershwin, Ira Gershwin)
© 1926 (Renewed) W B Music Corp.
All rights reserved. Used by permission.

Published 1990 by Bantam Press
a division of Transworld Publishers Ltd
Copyright © 1990 by C & J Films, Inc.

British Library Cataloguing in Publication Data
Gardener, Ava 1922-
Ava: my story.
1 Cinema films. Acting – Biographies
I. Title
791.43028092

ISBN 0 593-02191-6

Printed in Great Britain
by Mackays of Chatham, PLC, Chatham, Kent.

I was born Ava Lavinia Gardner on Christmas Eve 1922 in Grabtown, North Carolina. Not Brogden, not Smithfield, like so many of the books say, but poor old Grabtown. God knows why it got that name: there was no place to grab, and hardly any town at all. And wouldn't it just be my luck to be born a Capricorn. I've often thought of it as the worst sign, but no matter. It wasn't my style to let a little thing like the stars get in my way.

And speaking of luck, how about having to live through childhood with my birthday and Christmas Day being just about simultaneous celebrations? That meant I'd like as not be fobbed off with one present instead of the two I just *knew* I deserved. And the news got worse. It appeared that there was this whole other person, Jesus Christ, whose birthday a lot of people tended to confuse with mine. I was personally outraged. It was a long time before I forgave the Lord for that.

I came into this world at ten o'clock at night, and I've often thought that that was the reason I turned into such a nocturnal creature. When the sun sets, honey, I feel more, oh, alert. More alive. By midnight, I feel fantastic. Even when I was a little girl, my father would shake his head and say, "Let's just hope you get a job where you work nights." Little did he know what was in store for me. It takes talent to live at night, and that was the one ability I never doubted I had.

But that was all in the future. As a child, what I loved about my birthday was the Christmas tree with lighted candles on it and the fact that all the relatives came to *my* party. My older sisters and their husbands. Aunts and uncles. Lots and lots of children. And even when we were too poor to have two presents, Mama always made sure to bake two special cakes just for me. One was chocolate, the other white coconut. Mama understood how lonely just one present for Christmas *and* your birthday could be.

I was my parent's seventh child, always treated like the baby of the family and liking every bit of it. Two sons, Raymond and Melvin, had come before me, and four daughters, Beatrice (nicknamed Bappie), Elsie Mae, Inez, and Myra. At nineteen, Bappie was the eldest and already married, but she had the same tomboy nature as me. She'd climbed a peach tree during her pregnancy, which probably wasn't a good idea in the first place. Then, without stopping to think about it, she jumped down and suffered a miscarriage.

Growing up, I adored Bappie's husband William. He was big and strong and lots of fun. He'd hang me up by the back of my dress on a coat hook behind a door and swing me backward and forward like a pendulum. Or he'd take both my hands and swing me around in circles that soared higher and higher, with my small paws clinging to him like starfish. He was simply gorgeous. Mama loved him, too. But then Mama loved all the husbands and could be counted on to take their part whenever a squabble broke out.

Mama was Mary Elizabeth Gardner, but everyone called her Molly. Age 39 the year I was born, she was a real matriarch, a warm and neighborly woman who loved her family. Her father, Grandfather Baker, had been a feisty little redheaded Scotsman, a great farmer who swore he couldn't die happy until he had twenty children. Between Grandmother Baker and his second wife, he got up to nineteen before he died. So despite wearing those poor women out, I'm afraid Grandpa went to heaven brokenhearted.

Mama cleaned every room every day as though she were expecting Sunday visitors. With one exception. That was the kitchen, which always looked as though a hurricane had just swept through it. But out of that mess came the most wonderful food. When it came to hominy grits, nobody could touch Mama. Even her fried eggs were better than anyone else's. Mama owned only one cookbook, and even though it had the very distinguished title of *The White House Cookbook*, I'd be mighty surprised if any presidents' wives had so much as looked at it. Still, Mama swore by it, but her cooking was really the result of knowledge handed down from mother to daughter for generations.

Mama took after Grandmother Baker, who was evidently a very beautiful woman. Mama had dark brown eyes and magnificent creamy porcelain skin, which all we Gardner girls inherited. She had long, dark, wavy hair which she wore in a bun at the back. She was always a little chubby—great cooks usually are—and the pounds crept up as she got older. Though quite short (five foot three was as high as she got), Mama was very energetic and totally gregarious. She loved to chat, and, unlike me, she loved lots of people around her. And she was so kind, so interested in people and their problems. She encouraged everybody, especially her children.

Mama was obviously a strong woman, but what my father Jonas said was law. Mama loved him and would do anything he said. I remember one time in particular when it had snowed so heavily the night before that a huge pile of sawdust behind our house, a pile into which I used to practice high dives, had suddenly turned into a snowy mountain as high as the Alps.

I just couldn't wait to get through Mama's ham and eggs, grits, hot biscuits, and milk and start my glorious ascent. I had just about reached the top when I noticed Daddy looking up at me with a concerned look on his face.

"Daughter, come down from there at once," he said. "You'll hurt yourself."

Though he called my sisters by their Christian names, Daddy always called me "Daughter." But no matter what he called me, I wasn't about to come down. So I pretended not to hear.

Once more, Daddy made his wishes known in a quiet, reasonable voice, and once more I pretended not to hear. The next thing I knew, Daddy had grabbed me, hauled me down, and delivered two or three sharp smacks across my bottom. I was outraged. Daddy had never, ever, spanked me before. His method had been lots of good-advice lectures about what was right and what was wrong. So I raced, yelling, for the comfort of Mama in the kitchen.

"Daddy spanked me!" I screamed, the outraged innocent. "Daddy spanked me!"

If I expected Mama to enfold me in her arms and comfort me, I was in for a shock. The family disciplinarian, she could restore order with a quick cuff from either hand. Sure, she missed most of the time, but that didn't stop her from making her point. Now she turned from the stove and regarded me with cool eyes.

"Daddy's right," she said firmly. And I knew immediately that that was one argument I was never going to win. So I drifted out to play somewhere else, still turning this "Daddy's right" business over in my mind. It wasn't until years later that I really understood it fully, understood that right or wrong they backed each other to the hilt. It made for strength in their relationship, a strength I guess I was always looking for in mine.

I remember my father so well. He was tall and lean with soft black hair. A cleft in his chin and the green eyes that I inherited. But there was a sparkle in those eyes and a smile on his lips. He treated life as it came, and when the work on the farm was going well, he asked for nothing more.

On one level, there wasn't much to separate Daddy from the other farmers in Johnston County, North Carolina. He wore overalls hitched up over a plaid woolen shirt, with a short chunky jacket added if the season demanded it. He would have fit right in with those photos of pioneer farmers you see in every state museum. The ones of lean, rugged men with determined faces and weary, suspicious eyes. Eyes that had known hard times before and would know them again. There was never much happiness in those eyes, but, oh, God, they were indomitable.

Daddy, however, was different. There was enough of a streak of the lyric and romantic Irish in him to let you know that he was never ever going to make his fortune. I think that deep inside he would have loved to have gotten an education, maybe even studied the few well-worn law books that for some reason were always around the house. But that wasn't in the cards for him.

Daddy sharecropped. He farmed the land, and the deal he made was the traditional half and half. The landlord provided seed and fertilizer and they shared the profits, when there were any. Daddy was always a private man, shy and retiring to a large degree, and I inherited that trait from him. Even as a little girl, I could be pugnacious and combative on the outside, shy and nervous of people on the inside.

Daddy did everything slowly and deliberately; there wasn't an impulsive bone in his body. I can see him now, sitting at the kitchen table, making us lemonade. He'd rub the lemons for what seemed like hours so they'd be soft and the juice would literally pour out of them. Our tongues would be hanging out by the time that lemonade was made, but I've never tasted anything like it. No booze, honey, was ever so good.

One thing Daddy was not given to was quick anger and violent confrontations, no matter what the provocation. There was, for instance, the time my brother Melvin—everybody called him Jack, as they do with a name like that—stole into Daddy's tobacco barn to sneak a puff on a cigarette. Unfortunately, he dropped the match, and before you knew it, an almighty conflagration consumed not only the barn but the cotton gin behind it as well. In fact, one of my earliest memories is being held up to the window of our house to watch them both burn down.

Jack tore into the house and dove under the bed, fearing that Daddy's wrath would burst over him at any moment. But not only didn't Daddy take any action, he hardly even made a comment. He knew, of course, what Jack had done, but he also knew it had not been done deliberately. It was an accident, pure and simple, and you didn't brood over things like that. Punishing Jack would not have restored the barn or the cotton gin.

Daddy had faced hard times before, and gotten over them, but this was something else again. Since there was no insurance in those days, the fire left us without the money to stay on, and we moved out of our house and into a place called the Teacherage in nearby Brogden. Sitting on a green lawn under shady trees, the Teacherage was nothing more than a large clapboard house, with more rooms than I'd ever imagined, that served as a boarding-house for teachers.

You have to understand that in our part of North Carolina, there was no such thing as motels (and the only small hotels were in Smithfield, eight miles away), and respectability demanded that the young lady teachers for Brogden's Johnston County Grammar School be provided with room and board to suit their status. And with her skill in the kitchen, my mother was the ideal choice to run the place.

That grammar school, two stories high and made of red brick, looked suspiciously like a factory to me. But it provided elementary education up to the seventh grade for close to two hundred children. In fact, during the school term, Brogden was just about besieged by children. On foot, or bused from nearby farming neighborhoods, they poured in like a flood of puppies and kittens: girls and boys of all ages, jabbering, jostling, pushing, yelling, and squabbling.

Growing up in a Teacherage, with everyone focused on education, I sometimes wonder why I'm not a Greek scholar or something. What I did acquire, though, was an understanding of discipline, of the importance of doing your work properly and being clean and punctual. I got a good country education, and there's nothing wrong with that. It set standards for the rest of my life.

The only thing I didn't care for about school was having to force my feet into those hated, confining things called shoes. In those days, thousands of children throughout the South ran around barefoot for half a year and more. Shoes were expensive. Besides, I've always loved the feel of baked earth, green grass, soft mud, and stream water under my feet. It was a special sort of freedom, and to this day I try and recapture it every chance I get.

Sometimes, though, I felt a little left out of Brogden's comings and goings. I yearned to arrive on a bus like everybody else. And, my God, the status of showing up with your own box lunch. Part of me knew that Mama's lunches were much better, but I desperately wanted a lunch-box lunch. So I found friends who agreed to share their horrible biscuits and big repulsive slabs of ham, half an inch thick. That accomplished, I'd arrange to go home with them and spend the night. Then I could scrunch up in bed with a girlfriend and get the special joy of a bus ride there and back. I thought I was pretty clever, but I guess Mama saw through all my plots.

One adventure I had that even Mama didn't know about involved Al Creech. Al was my five-year-old nephew, the son of my older sister Elsie Mae and I was his self-appointed older and wiser protector in a world of rough, tough kids. So it was natural that I accompanied Al on his very first shopping expedition. We crossed the dirt road and entered the cool, dark general store, where, after proper deliberation, he walked away with his heart's desire: a handful of brightly colored marbles.

And what did the poor fool do? He marched off to the playground to join the big boys at marbles, eager to convince them that he was all grown up. But though I was a master marble flicker, Al was a total novice. The big guys took one look, recognized a sucker, and cleaned him out.

Al didn't have to tell me what happened. The end-of-the-world look on his face said it all. I was incensed. Al was my responsibility. More than that, I was pretty sure the big guys hadn't been above rearranging the rules to suit themselves. So I dragged Al back to the scene of the crime. The crooks were still hanging around, gloating. I stood over them and demanded, "You want to play marbles?"

The silence was total. No, they didn't want to play.

"Well, you're going to play," I insisted fiercely. "You're going to let me into this game . . . or else." What "or else" meant, I hadn't a clue, but it sure sounded threatening. And it had its intended effect. In five minutes, I'd won all Al's marbles back, and a few more for good measure.

I stood up and the marble gang stood up with me. This was war.

"We won his marbles fair and square," someone piped up.

"And I won 'em back fair and square. So what are you going to do about it? Want to fight? Who wants the first bloody nose?"

Nobody did. The triumph of virtue has never felt so sweet.

I certainly was a tomboy. I loved games, I loved action, and I could match most of the boys. Run just as quick. Climb just as high. Take as many risks. We played baseball with an improvised ball made out of a piece of coal wrapped around with used tobacco twine. A piece of wood cut into shape served as the bat. I played every position. I was inquisitive, adventurous—and occasionally jealous.

It all started with my love of dancing. In the Teacherage we had an old upright piano and I could swing around to any tune that was played. So when I heard that Myra, my older sister, was going to get piano lessons instead of me, my jealousy was overwhelming. Especially as Mama took me along with Myra for the weekly lesson at a place called Selma about five miles away.

The point was, I knew that Myra couldn't care less about having piano lessons, but I wanted them, desperately. So Myra would plunk away halfheartedly at her practice at the Teacherage, and when she was gone and nobody else was looking, I tried to bite the piano keys off. Literally. The piano stayed intact, but years afterward you could still see the little teeth marks on the innocent white keys.

From those moments on, music, especially *movement* to music, became a great passion with me. One of my greatest joys was the Holy Rollers. My parents' sedate form of religion didn't appeal to me, but Elva Mae, the sweet little black girl who helped Mama out in the kitchen, used to take me to the services at the Tee's Chapel. And I just fell in love with the singing and the preaching and all the rest of that good old-time religion.

It would start with everyone quiet and reverent. The preacher would warm up with a few quotes from his Bible. Then, out of nowhere, he'd catch fire and give everyone hell. I'm here to tell you, there ain't much forgiveness in that old-time religion. That particular savior was a mean son of a bitch. If you sinned, honey, he was going to get you, no doubt about it. "All of you down there in this congregation is sinners," the preacher would thunder. "And no sinner's going to escape hellfire and damnation. No sirree, no sirree."

Crouching down next to Elva Mae, I just knew I was one of the real dyed-in-the-wool sinners. Sinning when I broke a schoolhouse window during the summer so that Al and my friends could play in a classroom. Sinning when I hung out with Preston Lee and his brothers, boys who knew all the best cuss words and weren't afraid to teach me how to use them. Mama, though, would have a fit if she caught me saying them, so I had to be careful. Still, I got into the habit of using them, and they slip out to this day. They sure do give a satisfying jolt to a sentence.

And most especially I was a sinner at watermelon harvest time, when we raided our neighbors' fields. Not that we needed to. So many watermelons were grown that lots were left to rot in the fields. But we were thieves, we were excited by the dark notion of going out and stealing somebody else's. And it was hard work, too. When you're six or seven, the damn things weigh a ton— you could barely struggle along with one in your arms. But it was worth it when you got into the shade of a tree and started munching.

My private catalogue of sins was invariably interrupted by a "shouting." A woman in the congregation would suddenly leap to her feet and scream, "Oh, my Lord! Oh, my Lord! I'm in the arms of Jesus! I'm in the arms of Jesus! Let me pray in the arms of Jesus!"

That kind of outburst was like a red flag to the rest of the folks. All the sinners would go wild, shouting, praying, running down the aisles, leaping in the air. I guess it helped to drive the sinning out of them. I watched, holding my breath, my little eyeballs out on stalks. Then the frenzy would ebb out of them, the preacher would ease them back to normal, and we'd sing another hymn or two. Those lovely, surging, soaring spirituals sung in harmony and lifting the soul. Then we'd file out, peaceful and purified. And I'd plod home with Elva Mae, making pious resolutions about that watermelon-stealing stuff.

Though it didn't appeal to me, my parents' religion must have helped them when it came to the real tragedies of their lives. But even religion was not enough to help Mama get over something that happened twelve years before I was born, something that I'm sure left its tiny mark on me.

In those days, before electricity, everyone was up at first light. On this particular day, Daddy, in fact, had been up before daylight because he and some men were using dynamite to clear rocks and tree stumps from one of his fields. The dynamite sticks were ignited by firing caps, and those explosive caps and the dynamite had to be kept well apart.

The caps were kept in the house, in a drawer of the dining-room dresser. It was an important drawer, because Daddy also used it to store the money bag that contained the takings from the country store he was operating at the time.

Now, as Daddy was handing out the caps to the work team, one fell to the floor unnoticed. Mama came out of her kitchen a little later and began tidying up the hearth as usual. She swept odds and ends off the floor and into the fire, including, though no one knew it, the explosive cap.

Little Raymond, Mama's firstborn son, was up early, too. He had helped himself to one of her cheese biscuits and was standing in front of the fire munching it when the explosion occurred. The noise was horrific, and at first no one knew what had happened. But with a terrible intuition Mama dashed back into the dining room and found Raymond lying on the floor. She scooped him up and dashed out to the back porch, where she tried to stand him up on the ironing board to see the extent of his injury. Bappie, racing behind her, never forgot the look of complete despair on Mama's face. She clasped her small son in her arms and turned to look for help. But nothing was available, only a slow horse-and-buggy ride to Smithfield eight miles away. Raymond only lived until he reached the hospital there. He was two years, two months, and fifteen days old when he died.

I knew, as I grew up, that Mama always held a deep ache in her heart for Baby Raymond. And that ache helped forge the strong bond that kept Mama and Daddy solidly together through all those years. It was a bond that gave both their marriage and their partnership a dimension of strength, certitude, and continuity that I've never been able to find. All things considered, I think they were lucky. They belonged to a generation that made their vows and kept them.

TWO

In Johnston County, North Carolina, you couldn't be any kind of farmer at all without a mule. I can't remember if ours had a name, but I do remember that I loved him. And as much as he was capable of love, I think he loved me in return. When I was tired, I could hang onto his tail and he'd give me a tow. And though he could be ornery if other folks came too near, he never ever kicked out at me.

Our region was known as the Bright Leaf tobacco belt, a place where that bright yellow tobacco had grown and thrived since long before Columbus arrived. Ironically, Sir Walter Raleigh, the man who introduced the leaf to the British Isles, is also credited with bringing over the potato. And it was that crop's failure in Ireland in the 1800s that brought my father's forebears across the Atlantic and into the tobacco-growing business in North Carolina. But while Raleigh, the state capital, is named after that sterling gentleman, it was a Frenchman, Jean Nicot, who in the 1500s sent a package of the famous weed to Catherine de Médicis, the queen of France, and started the Western world on the smoking habit.

I don't suppose anyone as regal as a queen puffed tobacco through a clay pipe or wrapped it in a scrap of newspaper. But when me and my small gang wanted to acquire the taste, that's just what we did. We'd sneak into the barns where the tobacco leaves were hung to dry, tear off a bit, wrap it in newspaper like a cigar, and light up. Naturally, we got sick as dogs. That should have cured us of the habit, but we were nothing if not game.

Lesson two came when I was working in the fields toting water for the workers. My brother Jack called out, "Hey, sugar, bring the water across here and I'll give you a present." I did as I was told and was handed a black wad of tobacco.

"You *chew* it," said Jack, grinning at my puzzled look.

An old black lady a few steps away joined in the laughter. "You stick the plug in the back of your cheek, honey, and hold it there," she said.

Sound advice, but I was too young to take it. I swallowed the plug in one awful gulp and got sick all over again. Jack, being Jack, laughed his head off. Still, as my only brother, I just adored him and was proud to be his little servant, constantly cleaning his shoes and ironing his shirts. As a result, to this day I'm one hell of an ironer.

Jack, as you might suspect, was always getting into trouble. One time he had a great idea for making a little money on the side. He invested his wages in a load of fresh fish and traveled around our neighborhood, bartering the fish for farm products which he resold at a small profit. But on one trip, a smooth customer bartered Jack's stock of fish for crocks of corn whiskey. "You just pour the contents into screw-top fruit jars for easy handling," he told Jack. "This'll give you a bigger profit than vegetables."

So Jack, knowing that Daddy's away for a few hours, sets up this bar selling White Lightning at about five cents a shot. And seeing as how North Carolina was dry as a bone, he did a roaring business. Now corn whiskey is strong stuff, around one hundred and sixty proof. And if it hasn't been distilled properly, it's powerful enough to blind you or even kill you. So it's not surprising that when Daddy came home, he found fifteen of his friends and neighbors stretched out around Jack's bar, dead drunk. If Jack hadn't been too old to wallop, Daddy, who knew the dangers of that stuff, would have made mincemeat out of him. But he did close Jack's fish route and roadside bar. Permanently.

Ours was a neighborly and self-sufficient society. Families lived in white-painted clapboard houses dotted among the fields, with tobacco barns at the back and wicker rocking chairs on every porch. Back then, people raised most of the food they ate. Hogs were kept and the pork was home-cured. You'd go to the local mill and grind your corn for the cornmeal. Every housewife also had her stock of fruit and vegetable preserves. So if you ran short of bottled tomatoes, you could swap your jars of peas and peaches with a neighbor and get a fresh supply. And there were small local stores scattered around, like one Daddy ran for a while. They carried some canned goods, tobacco, sugar, seasonings, a few sweets, kerosene, and hardware for the fields.

Smithfield, the nearest big town, was only eight miles away. But because those eight miles were on narrow dirt lanes that frequent rains turned into muddy disasters, Smithfield might as well have been on some other planet. I mean, Smithfield had paved roads and built-up sidewalks and even *electricity,* things that didn't reach our neck of the woods until 1945 or 1946.

And Smithfield had one further attraction: an honest-to-God movie house. And Mama, bless her, became addicted. Which meant that if I had the pocket money for a ticket, I could always get a ride into town. I sat up in the balcony, where the seats were cheapest, and had as good a time as the law allowed. But if I ever thought even for a minute that somebody like *me* could ever end up up there, I surely don't recall it.

The best way I knew to earn that pocket money was to work in the tobacco fields, where I surprised myself by becoming fascinated by the intricacies of the growing cycle, a process that had as many challenges, failures, and successes as anything I saw up on that screen in Smithfield.

You'd start the tobacco off as early as the weather would allow, around January if possible. The seeds were real tiny so you mixed them with sand and scattered them in a prepared bedding plot. Then you put a big lightweight canvas over everything to protect the seeds from the frost. Once the sun started to shine regularly, you removed the canvas and watched the seeds sprout. The second half of April, when the sprouts were a few inches high and pretty sturdy, was the moment for replanting, or what we called, "puttin'-in-tobacco time."

This was the occasion when our mule really was in his glory, because the replanting was done with the aid of a mule-drawn contraption that, I swear to God, must have been invented by some demented genius way before the Civil War. The driver sat up front on top of a barrel of water. Not that he was really driving—the mule knew as much about the process as any human being, plodding slowly along the furrow until he reached the end.

During that walk, the driver would release a gush of water. Not much water, about a cupful. And the two planters, who'd be sitting backward in the back of the contraption with a pile of tobacco plants on their laps, would reach down and plug a plant in the wet spot. At least, that was the theory, though the process never seemed to work quite that way whenever I tried my hand at it.

Every year at this time, regular as clockwork, Shine would arrive. Shine was my black brother and dearest friend. Together with Al Creech, we were a threesome united against the world. Or at least against as much of the world as we could see. The three of us laughed, worked, and played together endlessly.

Shine was tall, skinny as a rail, and real midnight black. As far as I knew, he didn't know who his parents were, or where they came from, or even where *he* came from. He didn't seem to know exactly how old he was, either, but he knew he was very much in this world and he was enjoying it. He stayed in the house with us, ate with us, and was part of the family. And then one morning every fall, I'd wake up and Shine would be gone without a good-bye. I'd always feel sad at his departure.

Then, when I was about ten or so and Shine maybe three or four years older, Mama began to look at us with a sort of funny look in her eyes. In the Deep South, Mamas get very thoughtful about that sort of thing. All I knew was that the next "puttin'-in-tobacco" time arrived and Shine did not show up with it. I never saw him again, but I remember him and love him to this day.

By July, the leaves on the thick stalks would be turning yellow from the bottom up. You'd crop off the yellow ones—what's known as "ripe" tobacco—and come back in a week and keep going up the stalk. Just break them off with your hands and stack them up in your arms, that's the way I used to do it. Then I'd carry my stack to the nearest little truck that would be towed between the rows by mules. In case you haven't gathered by now, our Johnston County mules were *very* educated. You hardly needed to tell them, "Get up" or "Whoa!" If you did, they'd look at you as if you were out of your mind. They knew what it was all about. In fact, I'm surprised they didn't have a mule union to protect their interests.

Next, the bundles of leaves were strung up on tobacco sticks. This was skilled, swift work, and the ladies of the household would usually help out. At the end of the day, you'd take the sticks to the tobacco barns, where the leaves would be hung up to dry in the warm air that came off a wood-burning brick furnace.

Getting the proper temperature for the inside of the barn was the crux of the operation. At ninety to ninety-five degrees, you'd begin to see the yellow color you wanted. Then you'd build the temperature to about a hundred and twenty-five, at which point the little veins in the leaves would begin to dry. But the thick stems, the largest part of the leaf, would still have a lot of moisture in them. So you would let the heat run up to about a hundred and sixty to one hundred and eighty degrees to dry that part out, too.

To get all this right, you had to literally live with the tobacco. Night and day, you had to be there. I used to go and sleep nights in the barn with Daddy, and he'd point his finger at the thermometer and explain to me that if the temperature wasn't exactly right, the crop would be ruined. I thought it was all terribly exciting, and, what with the lamplight, the hot air and the sense of being *there* when everything important was going on, I guess it was.

Once the stem was dried and the tobacco cured—a process that took about six days—the leaf would be almost stiff; we called it "killed out." The next step was letting it come "into order," which meant opening the barn doors and letting the night air in to soften the leaf. That also needed a lot of experience, because if the leaf got too brittle, it would crumble.

At this point, everything would be graded into different classes, from the best to the worst. I can still see Aunt Ava, the only aunt I knew from Daddy's side of the family, sitting at the long grading bench, which was divided into little pens. She would inspect each leaf as carefully as you'd examine material for a fancy dress. The very finest leaf was first class, then came second and third and down to what they called the trash.

Finally, in the latter part of August, the warehouse would open up in Smithfield, and you'd start laying your tobacco out on the floor for examination by the auctioneers representing the various tobacco companies. It was a scary time, because the crop you had worked so hard on for all those months was out there taking its chances with everyone else's.

When it came to prices, I think the best we ever did was about twenty-five cents a pound, and that didn't last. I can remember how Daddy's hand gripped harder and harder in mine as the prices were called, and how the faces of some of the farmers were gray with anxiety as they left the auction hall. "Jesus Christ, all they're offering is ten cents a pound," they'd say. "God almighty, we were getting nine cents a pound when they first opened the auction halls in 1898. How do they expect us to stay alive?"

I was seven years old when the stock market crashed in 1929. I didn't even know what a stock market was, let alone a Depression. All I was curious about was what my older sisters were up to. Especially Bappie, who'd gotten fed up with William constantly chasing girls and had decided to divorce him. And, honey, was that ever a scandal. There had never been a divorce in either the Baker or the Gardner family, but Bappie just said, "Aw, what the hell, there's gonna be one now."

Not only did she get that divorce, she sailed off to get a job in New York City! She wrote regularly to Mama, though, and you didn't have to read far between the lines to know that Bappie was having a very hard time. She understood about the Depression, all right, even if I didn't. I had not even an inkling that during the next few months my world was going to collapse around me.

Daddy and Mama knew. Daddy knew because of falling prices and what was happening in the countryside. Mama heard rumors that soon became reality. The Brogden school authorities had to make cuts in line with the faltering economy. The Teacherage system was just too expensive. The seven teachers would have to find other lodgings, pay for their own accommodations, do their own cooking and cleaning, and drive or walk to school. So Mama was out of a job, and Daddy's tenant farming was not enough to make us a living.

But Mama had a good friend in Newport News, the huge ship-building port and navy base up North on the Virginia coast. This friend ran a boardinghouse that catered to shipyard workers, and she knew of a similar place that Mama could take over. There would be no shortage of boarders who were sure to love Mama's cooking and care, and Daddy might be able to get a job up there as well.

As if he could. Daddy was now fifty-five. He had been born in the country and raised to be a farmer. He'd lived and toiled on the land, loved its sunsets and sunrises and the friends it brought him. It didn't seem possible that he could tear up these roots and survive.

Mama, though, was different, and so was I. I really took it all in my stride. Of course I was sorry to leave my friends and the farm, but those twelve years of country life had left me with a naive kind of spunky confidence. I'd have to go to a new school, make new school friends . . . but so what.

What was more worrying was Daddy's cough. It had been persistent for quite a while now, even growing worse despite all the cough medicines Mama was always pouring down his throat. After a while, I just got used to hearing it.

THREE

When you are poor, dirt poor, and there is no way of concealing it, life is hell. In the country, where there is work and food and friends of the same age and background, you may never know you're poor. But when you restart life in a big city, oh, baby, does that condition begin to hurt.

When you are thirteen, fourteen, fifteen and you have to go to school every day in the same little green coat that Mama bought at a cheap sale, and the one skirt and the same sweater that you wash every other night and smooth out to dry, you know you are poor. For four years, one coat, one sweater . . . all I wanted to do was die. You're an adolescent, you're pretty, oh, how you'd give anything, hold your breath, for something pretty to wear.

I should have known that first day we set off in our old borrowed car to drive to Newport News that things were going to be difficult. It wasn't all that far—a hundred miles at the most—but crammed into the backseat and holding onto my dog Prince for dear life, it seemed like a thousand to me. Then, when we stopped for gas at a filling station, Prince leapt out and took off. I shouted after him but he didn't stop. We waited and waited but he didn't come back. I pleaded with Mama and Daddy to wait even longer, but they finally said, "Ava, honey, we've got to move on. He might never come back." And he never did.

We reached Newport News. It was a real city, a hell of a lot bigger than even Smithfield. Our boardinghouse stood on a side street near the James River. It was a big, three-story clapboard building, a bit run-down and in sore need of a coat of paint. Mama not only kept it spotless, she also cooked three meals a day for the dozen or more shipyard workers who were our boarders. And there was none of this "just orange juice and coffee" nonsense for these characters. They got bacon and eggs, grits and hash and hot biscuits for breakfast, and meals just as big for lunch and dinner. Once in a while, a marvelous black woman named Virginia would come in to help, but basically Mama did it all. She was so strong, and she worked so hard.

At my new school, I discovered soon enough that compared to the upper-crust tones of Virginia, my North Carolina twang was something fit only to be laughed at. On my very first day, the lady teacher called me out to answer questions in front of the whole class. After all, I was the new girl, this strange little hillbilly.

"Your name?"

"Ava Gardner." The accent was pure Johnston County, died-in-the-wool country. The teacher smiled, the other girls howled with laughter.

"And what does your father do?"

"He's a farmer."

Even more laughter. Imagine a farmer in a shipbuilding town like Newport News. I didn't think it was funny at all. In fact, my blood still boils when I think of how that teacher went out of her way to humiliate me. She could have taken me aside and asked me the questions quietly and sympathetically, but she didn't. And you never forget or forgive that kind of treatment.

One thing was true, though. There were no jobs for tobacco farmers in Newport News. For some reason, maybe boredom, maybe desperation, Daddy went off to spend some time with Bappie in New York. He came back to Newport News with his cough made worse by this terrible chest cold, and from then on, poor darling, he never had another well day. Looking back now I know that Daddy faced up to life and the bitter defeats it brought with a quiet courage. They say that the last enemy is death, and Daddy was facing him in his usual quiet, orderly way.

When he first got back, Daddy had to go into the hospital for a week or two. The doctors said he had a streptococcal infection of the bronchial tubes. There were no drugs for that sort of thing in those days and we had no money for hospitals either. When

Daddy came back home, Mama arranged for all of us to sleep in one little room about the size of a bathroom. For over a year, I slept on a pallet on the floor, until Daddy got so sick that the sound of his coughing kept us all awake. Then Mama had to take one of the rooms just down the hall, which she could have rented out to a shipyard worker, and moved Daddy in there.

I shall never forget Mama in those hard days. She'd given Daddy a little bell that he could ring if he wanted anything, and when that bell tinkled upstairs Mama would leave whatever she was doing and race up the stairs and open his door with a smile on her face. Not a fake smile, a real one.

I only saw my mother cry twice in her life. The first time was back in Brogden, when Daddy had had one white lightning too many the night before, and she probably figured that a few tears wouldn't do any harm in bringing home the seriousness of the offense. But the second time, in the kitchen in Newport News, broke my heart.

She came in from the markets with her heavy shopping bags and plonked them down on the floor. She sat at the table, put her head in her hands, and began to cry. She wept uncontrollably; her grief was endless. I didn't know what to do. I didn't know what to say. She told me she was crying because her feet hurt, but I knew it was because events had somehow overwhelmed her. I went and put my arm around her, and eventually she stopped crying, wiped her eyes, and smiled.

Mama had this lovely natural warmth, an enormous capacity for love and fun. She even loved all those shipyard boarders—she considered them all her children, just as all those young women had been when she was running the Teacherage. Coming from a household of nineteen, I guess having a large family was part of her heart.

My own feelings were different. I know now that our boarders were all hardworking folks, but at the time they seemed like terribly revolting old men to me. I hated their scruffiness and their newspapers all over the floor, and I hated their eyes as they looked at me. They never touched me, but they tried to flirt, and even though I was only thirteen years old, I instinctively knew what was going on. I wasn't ashamed of my parents, but I was ashamed of that house. I was ashamed of all those men who were always sitting or lying around. I couldn't bring a girlfriend home, and as for a boyfriend . . . that was potentially an even more embarrassing situation.

I was growing into adolescence in Newport News, and I have to say that Mama was not very helpful to a teenage girl. We may not have been very deeply into religion, but into sex we were not at all. Nothing was ever talked about; Mother never ever told me anything. Even having had seven children made no difference. The subject was forbidden. If it weren't for the older girlfriends I made at Newport News High School, my ignorance in that area would have been total.

In fact, I can clearly remember the moment when Mama finally realized I was growing up. I was in the kitchen with her; she was sassing me and I was sassing her right back. Now, Mama didn't take kindly to her young 'un being cheeky in her own kitchen, and she'd raised her hand to reestablish discipline. I was getting ready to duck when she looked down at me and, I swear to God, for the first time she noticed what was hapening to my figure. Well, she might not have blushed, but she sure was confused. She had a young lady here, and you don't take swipes at young ladies. Mama lowered her hand and covered her embarrassment with a gruff, "And what's more I'll put a bra on you, young 'un."

After that, Mama never lifted a hand against me as long as she lived. And Bappie intervened at some point and said, "Don't you put a bra on that child until I bring a proper one down from New York." In those years, breasts were considered slightly improper and had to be flattened out, and Bappie wanted to spare me one of the methods used in North Carolina: tying a baby's diaper around them and fastening it tightly behind with a safety pin.

With all this going on, you can imagine just how terrified I was on the morning of my first period. I knew you didn't talk about *those things,* especially not to Mama. So I flew to Virginia, the lovely fat lady who helped Mama out in the kitchen, whispering desperately that I was bleeding to death. Virginia hugged me to her and exclaimed at the top of her voice some of the most wonderful words I've ever heard in my whole life:

"Oh, Lord, honeychile. Bless you, bless you. Honeychile, you're a little woman now! A little woman!"

In a couple of sentences she'd restored my faith in the world, but there was more trouble in store. I had to go to the drugstore to buy Kotex, the man behind the counter handing me the package with a grave face, an ordeal I remember to this day.

Next came my baptism. It was considered very fashionable by all the girls at school; you simply had to do it. With my body changing the way it was, I was worried about the ceremony, so I went to see the parson. He wasn't in, so I confided my dilemma to his wife, and she—and I'll never forgive her—said in a lordly fashion, "Oh, don't worry, dear. God will take care of everything."

And God didn't take care of anything.

Unlike North Carolina, where baptisms often took place in a river near the chapel, our local Baptist church came complete with a sort of deep concrete bath behind the pulpit. That location meant, however, that everyone in the congregation could have a super view of what was going on. I was put in a thin shift and dunked deep under the water. When I came up, the fabric had turned sheer and stuck to me in such a way that my whole body was plainly revealed, and what seemed like a thousand shocked eyes were staring at me.

I felt humiliated, totally shamed. It was the worst experience I have ever had in my whole life. I hated religion for having exposed me in this fashion. And when I went around to this same preacher and asked shyly if he might perhaps come and talk to Daddy, because he was very lonely, he never did. Maybe we weren't good enough Christians for that.

So Daddy just lay there and slowly died. Daddy was never a complainer, so you wouldn't have known whether he was in pain or not, but I'm sure that racking cough must have been terrible. As often as I could, I went up to his room and read the papers to him. He loved hearing about politics, he adored President Roosevelt, and just being near him gave me a sort of peace and reassurance. But when he'd fall asleep while I was reading, I'd get angry, thinking: Why doesn't he stay awake and listen? But I suppose that was just the unthinking selfishness of childhood.

Daddy died in the hospital in Newport News, but we took him back to North Carolina and buried him in the graveyard where generations of Gardners lay. At the time I thought, I'll survive. It wasn't until much later that I found out how much I missed him, found out that some part of me lay in that grave with him. Years later, and another lifetime away, at Grace Kelly's wedding in

Monaco, I watched her strong, vibrant father walk her down the aisle and I couldn't help but think, If only I had a father like him to lean on. I still carry a deep sense of guilt because I feel I didn't do enough to help Daddy in those last sad days. I torture myself with having failed him, I truly do.

Whether I was prepared or not, though, my life was moving on, and it was as a sophomore at Newport News High School that I had my first date. And what girl ever forgets her first date! His name was Dick Alerton. Not only was he a senior, but he was handsome, a football player, and very bright to boot. He was also, and this was one of the things that was made quite clear in those days, from a different social class than me.

One of my girlfriends, who was also in his social class, brought him over to meet me one morning, so I guess he'd checked me out beforehand. I looked at him, and oh, my God, in one second, I was in love. He asked me for a date, and I said yes. That afternoon, I tried to tidy up the living room just in case I couldn't intercept him at the front door and he had to come in. I tried so hard. The shade over the front window, an old pull-down thing, was in tatters, so I took a pair of scissors and trimmed off the edges, but it still looked dreadful.

Dick had a car, a little Buick, and as soon as it pulled up I was out the door so fast I don't even think Mama knew I was missing. We went to the movies, which is what a date meant in those days, but I can't say as I remember the film. I felt so awfully shy I was shaking inside. I didn't know what to say—I didn't have anything _to_ say. Afterward, we went to a little drive-in joint for hamburgers, and as we drove along I read the neon signs as my attempt at making conversation: "Gulf Oil . . . Dairy Queen . . . Joe's Burgers." I couldn't have been much more than fourteen years old. If I hadn't been so shy and frightened, I'm sure Dick would have been very friendly. As it was, he never asked me out again.

The fact that I can't remember what film Dick and I saw tells me a lot about how confused my state of mind must have been, because at that time I adored films. And above all other actors, I adored Clark Gable. I'd seen him in _Red Dust_ with Jean Harlow. I practically swooned when he took off his shirt in _It Happened One Night_. I didn't even hold it against him when he let his eye rove over those Tahitian girls in _Mutiny on the Bounty_. And the fact that most of the women in the civilized world felt the same way I did meant nothing to me. I reserved to myself certain proprietary rights. Clark, I was sure, would understand my adoration.

And more than anything else, I wanted Clark Gable to play Rhett Butler in the forthcoming version of *Gone With the Wind*. Now novels, even big-selling ones, didn't usually find their way into my life, but, in a burst of intuition, our English teacher had announced it as the class literary project for the next semester. We fell on the book like small wolves, devouring it. I read it all, then I read it again. The image of Scarlett, Melanie and Ashley lounging on the veranda of Tara was etched in my heart. I could smell the perfume of the dogwood, see the blaze of lilac and azaleas, not to mention those bright dark eyes and divine smile of Mr. Butler. After all, the great plantation houses of Georgia had been just down the road a piece from North Carolina. And all us girls were Southern ladies at heart, just waiting for our own version of Rhett Butler to appear from behind a cloud of cherry blossoms. When Clark finally got the role, I felt that my fervent wishes just must have played a part.

Unfortunately, no fictional heroes were around to solve the problems facing Mama and me. And one fact was becoming increasingly clear. The boardinghouse income was barely enough to keep us going. We had no money. I had to go to work.

I approached Mama with my big decision. I'd leave school and get a job somewhere. Mama just about had a fit.

"Now listen here, young 'un," she said. "The most important thing that's happening to you now is your education. You're going to keep going to school here . . ." There was a momentary hesitation, and I knew that Mama had something else on her mind. She could no more conceal a secret than she could tell a lie. "At least," she added finally, "until the end of this semester."

"And then what?"

"We might go back to North Carolina."

That was exciting news, all right. "Back to Brogden?" I asked.

"No, but to the same sort of job. And to Wilson County, which is next door to Johnston. You've been to Wilson County. The place is called Rock Ridge. But you finish out your semester here first."

We did go back to North Carolina, as broke as when we left.

And when I returned to school there, I faced another dilemma. Back in Newport News, since I was on a secretarial track, I'd been allowed to bypass subjects like math, history, and French to concentrate almost entirely on typing and shorthand. But the authorities at the Rock Ridge Teacherage stated flatly that in order to get my diploma, I had to find room in my schedule for most of the subjects I'd abandoned in Newport News. Which meant I had to compress two years of study into one. That was one damn hard year, I can tell you.

But just when I felt I deserved a reward, my rascally brother Jack, who had a good job by then, came up with a surprise.

"Ava, honey," he said in that laughing, cheerful voice of his. "You're going to round off your education with a year at the Atlantic Christian College in Wilson. And I'm going to pay for it."

Atlantic Christian may not have been Harvard, but it was a fine college, and it included all the odds and ends that go with a college education: sororities, football and baseball teams, drama and debating societies. Once again, I concentrated on shorthand and typing. We still had no money, and I had to be driven in every day by a girlfriend who lived nearby, and driven back every evening.

And Mama, bless her, still ruled my private life with the strictness of a mother superior in the Carmelite order. Oh, yes, I was allowed a boyfriend, but hanky-panky of any sort was strictly forbidden. We stole a kiss or two between hand-holding, but that was it. I knew all the kids at school were necking like crazy in the backseats of cars, but I never did. Things like that, I'd been told in no uncertain terms, were beyond the bounds of propriety, and I was too scared of Mama to disagree. Mama did not approve of premarital sex *at all*. "If you know a man before you're married," she'd say to me like she meant it, "I'll see you six feet under the ground." My upbringing was totally Victorian; I grew up an old-fashioned, God-fearing girl, taught that marriage and motherhood were honorable achievements. And Mama was the eternal watchdog, intent on seeing that I *stayed* honorable until the bitter end.

I must have been seventeen. It was New Year's Eve and I had gone to a dance with a neighborhood boy I liked very much and had dated before. By the time we got back to the house and stood under the blazing porch light, it was one o'clock in the morning. As we said good night at the door, he took me in his arms and kissed me. It was a gentle kiss, not passionate, and I responded in kind.

We hadn't been there for more than two seconds before Mama crashed through that screen door like a bull out of a trap. Honest to God, I thought she was going to kill us both. That boy was scared shitless. She chased him back to his car and then came back yelling at me, "It's disgraceful! How could you do it? I will not have my youngest daughter behaving in such a wanton manner." And that was the printable part. The rest of the things Mama called me don't bear repeating. It's enough to say I never was so mortified in my life. I remember going to my room and scrubbing my face and hands over and over in an attempt to wash off some of the dirt I was sure I had contracted from that kiss.

Later on I thought: Gee, a kiss on the porch after a New Year's dance? It wasn't like we'd been sneaking around in the bushes, or even been necking in his car. But as I've said, Mama was pure Victorian, and when you see some of what's going on these days, maybe her ideas weren't all that bad.

FOUR

When people ask me about how I got into the damn picture business in the first place, I just have to smile. Because the truth is, if my sister Bappie hadn't decided on the spur of the moment to drop into Tarr's photographic studio on the corner of Fifth Avenue and Sixty-third Street in New York City, I probably would've ended up happy as a clam plugging away behind a typewriter somewhere in North Carolina for the rest of my days.

While Mama and I were doing the best we could back home, Bappie had been making her way in the big city. She was working at I. Miller, running her own section in the handbag and accessories department, in fact. She had a Canadian boyfriend who had gone back home for a short while to consider their future, and he'd written to Bappie asking for a photo to keep him company.

There were Tarr photographic studios dotted all over New York in those days, but the branch Bappie had chosen was run by Larry Tarr, one of the founder's sons. Larry took one look at Bappie, and she at him, and to hell with a photo to send to this Canadian guy. Larry made a big pitch for Bappie right on the spot, and they had a mad, whirlwind love affair and got married almost before the news had time to reach home.

Mama and I got our first taste of Larry when we went up to visit the newlyweds the first summer after their marriage. He turned out to be rather short, but very dapper. Not particularly good-looking but brash, confident, irrepressible, and irresistible in the way New Yorkers can sometimes be. He took a shine to me at once, which was pretty fortunate considering that I came back without Mama every summer afterward. A born promoter, Larry loved staying up late as much as I did, and it gave him a kick to take this impressionable kid to the kinds of nightspots that featured a dozen beautiful girls all about ten feet tall wearing nothing more than a handful of feathers. "Dollface," he liked to say. "You think you're beautiful. Look at that! Just look at that!"

It was in New York that I saw my first film star. I was all of sixteen, dressed just right by Bappie, carrying little white gloves and a little bag. The three of us were at a club that featured a live orchestra, and when I looked across the room, there was Henry Fonda, chatting with this very attractive woman. "See who that is?" I whispered excitedly to Bappie. "D'you think I could get his autograph? D'you think he'd mind?"

Larry overheard this and said, "Of course he wouldn't mind. Go on, Dollface, walk across and ask him." I approached very timidly across the floor, never having worn white gloves before and feeling handicapped by that little handbag. I got to the table, looked into Mr. Fonda's face and, fumbling with my accessories, dropped them all, one by one, onto the floor: first the pen, then the paper, and finally the damn handbag.

Henry Fonda, bless him, saw my total confusion and helped me pick everything up. Immediately knowing what I was after, he signed my piece of paper. And his friend was so sweet—she even asked me a few questions. Where was I from? Did I go to school? And then she said something I've never forgotten: "Oh, you're a lovely little girl. You should go to Hollywood."

I rushed back to tell Bappie what had happened, only to find that Larry, whose promoting instincts never took a day off, had been busy. Our table was close to the orchestra, and the bandleader, having watched me walk across the floor, had engaged Larry in conversation, something that was never hard to do. Big bands were the hottest thing going in those days, and it seems that the orchestra leader was eager to put one together and begin his move toward stardom. Only he needed a pretty girl singer to help him make the trip.

Isn't that a coincidence? says Larry. That little girl you've been watching—a nightingale! Ella Fitzgerald, the Andrews Sisters, might have had the same talent when they were young, but Larry personally doubted it. The young bandleader was suitably impressed. Could Larry see to it that she cut a disc of her voice? She sure did have the looks, and if she had a voice to match, the sky was the limit.

Now I have to admit that, like an awful lot of girls my age, the hope of my life was to stand in front of a big-band orchestra and have a crack at the microphone. Could I sing? Of course I could sing. Mama could sing pretty as a blackbird. If you're half Scottish and half Irish and you can't sing, there must be something wrong with you. So I left that nightclub feeling that my dream was about to be realized: I was going to become a singer. Addresses were exchanged. And within days Larry Tarr had found a studio with a pianist where a 78 disc could be made and offered to the band leader.

I told Larry that the only song I knew *all* the words to was "Amapola." That didn't faze him either. Just sing the song, and let's get the show on the road—that was Larry's philosophy. Which is how I found myself in that recording studio all alone with a pianist and a piano. Thank God he was a fairly understanding sort.

Where was my music sheet? he asked. Oh, dear, I didn't know I had to have one. I knew there were songs on music sheets—every piano top displayed them. But I hadn't brought one. Okay, that didn't matter. What did I want to sing? Amapola. Okay. What key?

That stumped me. Key? I didn't know what a key was. You opened a door with a key. That was about as much as I knew about music in those days. Somehow we got that worked out, too, and I piped out my little song. Larry handed the disc over to the bandleader. More addresses were exchanged. After he'd organized the band he was going to send me the lyrics to various songs and we'd be set to go. Oh, my God, the thought of it went to my head like the rarest champagne. Back at school, I shared this sublime secret with my special friends, and when they obligingly leaked the news, baby, did that lift my status.

I must have gone to our country mailbox at least a thousand times, but I received not a single note from that bandleader. Finally, the truth sank in. I was not going on tour. Period. Oddly enough, though, I did meet that bandleader one more time. He was leading an orchestra at a club in Los Angeles about eight or nine years later and I was already established in pictures. He was most pleasant—most impressed, in fact, with what had happened to me—and, I couldn't help but hope, torn with regret as well about his unfortunate lack of faith in the songbird from North Carolina.

Larry's next chance to exercise his entrepreneurial talents on my behalf came when I was at Atlantic Christian College. This is where a man named Barney Duhan, someone I only met once and that years later, became a key player on the team that launched me into the movies. Barney eventually became a New York City cop, but at the time he was an errand boy working in the law department of Loews, Inc. On his rounds, Barney often passed by Larry Tarr's showcase on Fifth Avenue, where Larry had put a picture of me. When he saw my face sitting under a fetching hat, he knew just what to do.

Because it seems that Barney had his own method of getting dates. Whenever he saw a pretty girl, he worked hard to get her phone number. Then, Metro-Goldwyn-Mayer being a part of Loews, he would call up and drop the magic words "MGM Pictures" in every second sentence, adding the vague suggestion "talent scout" wherever possible. How about a cup of coffee or a drink to talk things over? One has to admit that Barney in his way was every bit as good an entrepreneur as Larry.

Barney breezed into Larry's second-floor reception office and started his usual routine. "Gotta compliment you on that photo of that very pretty young girl you show in your window."

The receptionist was an experienced lady, very wary of smart young New York boys interested in pretty girls.

"Yes," she said coolly.

"You know MGM would be very interested in a girl with those looks."

"Would they?"

"Sure would. Now if you can let me have her phone number, I promise you it will get straight through to the right people. I have connections there."

"I am afraid that would not be possible. We do not give personal details and phone numbers of our models and clients to the general public."

"Oh," said Barney.

"But I will pass on your message to Mr. Larry Tarr when he comes in, and no doubt he will take the necessary action."

Barney knew when he had blown it.

"Oh, sure. Yeah. Thanks."

Barney left, having made his sole contribution to the launching of Ava Gardner into the film world. But without knowing it, he had lit the fuse that led straight to Larry.

When Larry heard about Barney Duhan's visit, he immediately got on the phone to Bappie, on fire with excitement.

"Gardner," he said, "do you know what's happened? MGM is interested in Ava. *MGM!* When can you get her up here?"

"Don't be silly, Larry," Bappie said. "Ava's in school, and Mama wouldn't hear about her doing such a thing."

Larry was undeterred. "Well, we've got to give them pictures," he said. "I'm blowing up everything that we've got of her. The whole staff is going to work all night. I'll take them over to MGM myself tomorrow morning."

It didn't take Larry long to discover that Barney Duhan was not exactly a big name at MGM. But he left the photographs anyway. Bappie telephoned me back in North Carolina to let me know what was happening and, honest to God, I was not excited. A singer with a big swing band? Now *that* was an idea with magic in it. But the thought of being a movie star? Sure, I loved movies, but being an actress had never been on my mind.

Larry must have been a hell of a photographer, because MGM liked those pictures. They said they would like to see me the next time I came to New York. I was to meet with a Mr. Marvin Schenck, in charge of talent and one of the big noises in the MGM outfit. So, on my next school break, Mama and I came up to New York. Mama wasn't very well at all, though I didn't know the whole story yet, so Bappie came with me on that first interview.

Mr. Schenck's office was normal enough: the usual desk, chairs, bookshelves, files. I sat down and he gave me some sort of a script with a male and female part. He read for the man and I was supposed to read for the woman. I'd never seen a script before, I'd never even read a scene before, but that was not my main worry.

I was terribly afraid that my North Carolina accent made me, as Bappie put it, "very, very Southern." She herself had been nicknamed "Dixie" when she first started working for I. Miller on chic Fifth Avenue, and whenever I'd visit and chat with the other salesgirls, I would see a great big smile creep across their faces every time I opened my mouth. People used to say I dropped my g's like magnolia blossoms, and I guess I did.

Mr. Marvin Schenck, however, was very sweet. He listened attentively to the first few sentences I said, and a rather abstract expression gradually drifted over his face. I don't think he understood more than three words out of the twenty I'd spoken. Finally, he gave up. "Well," he said, smiling, "I think a photographic test would be better. We'll arrange that for, say . . . tomorrow?"

The studio was quite a small place over on Ninth Avenue, and it had a tin roof. It was a boiling hot, humid summer's day, the kind New York seems to specialize in, but I didn't care. I sat in that studio spellbound at what was going on.

MGM was testing three people that day: Vaughan Monroe, a big-band singer who'd made himself famous with "Ghostriders in the Sky"; Hazel Scott, a celebrated black singer and piano player; and . . . me. I couldn't get over poor Vaughan Monroe. His ears stuck out, so they'd glued them back against his head and held them in place with a wire coathanger until they dried and stuck. I wondered about all the bother. Didn't my idol Clark Gable have ears that stuck out? He hadn't done so poorly, had he?

Those two were the important people they were testing, I was just someone in between. I remember I wore a dress that had cost Mama the enormous sum of sixteen dollars: a sort of greenish print, with a long, flared skirt. I wore a pair of Bappie's high-heeled shoes, because all I had were white saddle shoes, autographed all over by the kids back at Atlantic Christian College, wishing me luck. They were the only pair I owned, and since I'd had them for a long time, they were pretty turned up at the toes.

I watched the makeup people plastering everyone with this yellow pancake stuff. It was part of the procedure in those days—something to do with the lighting, they said. But poor Hazel Scott; it looked pretty horrible on her black skin. It took half an hour to get Vaughan's ears glued into place, and probably the same time to fix up Hazel, and I had a very hard time keeping my face straight during all this and not laughing out loud. When a guy's sitting there with his head in a coathanger, it *is* pretty hilarious.

Then it came my turn to go in front of the camera. They said, "Sit down," so I sat down. They said, "Look right . . . good. Now look left . . . good. Now stand up . . . good. Now walk across the room to that piano, pick up that vase of flowers, and come back here and place it on the table . . . good."

I didn't think it was good at all. It seemed like a complete waste of time and I hoped they knew what they were doing. Then they recorded what they called an interview test.

"What is your name?" And out came that rolling Southern accent, "Aa-vah Gahd-nuh."

"Are you at school?"

"Yes, I'm at the Atlantic Christian College in Wilson, North Carolina."

"What courses are you taking?"

"I'm taking a secretarial course in shorthand and typing."

A few more questions about my life and hobbies and that was it, all delivered in my broad dialect. The last question was: "Now we'll sign the contract, shall we?"

Once you'd had a test, baby, you got signed up. Immediately. It gave you no privileges to speak of, but it held you in their power. No other studio, hearing that someone promising had been tested by MGM, could nip in and do a doublecross. Pay? Fifty dollars a week for seven years. As an unemployed trainee secretary it sounded like a lot of money, but they knew what they were doing.

Because even if you were lucky enough to have the people in Hollywood ask you to come out, you still had to pay for your own food and shelter. And the first year of that seven years ran in three-month periods, so if you didn't match up to the studio's requirements by the end of the first three months, you were out on a limb and broke, a sure candidate to be back on the next train home.

The people in New York were shrewd; they sent a silent version of my test back to MGM. George Sidney, who later directed me in *Show Boat,* was in charge of selecting new talent, and he liked what he saw. I don't know whether or not George used the famous line, "Tell New York to ship her out, she's a good piece of merchandise," but that attitude was a good indication of the kind of treatment I had in store for me.

Movies may not have been a dream of mine, but I will admit straight away that when I compared the idea of a secretarial job in Wilson, North Carolina, with the chance of going to Hollywood and breathing the same air as Clark Gable . . . Well, the choice was not hard to make.

There were however, two grave difficulties in the way. Mama ruled my life completely. Would she let me go? More importantly, Mama was very ill and getting sicker every day. Could I leave her?

From the time we got back to North Carolina, I knew Mama was sick. For one thing, she was swallowing aspirin all the time, and I wondered what she was taking all that stuff for. Poor Mama, she'd had her seven babies, but never any medical attention to speak of except for a midwife. But she wouldn't talk about her pains to anybody. In those days you didn't talk about such things. It was only when my second sister, Elsie Mae, came down to visit us one weekend that Mama told her about the bleeding, and even then they didn't tell me. I suppose Mama thought I was too young to know about these women's complaints. But it wasn't just a complaint, it was cancer—cancer of the uterus, and it had been going on for three or four years. Mama hadn't wanted to complain or be a nuisance, or inconvenience anybody, so she'd just gone on working, looking after everybody else and hiding away her secret as so many women did in those days. We finally got her to Raleigh to see a doctor, but by then it was too late for her to have an operation. The cancer had spread too far.

When I took my screen test, I still didn't know the extent of Mama's illness. But Bappie did, and she remembers going with Mama to view the film. Now, as I've said, Mama was a great movie fan, and she fairly glowed when she saw her youngest up on the screen. "My girl's a beauty," she said to Bappie, and she smiled.

Now came the serious business. "I can't go with her," she told Bappie. "But she *can* go if you go with her."

Bappie wasn't so easily convinced. After all, she had a good job with I. Miller's; it had taken years for her to get to be head of her department. But Mama's word was still law, and when she said, again very quietly, "She can't go without you," that decided it.

So it was arranged that Mama would go and live with Inez and her husband in Raleigh. And Bappie and I would catch the Express to the West Coast and Hollywood. I had less than no experience, I didn't know anything about anything, but part of me had no doubt I'd end up a movie queen. And even if I didn't, I certainly didn't have a hell of a lot to lose.

MYRA GARDNER PEARCE

I was seven years old when Ava was born, and I remember it very well. It was Christmas Eve and my brother Jack and I were sent away from home for a little while. I still believed in Santa Claus back then, and I was worried, afraid he wouldn't come if we weren't there. I guess that was kind of silly, but at that moment Santa Claus meant more to me. I probably didn't realize what was going to happen.

We lived in Grabtown, right out in the country, and Ava was born at home. My father, who had a little country store, also owned a sawmill and sawed the lumber and built the house we lived in. It was a very nice-looking house, with five bedrooms, a living room, a dining room, and a little kitchen that came out from the side of the house. We needed a lot of room because my father's sister, Aunt Ava, who Ava was named for, lived with us some of the time.

My mother was just a wonderful cook; in fact, she was noted as the best cook in Johnston County. She made the best fried chicken around, and every weekend she'd bake two or three cakes, whip 'em up in no time. She was a very caring person, very interested in her children, as my father was. My mother was a bit more outgoing, and more of disciplinarian, and he was more easygoing.

We were a very close family. I always thought we had a good life. I didn't think of us as dirt poor, which has been written time and time again, until we are all sick of reading it. I can tell you now we were never dirt poor. We may have had some homemade clothes, but we always had plenty of good food. On Sunday, if we had company drop by, there was always enough food for everybody. We had a wonderful vegetable garden and had our own cow for milk. I know because I wanted to do the milking one time and failed. That seemed to be my brother's job.

Because there were seven years between Ava and me, I guess a baby was not expected when she came along. Because of that, she was sort of special, and everybody did dote on her. She had naturally curly hair that Mama had to brush every morning before she'd go to school, and Ava always hated that. But in the first year of her life, we thought she was never going to have any hair at all. She was kind of a baldheaded baby; she didn't grow a lot until she was about a year old.

Ava was sort of a tomboy, always climbing trees. When we lived over at Brogden, she got halfway up to the top of the town's water tank. Everybody was so frightened to see her up there. Finally, someone went up and got her down.

Ava was a pretty little girl, too, and everybody thought she was so cute and wonderful, but to me she was just my baby sister. We roomed together and we loved each other, but I never got the impression that she wanted to be in the movies. Mama loved to go to the movies, though, and she and some of the teachers from the Teacherage would get together and go to Smithfield to see one most every week. Mama especially liked Clark Gable. I wish she could have lived long enough to know that Ava did a movie with him.

FIVE

When Bappie and I stepped off the train at Union Station on the morning of August 23, 1941, we were immediately struck both physically and emotionally by Los Angeles' most enduring product: sunshine. It seemed to radiate off everything, even the sunglasses and smiling teeth of Mr. Milton Weiss. He held out his hand and said, "Welcome to Hollywood and MGM."

"Thank you very much," Bappie said. I said nothing. I was still overwhelmed by what I'd seen during our train journey across the country. I was green as a spring tobacco leaf, and trying to hide my nervousness behind a fixed smile.

Mr. Weiss, from MGM's publicity department, was a thin, sharp-featured young man. He wore a light gray tropical suit and a neat-looking Borsalino of the sort favored by Humphrey Bogart. With his pleasant, deep voice and his anxiousness to please, he was to be our shepherd for the next few days, breaking me into the system.

On the way to our hotel, in a company car, no less, I liked the bits and pieces of L.A. I managed to see, the tall palm trees and the beautiful houses surrounded by clipped green lawns. The hotel, the Plaza on Vine Street, was right in the heart of old Hollywood. Sunset, Hollywood, and Santa Monica boulevards were only a few blocks away. The intersecting streets were quiet and on the narrow side, shaded with trees and lined with small one- or two-story houses. The traffic wasn't all that heavy, there was no smog, only sunshine and clear nights full of stars. It was thrilling.

The next day began with a tour of the MGM lot in Culver City, a site that was definitely worth seeing. Twenty-three modern sound stages, great caverns of darkness as big as aircraft hangers, were spread out over a huge expanse of real estate that eventually grew to a hundred and eighty-seven acres. MGM had the world's largest film lab; MGM had four thousand employees; MGM had a railway station, a harbor, even a miniature jungle ready and waiting for a director who might fancy it. But most of all, MGM had stars. More Stars Than There Are in Heaven, one studio ad claimed, and I sure as hell wasn't about to argue.

Other studios might have better directors, or better writers, but MGM had the stars. Greta Garbo. My old heartthrob Clark Gable. The Barrymores. Joan Crawford. Spencer Tracy. James Stewart. Mickey Rooney and Judy Garland. Greer Garson. You name it, MGM had it. Louis B. Mayer, the man in charge, liked to think of the studio as one big family. You can guess who was the daddy, and who were the kids taking orders. A meeting with L.B., I soon came to understand, was to be treated as kind of a papal encounter.

In his own fashion, Mayer wanted to take care of his stars. MGM films were always the glossiest, with the biggest budgets, best technicians and glamour so thick you could spread it on a plate. The bigger stars were well paid (Clark Gable got a reported three hundred and fifty-seven thousand dollars in 1941), and the studio tried its hardest to live up to Mayer's dictum: "Make it good. . . . Make it big. . . . Give it class."

MGM succeeded often enough to make it the most famous—and most successful, in terms of both profits and Oscars—studio in Hollywood. In 1939, it had released my great favorite *Gone With the Wind,* and in this my first year on the lot it would turn out fifty-two films, potboilers like the Dr. Kildare, Tarzan, and Andy Hardy series along with the usual component of class acts like Spencer Tracy's *Dr. Jekyll and Mr. Hyde.* If I was going to be anywhere in Hollywood, this sure seemed like the place to be.

What I didn't, couldn't know at the time was that I was walking onto the MGM lot at the beginning of the end. Though she was at the height of her career, Garbo never made another film for MGM or anyone else after 1941's *Two-Faced Woman.* World

War II, which we were to enter just a few months later after the Japanese bombed Pearl Harbor, was crippling the industry's European markets. And something as funny-sounding as the consent decree was in the process of splitting MGM off from the hugely profitable Loews theater chain. I may have been taking my first nervous steps in Hollywood, but the studio system was about to totter onto its last legs.

While I didn't know any of that, I did know that I wasn't making the kind of money Clark Gable was, or even the hundred and twelve thousand that Deanna Durbin, just about my age, was pulling in. I got fifty dollars a week, and, courtesy of a little firecracker embedded in my contract, the studio had the right to impose an annual twelve-week layoff period during which my pay dropped to thirty-five dollars.

Clearly, on money like that Bappie and I were not long for the Plaza. The desk clerk there helped us find an apartment on nearby Wilcox Avenue: one room with a pull-down bed, a two-ring cooker, and a microscopic bathroom. Nothing classy, but we could afford it, especially after Bappie used an introduction from her New York boss to get a job at I. Magnin.

That same clerk worked out my bus route to the studio. Let me tell you, honey, you want to be a film star, you've got to be an early riser. I was stepping out into the cold dawn of Hollywood at five A.M. I walked to the bus terminal about three blocks away and took the first bus out of there to Wilshire Boulevard. A second bus took me close to Culver City and a third one dropped me off in front of the studio.

The nice men on the gate, who had obviously seen a thousand white-faced kids go through in their time, told me the way to makeup. That was my first destination. I held a piece of paper giving me my orders—the call sheet—which informed me that I had to report to a stage where I'd be an extra dancing in a ballroom scene. It sounded very pleasant. But first the makeup department. I was terrified.

As soon as I walked in through the white coats and the bustle and announced shyly, "I'm Avah Gardnuh. I was told to come here," I realized that my statement did not electrify anybody. Nobody had ever heard of Avah Gardnuh. Nobody cared if they ever saw Avah Gardnuh again. Oh, they were busy all right, but eventually Jack Dawn, who was head of makeup, was told of my arrival, and he came out to see why I was lost. He was very brusque. "You are in the *wrong* department. You should be down in the *extras'* makeup department." His tone indicated that the extras' makeup department was a sort of leper colony reserved for juveniles like me.

Confused, I held out my piece of paper and said plaintively, "But they told me to come *here!*"

"Wrong place," insisted Jack. "*Extras'* makeup." Of course, hindsight would later tell me that I should have told them I was under *contract,* that magic little word that makes all the difference between officer class and the lesser ranks.

I think Jack Dawn decided to be nice, for he pulled out a piece of paper and went on, "Now here's a list of the makeup you'll need *down there,*" making it sound like the last circle of Hell. And, as my eyes popped out, he went on: "Pancake makeup." What the hell was that? "Mascara." I'd never heard of it; it sounded like a disease. "False eyelashes." I needed artificial eyelashes like I needed another head. Plus a lot of other things. I stood looking down at the list thinking, "How am I going to afford this on thirty-five bucks a week, plus fares, plus rent, plus food . . ."

I went to the drugstore and used up all my money, except for the three bus fares home. Bappie looked at my purchases very suspiciously and made rude noises. Especially about the pancake makeup. She was right. In those days it was terrible stuff, a bright-yellowy-colored cream. You dabbed it on with a sponge. When you smiled everything cracked. Even Garbo would've looked like Mrs. Frankenstein.

As a matter of fact I didn't use any of it. Somewhere in makeup they finally got the message that this kid was a contract player, not an extra. The cosmetics were on the house, paid for by Louis B. Mayer. And the next time I went in I was passed to Charlie Schamm, who was a sweetheart and did my makeup for years afterward. Only once did I have to put my small North Carolina foot down. Over the eyebrows. They wanted to pluck every one out! I said a loud *"Nooo!"* I would have added, "If anyone tries it, I'll kick his teeth in," but I'd already made my point.

In Hollywood in those days they either shaved off or plucked out the eyebrows and replaced them with a thin pencil line. Lana

Turner, poor darling, suffered from this because they plucked out her eyebrows, shaped them, and waxed them until all she could do afterward was use a pencil.

I did let them have their way with my lips, turning them into sort of a huge Joan Crawford scarlet blur. In fact, when I looked in the mirror afterward I had a hard time knowing if it was me. But that was Hollywood's standard starlet treatment in those days: orders were to turn out a series of look-alike china dolls, and everybody followed orders.

One member of MGM's staff who was certainly not into that assembly-line routine was Sydney Guilaroff. He was a master hairstylist, but my first meeting with him was awful in a way I don't think I'll ever forget.

I was crouched in the hairdressing chair in Sydney's salon, waiting my turn for his attention with about three or four other girls. We were only too happy to wait, because Sydney was an artist. He had been Joan Crawford's hairdresser, Greta Garbo's hairdresser, God knows who else's hairdresser. But that day he was creating hairstyles for our group of starlets. All of us were playing walk-on parts, but on different sets. Some needed an in-town styling, others an office or country look. And Sydney could effortlessly handle them all.

What he couldn't handle, however, was the sound of someone chewing gum. Now you have to understand that chewing and cracking gum are like breathing in North Carolina, part of the normal pattern of living. I was chewing away, trying to keep calm, when, without thinking, I cracked my gum.

I paused, frozen, but it was too late. To Sydney, it had echoed as loud as a pistol shot, and he reacted as if he'd been struck in the neck by a pair of hot curling irons. His voice was loud, cold, and clear.

"Who is the girl who is chewing gum in here? Take it out of your mouth this minute."

Had I known about Sydney's diabolical hatred of chewing gum, I never would have dared chew at all. But now it was too late. I did the only thing I could: I swallowed it, cowering even lower in my chair, trying to cringe so far down that nobody could possibly see me. My face could have been bright scarlet for all I knew. And I couldn't say a word, not a single word.

Sydney stalked around, looking for his victim. All the girls looked innocent. I looked like someone on the way to Death Row. He paused behind my chair. Instinctively, he knew he was right. But he'd made his point, and no more humiliation was necessary. He did my hair beautifully and gave me a friendly pat on the shoulder as I left. I'd survived, and at this stage of my career, if you can call it that, survival was the best I could hope for at the end of every day.

Because the truth was, even in those first days at MGM, even when all I had to do was walk on the set and hide in a crowd of extras, I was terrified. Then I discovered that on every set there was someone called the prop man. And the prop man had everything that might be needed in a film scene, and I mean *everything*. Including all kinds of drinks: coffee, tea, soda, and the real thing. All I'd have to do was sidle up and raise my eyebrows, and something would be handed to me in a paper cup. I never knew what it was, and I didn't care. I never liked the taste of any booze, and I didn't start drinking seriously until I was in my thirties. All I knew then was that with two big chugalugs inside me, I could calm the rising panic.

Once I got used to things, I just loved working with the extras, especially the dress extras. Oh, boy, they were quite a superior class of folks. They provided their own evening clothes, which meant tuxedos or white tie and tails for the men, a variety of evening gowns for the ladies. And no matter how old or crippled or gray they got, they were always buoyed up by enormous hopes. One of these days, with just the right bit of luck, being in the right place at the right time, the right word from the right director, they would emerge like Cinderella, ready for stardom and all its perks.

My ambitions were nowhere near as high. I spent an awful lot of time in what was called the Picture Gallery, run by a great portrait artist, Clarence Bull, and his team. But great portraits weren't what they had in mind for me. My specialty was what was called "leg art," publicity stills of the cheesecake variety intended for use and reuse in newspapers and magazines around the country. It was not my favorite activity.

I don't know—I don't think anyone knows—how many hundreds of those shots I posed for. You could have carpeted Hollywood Boulevard from curb to curb with my pictures. I don't remember how many swimsuits I wore out, without getting near the water. I shot enough sultry looks around the gallery to melt the North Pole.

Often the idea was to get pictures to match holiday seasons: I was always a smiling Easter bunny, or a roguish lady Father Christmas or at least one of his reindeer. With other starlets, I began to load hay, round up chickens. "And Ava! You mean if we got a cow you could actually *milk it*? Come on. I don't believe it. Ava, I bet you don't know one end from the other. . . ." I think some of those guys working for Clarence Bull thought that milk came from some underground spring and was packed into cartons at the source.

They produced a cow. Fortunately, someone knew the difference between a cow and a bull. It was a milking cow and I milked her. MGM was overjoyed. They'd actually got a starlet who could milk a cow. Even Mr. L. B. Mayer couldn't do that.

I especially remember a record heat day in Los Angeles when somebody said, "Okay, let's get somebody who's got good legs and knockers and put her in a bathing suit on top of this enormous block of ice." And the block they got really was enormous; it must have weighed a ton. A huge crane was needed to get it into position outside the Picture Gallery. And who was chosen for the honor? Ava G. I wore a red candy-striped bathing suit, and they heaved me up to the top. I held an ice cream cone and smiled happily as they turned on a fan so my hair blew in the wind as my bottom froze. It made all the newspapers. No one ever called it an intellectual profession.

There were also lessons in voice production, in elocution, in drama. One thing I was very determined about. That North Carolina accent had to go. Not only because they laughed at me—I was sick and tired of being teased about it, it made me shyer than ever. If ever I was going to speak a single line in a movie (which I doubted) a voice from the Deep South was not going to help. Today, you can talk any damn way you like in pictures, but in those days it was very important to speak the way *they* wanted.

The great Lillian Burns was the MGM drama coach in those days. In principle, she was responsible for everyone and everything, from starlets like myself to Lana Turner, but in practice she worked with you only when you had a specific part to master. Since I wasn't in that league yet, I was sent to Gertrude Vogeler, the vocal coach, a woman I came to love very dearly.

She was a beautiful old lady, very old, very gray-haired, very overweight, with a million cats—well, it seemed like a million anyway—and an ancient Chinese cook who was funnier than anything ever seen in the movies. Lillian Burns had this fabulous office, but poor Gertrude was way off in the back of the lot. She also worked out of her own house on Whittier Drive, a sort of cottage where she adopted everything that moved. The cat union was the first to discover this and move right in, but she also adopted us kids—the starlets. A lot of them had less money than I did and a lot of those were sending what they had home to small towns in places like Idaho, Nebraska, and Louisiana. Gertrude would take in some of these, and she'd also smuggle in other young kids who were trying to be actors. They'd bed down somewhere, the cook would feed 'em, the cats would sit on 'em, and Gertrude would teach 'em.

Gertrude had a hard time with me, but she was so loving and skillful. I can remember her sitting opposite me, her motherly bosom going up and down, trying to get my voice a couple of octaves closer to my navel. "Sit on it, Ava!" she'd say. "Sit on it, my beauty! Make your voice come up from down there—down *there*. That's good, that's good."

Gertrude had the most beautiful voice herself. And she was not just a voice coach, she was an institution. She'd give you a page of dialogue to work on, and if she hadn't enough time, you'd go back to the cottage, and by God you'd find you were into yoga exercises and breathing and all kinds of stuff. You were not going to breathe just from the throat, you were going to speak from down there—down *there*. Every time I went back to Los Angeles for years after that—as I'm sure so many other of her pupils did—I went back to kiss her on the cheek and say thank you.

One thing I wasn't thankful for, then or ever, was the goddamn MGM contract I had to sign. I had to accept any and all roles assigned to me. I had to make personal appearances for publicity purposes, or for any other reason they could think up, anywhere they chose. Travel anywhere MGM felt like sending me. But I could not ever leave Los Angeles, even when I was on vacation, without their permission.

And the standard morals clause. That was worth a few laughs. I solemnly agreed to conduct myself "with due regard to public conventions and morals" and not "do or commit any act or thing that will degrade her in society, or bring her into public hatred, contempt, scorn, or ridicule, that will tend to shock, insult, or offend the community or ridicule public morals or decency, or prejudice the producer or the motion picture industry in general." My God, if we so much as were photographed in a night-club with a cigarette, the studio would insist that it be airbrushed out.

I decided from the very first that the contract abused my sense of personal human rights. We were told what to do, when to do it and how, and we were paid very little. I used to joke that we were the only kind of merchandise allowed to leave the store at night, but it wasn't a very funny situation. And this particular piece of merchandise was female, Southern female. I decided from the first that I had the right to act according to my own principles. And if mine clashed with theirs, and they didn't like it, that was not going to be my problem.

SIX

It started on my very first day at MGM. Milton Weiss was taking me around the lot and I was making a great effort to keep my mouth from dropping open. The final sound stage we visited was full of music, noise, and bustle. *"Babes on Broadway,"* Weiss whispered to me. "Mickey Rooney and Judy Garland!"

I was trying to figure out an appropriate response when I saw someone detach him or herself from a crowd and walk toward us. Whatever *it* was, it looked an awful lot like Carmen Miranda, the Brazilian firecracker who always seemed to be living through a perpetual fiesta. *It* wore a bolero blouse, a long and colorful slit skirt, enormous platform shoes, and the biggest fruit-laden hat I'd ever seen. The mouth smeared with thick scarlet makeup opened and a voice said, "Hello, I'm Mickey Rooney."

Thank God for Milton Weiss. "This is Miss Ava Gardner," he said, giving me a minute to recover from the shock.

"Hello," I said. I may have managed a smile. What the film was about I never discovered, but everybody in America knew Mickey Rooney. Only two years older than me—and considerably shorter—Mickey was the most popular star in America, earning five thousand dollars a week, plus bonuses. Almost literally born in a trunk to a pair of vaudevillian parents, Joe Yule, Jr. first toddled onstage at age fifteen months, made his film debut at six (playing a midget!), and was so successful making some fifty Mickey McGuire two-reel comedies that he changed his name to his character's.

When he was fourteen, Mickey changed it again, this time to Rooney, and played the plum role of Puck in a glossy Hollywood version of *A Midsummer Night's Dream*. He shared a special Oscar with Deanna Durbin in 1938 for "bringing to the screen the spirit and personification of youth" and he'd made a whole bunch of Andy Hardy movies, playing a peppy son always in need of advice from Lewis Stone's kindly father. No wonder these were Louis B. Mayer's favorite films. Mickey had already been through it all, and I hadn't even begun my career.

Not that that bothered Mickey. When Bappie and I returned to the Plaza Hotel that night, the phone rang and a voice said, "Hello, Miss Gardner, this is Mickey Rooney. What about dinner tonight?"

I was flustered and I reacted instinctively. I played it like a little lady, a little Southern lady.

"I'm busy," I told him. Busy! I didn't know a soul.

I soon found out that Mickey Rooney never took no for an answer. Every night during those first two weeks in Hollywood the telephone rang and it was Mickey Rooney. Sometimes Bappie would answer and cheerfully make the excuse that I was out, or I was tired and had gone to bed early; sometimes I had to do it myself. At eighteen, you obey the S.L.C., the Southern lady conventions, and you don't go out at the drop of a hat when a gentleman invites you to dinner. A Southern lady has to be courted, and a *gentleman* has to be gallant, chivalrous, and patient. After all, I hadn't read and reread *Gone With the Wind* for nothing.

Bappie, however, thought I should give him a chance, that he wasn't going to keep calling me forever. But he *did* go on calling—forever! At least it felt like forever to me. One evening, when I'd used up my last excuse, I said in exasperation, "Now listen, Mickey, I've got my sister Bappie here. I just can't leave her here by herself." Not missing a beat, Mickey made one of the greatest sacrifices known to man and said, "Well, let's take her out, too."

We went to Chasen's, one of Hollywood's landmark restaurants. Full of the people who made Hollywood spectacular, and they all welcomed Mickey as if he owned the place. Taking me by the hand, he towed me around from table to table, cracking gags and introducing me. It was so swift and spontaneous I didn't even have time to feel nervous. I had to say one thing for him: he sure had energy.

After that, Mickey and I started going out on a regular basis. At first Mickey's shortness kind of stunned me, but he was charming, romantic, and great fun, and I began to miss him when he wasn't around. I was reared in a Southern tempo, and Mickey had so much speed it was dazzling. His kind of courtship was as foreign to me as the caviar we had at Romanoff's or the zombies we downed at Don the Beachcomber's.

And like those zombies, Mickey had a powerful effect. He was the original laugh-a-minute boy, and even the second or third time around his stories, jokes, and gags were funny. There wasn't a minute when he wasn't onstage. He loved an audience, and I tried to be as good a one as I knew how. Occasionally, a voice would sound in my brain warning that maybe life with Mickey would be like life on a sound stage. But whenever the warning sounded, Mickey drowned it out with a new joke.

And those were not the only fears I had. Mickey was so different from me. He was enthusiastic, sure of himself, and good at everything he tried, from acting to golf, tennis, and swimming. I may have been close to my nineteenth birthday, but I hadn't changed all that much from that tongue-tied country girl out on her first date who had tried to fill in the silences by reciting the names on the brightly lit signs as we drove by. I may have seemed like a cool customer, but that was just the constant fear and shyness I tried so hard to conceal, the front I put on when I was terrified of things.

I loved our nights out, dancing at Ciro's or the Trocadero, eating at smart restaurants, and all the new acquaintances I made through Mickey—people like Lana Turner, Judy Garland, Esther Williams, Kathryn Grayson, Elizabeth Taylor, and a young English actor, Peter Lawford, who remained a good friend for years.

But no matter how much fun I was having, I was not going to bed with any man until I was married to him. Sex before marriage was definitely out; in Mama's terms, even a couple of kisses before marriage were a kind of prostitution. I was a very old-fashioned girl, as Mickey found out after a couple of wrestling sessions in the back of his car.

One night, Mickey said, "Let's get married. Now." Just like that.

Corny as it sounds, that took my breath away. But I reacted, immediately and very loudly: "No!"

"Why not?"

"Because I'm too young and you're too young. No."

Mickey, as noted, did not understand the meaning of the word. He thought I was being coy. I wasn't. He asked me every night. Sometimes several times a night. "Please don't start that again," I'd tell him. "You're crazy. I don't want to marry anyone until I'm positive it will work out." But he kept persevering. First he won over Bappie, who, like Mama, was always on the man's side. Finally, I said yes as well, with one proviso: not until I'd passed my nineteenth birthday.

"Great!" Mickey said. "We'll throw a birthday party for you at Romanoff's on Christmas Eve and we'll announce our engagement there."

Now came the next obstacle. "Ava, if we're going to get married, you've got to meet Ma."

Meet my future mother-in-law? I had never even considered that a mother-in-law came with the package, and the idea terrified me. Mickey's mother was divorced from Joe Yule, remarried, and living in a huge house in the San Fernando Valley. "We'll just drop in and give the happy news," Mickey said, bubbling away.

Bappie took me down to I. Magnin and we bought a pretty black dress and all the accessories. I sure hope we got a discount.

Mickey picked the evening. He didn't telephone to break the ice, or forewarn Ma. We just arrived. Me quaking.

We breezed into the house and Mickey marched me through to the sitting room. There was Ma sitting cross-legged on this enormous sofa. At that time a famous newspaper comic strip was running called Maggie and Jiggs. Either Maggie had been based on Ma or the other way round. She was a complete look-alike. The size, the glasses, the mop of frizzed hair.

Ma, with her legs tucked up under her, was reading the *Racing Form* with fierce intensity. At her elbow on a small table was a tumbler half full of bourbon and a bottle behind the glass as backup.

"Ma," said Mickey proudly, "I want you to meet Ava. We're gonna get married."

I was standing there, feeling like a complete dummy. Ma stopped reading the *Racing Form,* slightly adjusted her glasses, and stared over the top of them. She took a few seconds to reach her verdict.

"Well," she said slowly, "I guess he ain't been into your pants yet."

I was mortified. The big occasion. A great moment in a girl's life. How could she? At the time I didn't know whether to laugh or cry. I was just dumbfounded. And that was my meeting with Ma.

Since then I've laughed about that night hundreds of times. And let me add I eventually got on marvelously with Mickey's Ma, who knew more cuss words than my entire childhood gang put together. In fact, I got along with the mothers of all the men I married, all of them strong, assertive women. If only I'd gotten along half as well with the husbands, I'd still be married to as many of them as the law allows.

The next hurdle was a meeting with Louis B. Mayer. We had to get his permission to get married. It was in the contract. Metro owned both of us, and did not look kindly on any change in Andy Hardy's status. We arrived at Mr. Mayer's office together, but Mickey went in alone. He was weeping because he wanted to get married, and Mr. Mayer was weeping because he didn't want him to. Father and son stuff, just like in the movies. It must have been a great scene, because Mr. Mayer and Mickey were rated the best criers in Hollywood.

While all this weeping was going on, I waited in the outer office with Mr. Mayer's elderly and very disapproving secretary. When I'd had my screen test I'd been asked, "Which would be more important to you—your career or love?" I said, "Oh, mah cahreah, of cawse!" And then the first thing I'd done when I'd gotten the damn contract was to marry Mickey Rooney. No wonder that secretary was not at all pleased. She told me icily that it was not possible for a leopard to change its spots. I was quite hurt at the time, knowing it was a nasty statement but not being sure exactly what the hell it meant. I found out soon enough.

Mr. Mayer gave in; Mickey, as you may remember, was a very

determined young man. The wedding would go on, but Metro would set the rules. Les Petersen, Mickey's personal publicist at the studio, was put in charge of all the details, and he sold Mickey on MGM's plan for a nice quiet, unpublicized little ceremony. And, as a dutiful wife-to-be, I agreed with my future husband, even though it ruined my dream of getting married at a beautiful ceremony dressed in a white wedding gown. I didn't mind missing out on the big wedding, but I did miss the dress.

Mickey and I were married on January 10, 1942, in Ballard, a town near Santa Barbara in the foothills of the Santa Ynez Mountains. The wedding party consisted of the two of us and five guests: Bappie, Mickey's father, Ma and her new husband— and Les Petersen. An official photographer from MGM took pictures. I wore a simple blue suit and a corsage of orchids, Mickey a dark gray suit, a polka-dot tie, and a white carnation. Presbyterian minister Reverend Glenn H. Lutz (who later moved on to bigger audiences in Las Vegas) conducted the services with a beaming smile, and Mrs. Lutz banged out the wedding march and "I Love You Truly." Mickey fumbled with the wedding ring, inscribed "Love Forever," which was probably some kind of portent, given that he racked up eight marriages altogether and I managed another two. No one shed any tears.

The wedding over, the pictures taken, Mickey and I got into the getaway car that was to whisk us to our intimate honeymoon retreat near Monterey—and Les Petersen got in with us. What the hell Les was doing with us only L. B. Mayer could possibly know. Actually, I know exactly what he was doing there. He was personally responsible to Mr. Mayer for keeping the name of Andy Hardy pure and unsullied. And as Mickey loved booze, betting, and girls, not necessarily in that order, that was quite a job, and I have to add that I forgive dear Les completely for what he had to do.

Our little place by the sea turned out to be the enormous Del Monte Hotel near Carmel on the Monterey Peninsula. It is also only a stone's throw from one of the most famous golf courses in the world, Pebble Beach. And I was soon to find out that by some strange coincidence Mickey had a completely new set of golf clubs, his wedding gift to himself, in the trunk.

The suite in the hotel was great: huge fireplace, a lounge

that stretched for a mile, a big bedroom, champagne everywhere. But by now I was cooling very rapidly about this honeymoon deal. I realized that it was a bit late for the bride to default, but I wanted to keep the moment of truth off as long as possible.

Drinking seemed to be the only way of doing that. "Les, let's have another glass of champagne. Plenty left. Let's have a party." Every glass delayed procedures. Invisible masculine signals were now beginning to vibrate between Mickey and Les. I couldn't care; no one felt less inclined to honeymoon activity that night than I did. Nothing to do with Mickey. I loved him, but I needed time to think this thing through. I had been brought up by Mama, after all, and I had not been briefed about this next bit. This business of sex was going to ruin the entire marriage.

I clung to Les Petersen's arm as if he were the Rock of Gibraltar and I was in danger of being swept away by a raging sea. "My glass needs a refill, Les. We've got all night, haven't we? What's the champagne there for, anyway? Bridal celebration!" Les was shocked. Brides did not behave like this. Especially when they had publicity men with them.

The male signals were now audible.

"Well, see ya, Les."

"Oh, sure, Mick, see ya, Mick."

"There's a lot of champagne left," I wailed, but I knew that sooner or later Les was going to unhook my arm and abandon me. Why wasn't it like the movies . . . the embrace and kiss, the slow fade, the dim lights, the soft music?

Let me say at this point that I approve highly of the physical side of relationships between male and female. Not only does it make the world go round, it's marvelous. In that respect all my three marriages were perfect; I loved each one of my husbands just as much when I left them as I did when I married them . . . but that honeymoon night in the Del Monte Hotel I just wasn't ready.

Oh, it worked all right, and I was agreeably surprised. Even when next morning, damn near as soon as the sun came up, Mickey was out of bed and heading for the golf course. He'd got a game fixed up with three of his buddies. That was Mickey. He spent most of our honeymoon on the golf course, leaving you know who to hold the bag. When you came down to breakfast, he was there. When you had your dinner, he was there. When you went to bed, he was damn near there as well. Poor Les.

By this time, World War II was on in earnest and after only a week of golf widowhood Mickey and I were put on a war bond tour. We were to drive north to San Francisco, take a cross-country train to appearances in Boston and New York, then go down to Fort Bragg and finish up with a big show with a lot of other stars for the President at the White House. And since Mickey had just finished *Life Begins for Andy Hardy,* publicity for that picture could be included in the tour. MGM never missed a trick.

On the way to San Francisco we heard the tragic news about Carole Lombard, Clark Gable's wife. Flying back to Los Angeles after a war bond appearance in Fort Wayne, Indiana, her plane had crashed near Las Vegas. There were no survivors. It horrified us all. Poor Clark, I thought. Oh, God, poor Clark. And it drove home the point: there was a war going on.

No one took much notice of me in San Francisco. We checked into the Palace Hotel—and got the presidential suite. I don't think anyone revealed until later that it was the suite that President Harding died in. Mickey was interviewed, and I was included in some of the photographs. Me sitting in an armchair, and Mickey smiling on the arm because of the height difference. But Mickey was the lion. Who'd ever heard of me? I was just another pretty girl.

Next morning we were off on the Union Pacific heading for Chicago, an overnight stay at the Ambassador East, and Mickey giving more interviews to promote his new picture. On again then by Twentieth Century Limited to New York. This time we stayed at the New Yorker, and Bappie came in from Los Angeles to stay with me. It had been plain to Bappie, if not to me, that her marriage to Larry Tarr had been rocky and on the point of shipwreck for some time now. As I've said, Larry was lovable but impossible.

Boston, where the mayor had laid on a luncheon in our honor, was nerve-racking. It was a terribly elegant meal, in a terribly elegant and beautiful old house, with a terribly elegant guest list. Oh baby, this was the first time in my life I'd ever been to a real banquet—even seen a table laid out for a banquet—and my knees shook under the tablecloth. It was nothing like Mama's boardinghouse. I can't tell you the size of the plates, and the silver lined up in rows on either side, and the crystal—all those glasses—oh God, which one did you use first? I really suffered through that meal, and as a kid, I was not drinking. (We won't go into the bridal night champagne; that was pure self-defense.) If only I'd been older and more experienced and managed a couple of quick drinks I might have enjoyed it.

Next stop Fort Bragg, the huge North Carolina military establishment, where Mickey was again given the royal treatment. And now, en route to Washington, we had a chance to take a side trip to Raleigh, where Mama was being cared for by my sister Inez. There was a pleasant sun room where every afternoon Mama rested on a little sofa. And Mama had made herself pretty. She'd got herself dressed to the nines to meet her famous son-in-law. We had all the aunts and uncles and cousins and kids, and fried chicken, a real Southern feast. And the house was filled, which couldn't have made Mama happier because she loved people around her. And Mickey liked that sort of situation, too, and in my terms gave the greatest and most heartwarming performance of his life. He entertained Mama, he hugged her, he made her laugh, he brought tears to her eyes. He did his impersonations, he did his songs and dances—it was a wonderful, wonderful occasion for Mama, who we all knew was slowly dying. Although I had loved Mickey from the start, that show he put on moved me beyond words.

So on again to Washington for a very special occasion. To observe the President's birthday he and Mrs. Roosevelt were meeting a group of Hollywood stars and entertaining them at the White House. And Mickey and I were to be part of the group. I've still got the newspaper clipping and the picture of all the stars: John Payne, Gene Raymond, Pat O'Brien, Jimmy Stewart, Rosalind Russell, Edward Arnold, Gene Autry, Jackie Cooper, Betty Grable, Douglas Fairbanks, Dorothy Lamour, William Holden, and Mr. and Mrs. Mickey Rooney joining that world-famous contingent. And I think because we were so young—and I was certainly so shy it hurt—the President and Mrs. Roosevelt singled us out for a little special attention. My thought was: six months ago I was in Wilson, North Carolina, worrying about what sort of secretarial job I might get, and here I am in the White House being introduced to the President of the United States and the First Lady. It was unbelievable—absolutely unbelievable!

When we returned to L.A. we moved into an apartment good old Les Petersen had found for us in the Wilshire Palms near Westwood. With two bedrooms, a living room, kitchen, and bath, it was a great improvement over the room Bappie and I had been sharing, though I can't say I was crazy about the way it was decorated. White walls, white carpets, pieces of fake leather furniture scattered around at random made it almost as inspiring as the average hotel suite. Not that we were there that much: I don't think Mickey and I had more than a dozen dinners at home during our entire marriage.

Marriage. I'd wanted to get married, all right. I loved the idea of being married. But, really, neither Mickey or I had so much as a clue as to what that word really meant. We had no idea that marriage involved a meeting of the minds. That it involved sharing of problems, planning together, making a life together. Although Mickey had been brought up in show business and was very sophisticated in a way, he wasn't ready for it. He'd be the first to admit that he looked on marriage as a small dictatorship, with you know who as the one in charge.

But I really can't say our breaking up was Mickey's fault. He was just made the way he was and I didn't find out until it was too late that I wasn't the right girl for him. We weren't compatible. For one thing, with my parents as an example, I'd been brought up believing that marriage was a very sacred and final thing. I like domesticity, and though it's out of fashion to say so, I liked the idea of cooking for a husband who came home every night.

Well, forget that to start with. Mickey wanted to be on the go every minute of the day, with parties, clubs, and nightly dinners out. I didn't mind going out—I loved it—but even for me there were limits, like always having a bunch of Mickey's friends along with us. And when we'd wake up in the morning, if Mickey didn't have to be on the set at Metro at dawn, two or three guys would arrive and off they'd go to the golf course. Mickey's role in life was to amuse the world, and he tore himself apart doing it.

Mickey clearly thought, if he thought about it at all, that a marriage could run concurrent with his normal lifestyle: boozing, broads, bookmakers, golfing, and hangers-on, not to mention the heavy involvement of studio work and publicity. Honey, let's take bookmakers for a start. Mickey was the guy they'd put a telephone under the stage for so he could be in hourly contact with his bookies. Usually he lost far more than he'd won; that's how bookies manage to spend winters in the Caribbean. Occasionally he won a big lump of money from the track, and I'd get a lovely present, usually jewelry. I especially remember a beautiful ring, but, by God, Mickey wanted it back the next week to pay off his gambling debts.

For a while I felt, if you can't beat 'em, join 'em. If Mickey was going to involve himself in a thousand activities, so would I. I took golf lessons, I took tennis lessons, I took swimming lessons from Esther Williams, a sweet girl in my starlet group and an Olympic champion. What I finally couldn't take, though, was Mickey's other girls. Talk about playing the field. Jesus Christ, Mickey played all the fields known to man.

We'd been married about two months when I woke up in the middle of the night with these awful pains in the stomach. They were so excruciating that I was rushed to Hollywood Hospital, where they found I had an inflamed appendix and operated at once. Convalescing, I sat up in bed, looking pretty and receiving guests. Mickey rushed in and out bearing gifts and books and spraying kisses. Then I came home, happy and contented and, God almighty, it was clear to me he'd been entertaining girls in my bathroom and bed. My bathroom! My bed!

I screamed to Bappie for help and she tried to console me. I screamed at Mickey and he lied as only Mickey can. No, that's not true. Two of my husbands were the best liars in the world. They lied with a smile on their lips and a shine in their eyes.

I know that men who've been married for five, ten, fifteen years make the occasional slip—I suppose some of them make it every five minutes. But when you're just married, and your wife is young and beautiful, and she's been away in the hospital, to behave that way in your own home and your own bed, that's inexcusable. I did not believe in cheating. I don't cheat and I don't want anybody cheating on me. Maybe I'm stupid because I know every man in the world is going to do it. But in those days I was more trusting.

There was no competition between Mickey and me about our careers. Mickey was at the top of his profession and I was doing publicity photos for Metro and small walk-on parts in forgettable films. I came home and cooked and cleaned and decorated the house, and waited for Mickey. Besides golf he usually had "a coupla things to do" and would be "a bit late" or "work out a few things with the director" or "slip out to the track to back a certain winner."

MGM decided that with the wedding an established fact, they might as well cash in on reality, and made *The Courtship of Andy Hardy*. But film romance with Andy Hardy and real romance with Mickey Rooney were miles apart. We had constant rows and reconciliations. We moved to a larger house on Stone Canyon Drive in Bel Air. And I suppose my spirit of independence and confidence was increasing. The quarrels continued. Eight months after we married and after a noisier row than most, Mickey went home to Mom and I returned to the Westwood apartment. Mickey was working on his new film, *A Yank at Eton,* on location in faraway Connecticut. He called a lot of times, and I decided we should try again.

It didn't work, and the main reason was Mickey's inevitable philandering. Mr. Mayer's secretary was right after all—this leopard couldn't change his spots. Finally, it was Peter Lawford who revealed that Mickey in his golf cart, and some little babe in hers, were having a series of secret rendezvous, which were not secret at all but fairly common knowledge. Peter and I dated a lot, and danced a lot, but we never had any sort of affair. A kiss on the cheek, a hug, and lovely friends, that's all we ever were. As I say, I never cheated on a marriage.

I remember that final night when it became clear that life with Mickey would always be impossible. We were at the Ambassador with a party of Mickey's cronies. The drinking got heavy, Mickey got drunker, and the cronies began egging him into doing silly things. "Come on, Mickey, where's your little book, with all the babes' telephone numbers? Share it with your friends."

And Mickey, too drunk to care, pulled out the little notebook with his list of conquests and began to recite them right in front of me.

I left. One year and five days after the ring marked "Love Forever" was slipped on my finger, the marriage was finished and the lawyers took over. They came up with the usual grounds, "grievous mental suffering" and "extreme mental cruelty," and I had to testify in court that Mickey did not want a home life with me and remained away for long periods of time. I paid my own legal fees and waived the claim I had on half of Mickey's property, settling for twenty-five thousand dollars. I didn't want his money. We were babies, just children, and our lives were run by a lot of other people. We hadn't had a chance.

The divorce decree was granted on May 21, 1943. A very sad occasion made even sadder because Mama died on the same day. We'd expected it, known it was going to happen, but that didn't make it any easier. You can get over pain, loneliness, disappointment, and love, but you never get over grief. That lasts forever.

SEVEN

In the period between 1941, when I first arrived in Hollywood, and 1946, when I did *Whistle Stop* and *The Killers*, I appeared in seventeen films. No one noticed. The films were barely memorable and you'd need a magnifying glass to pick me out of them. I was there all right, married to Mickey, arriving at the studio every morning right on time, a face or figure in the crowd. I might be swirling on a dance floor, joining a gang of kids outside the drugstore, or splashing in the water on a crowded beach. Invisible, but there.

While people have speculated that being married to Mickey may have helped me get my first sequence of walk-on parts, the plain facts are that being Mrs. Rooney *never* gave me a single boost in the direction of stardom. Mickey *never* tried to make me an actress, *never* taught me anything, and *never* got me an acting job.

Not that I couldn't have used some help. I was greener than grass about everything. I'd never acted or been photographed; I was awkward and scared stupid. Half my time on the set I was trying not to bawl because I didn't know how to do what they wanted.

My very first feature came in 1942. *We Were Dancing* wasn't memorable because of anything I did but because it was one of the last films Norma Shearer appeared in at MGM. Once billed as The First Lady of the Screen, she was a five-time Oscar-nominated actress who'd been married to Irving Thalberg, the studio's boy genius. But after Thalberg died in 1936, Shearer's star waned, as did her judgment—she turned down both *Gone With the Wind* and *Mrs. Miniver*—and she ended up finishing her career in my forgettable debut. You had to be pretty sharp-eyed to spot my few seconds walking across a hotel lobby. Not surprisingly, my name was not included in the credits. In fact, I barely remember being in the damn thing at all.

That same year I appeared in a picture I won't ever forget. It was *Calling Dr. Gillespie,* the umpteenth of a series starring Lionel Barrymore as that lovable fussbudget of a doctor who so captivated audiences that people actually wrote him letters about their medical problems. The film was directed by Harold Bucquet, but I think it was an assistant director who picked me out of my usual crowd late one afternoon and said with a grin, "Ava, this is your big chance. Eight words." The doctor would say, "What is it, my dear?" I would respond with something like, "Doctor Gillespie, the other patient has just arrived," to which he would reply, "Just show him in, will you?" Not the most deathless of exchanges, but I wasn't in a position to be choosy.

The Dr. Gillespie films were quickies, filmed with a minimum of fuss on the studio back lot. Mr. Barrymore was pretty old and sick at the time, and because of that he'd been given a special dispensation (which only he and Clark Gable received) to go home when the clock struck five. It was about that hour when the time for my big line came around, and who should come trundling up, wheeling himself along in his wheelchair, but the great man himself.

Someone said to him, "Oh, Mr. Barrymore, it's past five. I believe you're supposed to be on your way home by now."

What did Mr. Barrymore do? He smiled across at me and said, "Leave that young lady with no one to look at her, no one to respond to her line? Of course not. That would be unkind."

And even though I was terrified at the idea of opening my mouth and having to produce words, I thought, What a wonderful old gentleman . . . and what lovely old-fashioned manners.

Mr. Barrymore taught me something I never forgot: he taught me what "respond" really means to an actor. When you've got a close-up to do or lines to speak, it's best if you can react to another performer, to his or her facial expression or voice. That reaction helps you to play your own part. But it isn't absolutely necessary that they stay—a script girl can read in the line for you and her voice will be cut in the editing.

So a lot of actors don't stay; they go back to their dressing rooms or wherever. But the good ones, the great ones are always there, because they know what that support really means. Clark Gable and Richard Burton were always there, and let me tell you, if you're playing a scene it's a damn sight nicer having Clark or Richard giving you the line, or the smile, or the scowl, instead of some disinterested script girl who's filling in for them. I was, and still am, so grateful to Mr. Barrymore for staying after hours, grateful for the presence and support he gave me in my first-ever spoken line in movies. It made all the difference in the world.

In the next picture, *Kid Glove Killer,* directed by that very famous director of the future Fred Zinnemann, I played a carhop with a screen time exposure of at least ten seconds. But that film is important to me because I met another young actor, Van Heflin, whose beautiful wife Frances remained a firm friend for years afterward.

Many months later I played in another Dr. Gillespie film, and this time I had more of a part. It was called *Three Men in White,* a really silly story, but Hollywood was awash with quick, silly stories in those war years. This time it was Lionel Barrymore's mission to check out the credentials of his very promising intern, Van Johnson. Could he really become a doctor of integrity and character? Would he be able to resist the temptations of pretty nurses and patients who would waste his time and drag him away from the stethoscope and rigorous medical procedures? I'm sure Dr. Gillespie's eyes were gleaming behind his glasses at the idiocy of such a plot.

Marilyn Maxwell and I were chosen from the studio's starlet pool as potential seductresses, primed to test Van Johnson's resolution. These days, given a theme like that, the titillation factor would certainly be emphasized. In those days, with the eyes of the Hays office everywhere, we had to play it strictly for laughs.

I remember in one scene I had to pretend to be a sexy clinging lush who was still sober enough to make a pass at Van in the emergency room. The audience, of course, already knew that I was *really* a sweet young thing supporting my invalid mother.

Van Johnson—I hope to his intense regret—resisted all the efforts of Marilyn and myself to drag him into bed. He proved himself a worthy successor to Dr. Gillespie, and everyone lived happily ever after.

And for the first time film critics became aware of my existence. The *Hollywood Reporter* decided that Marilyn Maxwell and Ava Gardner, "two of the smoothest young sirens to be found," were "superb, and should delight the studio with their histrionic conduct here." This was the first film I received any kind of critical notice in, and, believe me, it was nice to be noticed for something besides being Mrs. Mickey Rooney.

Yes, I was still seeing Mickey from time to time. He was certain that this divorce business was purely a temporary affair, that we would soon be back together again. We were seen together at various clubs, and the columnists, helped by Mickey's constant assertion that reconciliation was a sure thing, put two and two together. And in truth, on several occasions during that period Mickey and I did end up in bed together. But I made it very clear to him that he was very much my *ex*-husband. "As a husband, you were a pain in the ass," I told him, "and as a wife I was probably a disaster. Two disasters don't make for a marriage. It's over. Period." Mickey went on making sad noises about us until almost the end of the war, when he bumped into a beauty queen in Birmingham, Alabama, and made her wife No. 2.

In between those two Dr. Gillespie epics, I made the only other of my early films that made any kind of an impact on me, even if it didn't do much for anyone else. Though my Metro salary had by now risen to the great sum of one hundred dollars a week, MGM had decided that they could recoup that hundred and more by collecting a fee for loaning me out to another studio, whether I wanted to be loaned out or not. I got sold like a prize hog as often as the studio could manage it, and, honey, I hated that from day one.

This first time, though, being loaned out did have some compensations. I was shipped out to a Poverty Row company called Monogram, and, playing a sweet young thing named Betty in

Ghosts on the Loose, I got my very first credit in the billing. For some obscure reason, Betty had been kidnapped by a gang of villainous Nazi saboteurs led by that archfiend Bela Lugosi. In real life, Bela was a gentle man who wouldn't frighten a nervous kitten, but as Dracula, honey, he'd filled every movie house in the country.

If you think the U.S. Cavalry rode to my rescue, you must be in the wrong movie. It was Leo Gorcey and the intrepid East Side Kids, a gang of slapstick teenagers who favored baggy pants and big caps worn sideways, who saved me from Bela's clutches. I remember in one scene everyone had swastikas painted all over their faces, so they could say they had German measles: that was our standard of comedy. I don't remember much else about the film because it was shot at such enormous speed. We had one film stage and it took one week. Action—film—print! Even the little experience I'd had with Metro told me that this was *not* a quality film. In one scene the hero accidentally stumbled over a prop and fell. Nobody cared. No retake. Print it! All part of the glorious fun. The film is still shown occasionally on television, even these days, and I believe people still laugh at it. Ric Vallin, the hero, took me out to dinner one night and I liked that. We both knew we were not in the running for the Academy Awards.

Ghosts on the Loose was a piece of sweet, unsophisticated rubbish. But it did give me one sudden thrill that I've never forgotten. And although it's happened a hundred times since then, the feeling of that first wonderful moment never returned.

Bappie and I were walking in an area of Los Angeles where the theaters didn't show the best of movies. I don't think they even showed B pictures—the movies they played were of the XYZ variety. But suddenly Bappie gripped my arm and said excitedly, "Ava! Look!"

High up, outside one of the movie houses, there was this huge blazing sign in electric lights:

Ghosts on the Loose
With Ava Gardner

Oh, my God, I couldn't believe it. Who in the world had decided to put those words up there I'll never know. Perhaps it was because I'd been married to Mickey; I certainly didn't have any star status of my own. But at that moment I didn't really care about the hows or the whys. My name was up in lights for the very first time in my life. I've got to say it was a thrill. Then it wore off, and I've never had that feeling again. Ever.

EIGHT

hat can I say about Howard Hughes? A world-famous aviator, a multi-multi-millionaire, a very complex man, courageous, bold, and inventive? You bet. But also painfully shy, completely enigmatic and more eccentric, honey, than anyone *I* ever met. For God's sake, he and I were born on the same day, and if you think that Capricorns fall into the same category, you know what that means. I was never in love with him, but he was in and out of my life for something like twenty very remarkable years.

One of the main reasons Howard and I got on for so long was that Howard knew he could trust me. No matter what happened, and boy, did a few things happen, he could be certain that what went on between us was confidential. No gossip columnist or newspaper would report a word of it.

A mania for secrecy was hardly Howard's only eccentricity. His taste in food, for instance, was bizarre to the point of absurdity. I never saw him eat anything for dinner but a steak, green peas, perhaps a few potatoes and a small salad, followed by ice cream topped with caramel sauce. Night after night, year after year.

And Howard was more than ultraconservative politically. I would say he was a racist and a bigot. Only WASPs were on his payroll; no Jews or blacks were allowed to work in his plants. He once explained to me his attitude toward our political system: "It doesn't matter to me which party gets in. I contribute equally to both of them. So whatever happens, I get what I want."

Money was the root of Howard's influence. His father, the founder of Hughes Tool in Houston, Texas, had come up with a shrewd redesign in the drill head used to burrow for oil. His new tool went through layers of rock as if they were cheddar cheese. As a result, when the old man died, Howard at eighteen or nineteen was on his way to becoming one of the wealthiest men on earth. And for the rest of his life, he was enthusiastic about only four things: money, movies, aircraft, and beautiful young women with beautiful breasts. Which, obviously, is where I came in.

Howard first made his presence felt early in 1943, when I'd separated from Mickey but still hadn't gotten my divorce. I was pretty lonely, and when a neighbor I was friendly with said, "You know, Ava, Howard Hughes is a friend of mine and he'd love to meet you," I said, "Okay, invite him around to your house for a drink and we'll see how we get on."

Now, for some inexplicable reason, though she had said Howard Hughes, my mind slipped and thought she'd said Howard Hawks, the famous film director. But neither Howard arrived for that first meeting. Instead, a man named Johnny Meyer did. He was fat and bald but personable and a nice guy; I didn't find out until much later that one of his jobs for Howard was sizing up potential girlfriends.

Meyer apologized for the absence of Hughes/Hawks. He'd been called away on urgent business. Something to do with the production of airplanes. Oh, I thought, he's making an airplane picture. But he added, "I know that Howard is dying to meet you. Can he call you and fix a date?"

I said, "Sure. I'm usually back from the Metro lot by six or seven."

Next evening the phone rang and the voice said, "This is Howard. I think you met my colleague Mr. Meyer last night—"

"Yes."

"Perhaps we could have a drink and talk?"

"When?"

"Now."

"Oh. All right. Why don't you come round here and have a drink?"

Howard arrived on the front doorstep. He was well over six feet tall but couldn't have weighed more than a hundred and fifty pounds. Thin, bronzed, a small mustache. Eyes dark and searching. A male man. Secure. Private. But a nice smile in a long, serious face. He reminded me a bit of my father. And I guessed he was at least fifteen years older than I was.

We went out to dinner at a little place he knew and I went on saying Mr. Hawks this, and Mr. Hawks that, as we chatted about airplanes. I guessed if he was going to make an airplane picture, we should be talking about it. Eventually he said, "You know, my name's not Hawks, it's Hughes."

"I thought you were making a picture about airplanes."

"I've made that one," he said.

"What's it called?"

"*Hell's Angels.*"

That stopped me in my tracks. I knew about *Hell's Angels*. The story of American pilots in World War I, it had taken almost three years to make before its release in 1930 and it had cost more than three and a half million dollars, a pretty colossal sum in those days. It also nearly cost Howard his life. When his stunt pilots said that some of his flying ideas verged on madness, Howard went up to show them how it was done. The stunt pilots were right: Howard crash-landed and had to be yanked out of the debris unconscious and rushed to the hospital with multiple injuries including a smashed cheekbone.

The upshot of it all was that I liked him, and within a week Howard and I were good friends. He was a straightforward, no-bull Texan, direct and terribly helpful in practically every way you could imagine. As soon as he heard that Mama was very ill with cancer, he told me he'd get the best cancer specialist in the U.S.A. to visit her. And he kept his word. And when Mama died and Bappie and I couldn't get on a flight home because of the war, Howard threw a pair of desk-bound four-star generals off the plane so that we could get to Mama's graveside. After all, he did own TWA.

And for as long as Howard and I remained friends, he continued to make things easy for me when I wanted things easy. Let's say I was in Palm Springs and I wanted to go shopping in Mexico City. All I had to do was call Howard and within minutes a chauffeur was waiting outside to take me to the airport. A plane would be standing by just to take me, and once I arrived I was met by another chauffeured limo and driven to the best hotel in town, where a suite was waiting for me. If you wanted to be quiet and left alone, no one could arrange it like Howard.

Let me emphasize right here that *friend* is the word for our relationship. Howard didn't make any extravagant passes, in fact made no demands on me at all. A kiss on the cheek after about our tenth dinner was as far as he went. He made it clear that he was interested in me emotionally and romantically, but he was prepared to be very patient. (For my part, sharing a bed with him was always one length I couldn't imagine myself going to.)

Not that this, or for that matter anything else, deterred Howard. When Howard Hughes wanted something, he went after it with tunnel vision, and he saw no reason not to use the same tactics on the gentlemanly seduction of me. He was, someone once said, like a spoiled child when he couldn't get what he wanted, whining and wailing about it until he did. He could also be determinedly vengeful if anyone crossed or opposed him.

Even in those early weeks I discovered just how private Howard wanted to be. He didn't trust many places. One of the ones he did was the Town House, where he could get his favorite steak, and the Player's Club on Sunset Boulevard, run by the famous movie director Preston Sturges. Preston would keep it open with an orchestra in attendance just for Howard and me. Because Howard loved to dance. Unfortunately, Howard was a lousy dancer. There are four sorts of dancers: the good dancers, and the hoppers, jumpers, and pushers. And with the exception of Mickey, I've never had a husband or boyfriend who was a good dancer. Frank Sinatra and Artie Shaw were useless on the dance floor. I have an idea that being musicians they were always a fraction ahead of the beat, never quite right on it, so you followed hopefully and got dragged along. And Howard clutched you so hard it was like he was afraid he might lose you in the crush. As we were all alone on the Player's Club dance floor, that was always a bit odd. In fact, he nearly squashed me to death.

Being low profile also extended to Howard's ideas of appropriate dress, which in practice meant looking very much like a tramp. What other multimillionaire could get tossed off a yacht he was about to buy when one of its officers came up and tersely said, "Get ashore, bud. We've hired all the crew we need."

Clothes also figured in another one of Howard's spectacular plane crashes. Bappie and I were staying at the Desert Inn in Las Vegas with Howard when he decided to make a farewell test flight over Lake Mead in his Sikorsky amphibian plane. The war was still going on, and naturally the Air Force wanted to requisition the thing and test it for themselves. Howard, however, being Howard, was reluctant to part with one of his favorite planes and asked for that one last flight.

With four government officials on board and Howard at the controls, the plane clipped the water with a wing as it attempted a landing and went straight into the lake. Two of the government men were killed and Howard, copilot Glenn Odekirk, and the other two were fished out just in time, escaping with little more than bruises.

Howard, however, had lost almost all his clothes. The first thing he did was borrow a tweed jacket from his copilot, which was a mistake to begin with because Glen was a short, powerfully built man and Howard was a six-foot-three beanpole. And then he marched into the J. C. Penney store in Boulder City, Nevada, and bought a pair of khaki trousers for around a dollar ninety-eight, the cheapest pair he could find.

I'll never forget seeing Howard in that outfit, the pants starting six inches above his ankles and the jacket sleeves starting six inches above his wrists. It was no use telling him about it; to my knowledge he wore that same outfit night and day for at least five years. He was someone who would spend hundreds of thousands of dollars dredging the amphibian from the bottom of the lake but wouldn't go over a dollar ninety-eight for a pair of pants. Say what you like about Howard, he was his own man.

One day, out of the blue, Howard suddenly suggested we spend a few days together in San Francisco. Marvelous! I was always happy to go anywhere with Howard. And Howard had always been the gallant Texas gentleman, always responsive to a lady's no. So how was I to know that Howard was in a rare Don Juan mood, working on a plan called How to Seduce a Girl with a Few Samples of Everything She Adores.

Bappie thought it was a great idea. Bappie was totally convinced that any girl who had the chance to become the bride of the "richest-man-in-the-world" was crazy to even think of taking evasive action. I knew this because sometimes when I was away Howard would come to the apartment and sit there talking with Bappie for hour after hour, and his romantic intentions would inevitably surface.

Anyway, I loved San Francisco: its up and downs, the Golden

Gate Bridge, the clanking cable cars, the marvelous restaurants and little clubs where you could dance the night away. And Howard and I were going to be traveling on the Santa Fe first class, two sleeping cabins, champagne, the lot. I decided to be at my chicest, to bring the best and most expensive clothes I owned: a navy blue outfit from Irene, one of the great designers at Metro, a really smart tailored suit for traveling, very high heels, the perfect bag, just the right gloves. After all, Bappie worked at a store that specialized in such items, so I could afford to be very high class.

Howard was picking me up and driving us to the station, and Bappie, who wasn't going with us, was looking out of the window waiting for him. I heard her murmur something and I hurried across to see what'd happened outside, took one peek out the window, and screamed, "In that? I'm not going in that!"

That was Howard's so-called *car* from which he was in the process of emerging. I could bear the way he was dressed, in his shiny blue serge suit, the trousers held up by a tie, the sort you usually wear around your neck, the coat slung over his shoulder, his shoelaces undone. I'd borne it for weeks. I'd even be willing to bear it on the Santa Fe. But taking that car to the station? No way!

Later I learned that it, the vehicle in question, belonged to Howard's cook, Eddie. Howard had just borrowed it. It was not a car, it was a wreck—battered, filthy, and worst of all, it had no hood to conceal the nasty-looking engine. I'd never driven in a car without a hood before and I wasn't eager to start.

I said, "Here I am dressed up like a thousand dollars and he expects me to be driven to the station in an old jalopy without a hood!"

"It's not far," said Bappie soothingly. I said, "I'm dressed pretty, and I'm not about to sit in that wreck! We'll drive in my car."

Bappie was disbelieving. "He's the richest man in the world, and you're going to refuse to travel in his car?"

I said, "That's not a car, that's something from a wrecker's yard."

I'd said over and over again to Howard, "Please get a new suit, please get something. I'll even buy you one if you can't afford it." And now I could see, piled in the back of that dreadful vehicle down below, Howard's usual assortment of custom-made white cardboard boxes, all constructed to his specific instructions. One held clean shirts, another had underclothes, a third toilet articles. That was Howard's idea of luggage.

Howard arrived in the apartment and we discussed the whole matter. Bappie was totally on Howard's side. She always was. I don't blame her. Here was her daft kid sister who had a chance of catching a tycoon as wealthy and powerful as Howard. Why didn't we let her drive us to the station in *her* car if I didn't like Howard's?

I said savagely, "Howard's probably entering his for the 'Heap of the Year' award."

Howard wasn't put out. Didn't really know what the girls were arguing about and what I was complaining about. By this time we were approaching train departure time, and I had taken alcoholic refuge in a couple of large drinks. So my better judgment got fuzzy and, helped by the booze, I started to see the funny side of the situation. I agreed to go in Howard's heap, avoiding all the odd looks when we finally reached Union Station. We were shown to our sleeping compartments, mine next door to his, and the train began chugging up the California coast.

One little thing that happened soon after we started did surprise me slightly. After I closed the door to my compartment, without thinking about it I closed the latch. About three seconds later there was a knock on the door, and a very sad-faced Howard stood there saying quietly, "You didn't have to do that." This was a man who supposedly had been deaf since he was a kid, someone I'd seen hold a hearing aid in his hand and switch it on and off when he felt like it. But before I could ask him how he could possibly hear such a tiny click, he said, "Why don't you go into the bar? You'll find a nice surprise there. I'll join you in a few minutes."

Off I went. Those bar cars, with those magnificent black waiters absolutely impeccable in their smart uniforms, made train journeys in the forties a great experience. I sat alone at a small table, conscious that everyone was eyeing me and wondering who this unescorted young woman might be. I was ready to be patient; when Howard said he would see you in a couple of seconds, it could be a couple of years. Then one of the waiters arrived bearing one of Howard's larger-sized white cardboard boxes and laboriously began to undo it. He extracted wads of newspaper. Everyone in the car was enjoying Howard's surprise, especially the newspaper wrapping. And out came a bottle of the finest vintage champagne, perfectly chilled, perfectly wonderful. Why the hell he couldn't have asked the waiter to bring it over to me unwrapped, let me examine the label, and then hand it over to the barman to serve, only Howard knew. Perhaps he thought there was something magical in white cardboard boxes. I'd love to have heard a psychiatrist on that subject.

The champagne certainly was magical. Two glasses and I was smiling at anybody who wanted to smile back. A third and I was almost prepared for Howard. Almost.

Through the doorway, almost mincing toward me, came Howard. The rejuvenated Howard, the resplendent Howard, pleased as a little boy exhibiting his first grownup suit. Except that it wasn't a new suit; it was an ice-cream-colored affair that he must have worn at some high school or college function about twenty years before. Howard, the shy one, the invisible one, pirouetting like a goddamn male mannequin, oblivious of the belt in the back and *pleats* that must have gone out with dueling. As usual the sleeves were four inches too short and the trouser legs six inches above his socks, but he had put on a splendid white shirt and a tie. Now I was getting it. This was the *surprise*. That wreck of a car and those old clothes had all been a bluff. Emerging now was the dandy, the toast of Phi Beta Kappa, the sharp dresser, the man who could impress Ava Gardner in the flash of ice-cream-colored linen . . . and he was deadly serious. The inhabitants of the club car were transfixed. Stunned into silence, they could not believe the performance. I did my best to look appreciative, choking back the words, "God almighty, Howard, which trunk did you dig that out from?"

Thank God for the champagne. Howard chanced a glass and I drank the rest, which made me glow and beam at Howard as if I knew intuitively that he'd spent at least a week selecting this elegant outfit at Brooks Brothers. By the time we puffed into San Francisco the next day, Howard was looking as if he'd just won an Oscar.

Our hotel, the Fairmount, sat magnificently on the top of Nob Hill, and our suite was glorious.

I say *our* suite because Howard had allotted himself just a

small room next door to my magnificent drawing room, bedroom, and bathroom. There was however, a connecting door,
which I immediately locked to make certain there weren't going
to be any misunderstandings, whether Howard was sad-faced or
not.

More champagne was waiting in the drawing room, this time
in a silver bucket, thank God. But now Howard was in a hurry.
"Let's go shopping!" he said with a laugh and the knowing look
that a husband gives his wife when she knows this is an opportunity not to be missed. Trouble was, I must be one of the few
women in the world who could miss shopping without a single
regret. "Why don't we have cocktails, drink some more champagne, have a bath, think about dinner?" I said.

"Shopping first," replied Howard adamantly. "The rest is all
arranged."

A taxi was waiting and we were driven off to the town's best
department store. I didn't know a thing about San Francisco
shopping, but the place was huge, holding all the goodies in the
universe. We got out and Howard said, "Now, I want you to go
in there and buy whatever you want. I'll come back and pay for
it. Whatever you want—remember that."

On later reflection I suppose I should have come out bearing a
sable coat over one arm and wearing a diamond bracelet on each
wrist, or, if I was modest, at least a new toothbrush, as the offer
from the "richest-man-in-the-world" was plainly genuine. But all
I did was wander miserably around the store. I remember they
had some wonderful jade, which was fantastically expensive.
Now, I love jade, and occasionally these days I think: Why, oh,
why didn't I do as I was told? But I wasn't feeling that way then.

Naturally, no sign of Howard, and I got so bored in the store I
went and waited for him outside. I probably waited for forty-five
minutes, maybe an hour, and suddenly there comes Howard
walking down the street carrying—oh, God help me—another
white cardboard box. If I'd known what was in it I might have
dropped dead!

Back at the hotel I dressed for dinner in my chic cocktail dress,
not knowing quite where we were going because Howard was
being cagey about his plans. Knowing him, I knew we were just
as likely to end up in some greasy spoon where he could eat his
eternal steak and peas followed by ice cream and caramel sauce.

And my expectations were not raised when I saw that Howard had abandoned the vanilla suit for the original dark blue shiny one. But I was wrong. Before we left, he presented me with an exquisitely made gold ring set with sapphires, and for dinner and dancing we went to a wonderful restaurant with a marvelous band. Howard and I were on the floor within seconds, and Mr. Bear-Hugger was holding me so tight that I sometimes wondered if my feet were even managing to touch the floor.

More booze, a lot of laughter, and then on to a cabaret club that was totally unlike anything I'd ever been in with Howard before. This was a gay club, and though usually with Howard we were tucked away in back, hidden from everybody's eyes, now we had seats in the front row. The show was hilarious: all these drag queens in wigs and gowns, lipsticked and mascaraed, a lot of them looking like Dracula's mother, told absolutely out-rageous jokes. It was so funny I was falling out of my seat, and Howard was laughing, too.

It was very late when we left. In the hotel we were alone in the elevator except for the piles of Sunday newspapers awaiting dis-tribution later that morning. Casually I picked up the section with the funnies. I was smiling at them even as Howard was un-locking the door of our suite.

There was another bottle of champagne chilling in the ice bucket, even a bottle in my bedroom awaiting attention if neces-sary.

But the evening was over as far as I was concerned. I'd had a gorgeous time and now I sat myself down to laugh at the funnies. I didn't notice that Howard was growing colder by the minute.

Now—years later—I can understand his feelings. He had done his best, thrown caution to the winds, exhibited this brand-new free-wheeling, devil-may-care Howard, the snappy dresser, the champagne drinker, the dancer, the man who could show a girl like me a really good time. "I'm going to please this girl if it kills me." If only he could have understood that I'm so much simpler to please than that. *Now,* I can understand. The perfect woman of Howard's dreams should have been falling into his arms at that moment.

Howard opened a bottle—the pop didn't even disturb me— and came across to me with a glass. I said, "No, thank you," and chuckled at some dumb item I was reading.

Howard took the glass away, and came back and stood over me. Then, suddenly, he swooped down, violently tore the paper out of my hand, and threw it on the floor.

I couldn't believe it. I was outraged. A marvelous night like this and he had to spoil it with one rude, dramatic gesture. I kicked off my shoe so hard it left an imprint on the ceiling.

No screams of anger from me either. I was up and into my bedroom within three seconds. Door shut, bang! Door locked, click! Check that the connecting door between rooms is locked and bolted. Good! I'm sure if I'd had a hammer and nails close at hand I'd have nailed up the windows.

Then I sat on the bed. Totally miserable. What was the matter with the man? What had I done wrong? And now what was I going to do? How was I going to get out of there? I wanted to go home. I wanted to be safe in my little apartment in Westwood. What had started so well had turned into a terrible, terrible night. Even when I pried open the champagne to see if that would help, it didn't.

I must have fallen asleep, for I was awakened eventually by a knocking on the door and a voice calling, "It's Bappie, it's Bappie. Open up."

Bappie? I let her in and asked, "How the hell did you get from L.A. to San Francisco so quick?"

"Howard rang me at dawn. Said there was a private plane waiting for me at the airport, that I had to catch it—it was urgent."

I told her, "What's urgent is getting me back to L.A."

Bappie led me back to the stupendous bed, propped me up against the silken pillows, patted my hand, and tried to calm me down. I could tell she was very excited about something. "He gave you a gold ring last night?"

"Here it is. Give it back. He wants it back, I expect."

"Ava, are you out of your mind?"

I glared. She'd come all the way from Wilshire Boulevard to tell me I was out of *my* mind? Yes, I was out of my mind to trust Howard Hughes. "He's humiliated me . . ." I began.

Bappie cut me off. "Ava, do you know what he's got in a card-board box in there?"

"I couldn't care less."

Bappie's eyes and voice were bright with excitement. "It's full of the most wonderful jewelry I've ever seen. A million dollars' worth. He bought it yesterday from Tiffany's or somewhere."

I thought, so that's what he was doing when he left me marooned in that store.

Bappie was practically drooling. "I've been talking to him for an hour. He's desperate. He's shown me some of the pieces. I've just held in my hand a brooch—solid gold, encrusted with diamonds, emeralds, and rubies . . . God almighty, Ava, in all my life, nowhere have I seen such jewelry. I'm going back to get you a piece to look at—"

I said, "I don't want to see his goddamn jewelry, I want to go home."

"Ava, you can't. Don't you understand this is his way of getting engaged? For a whole seven days he is going to give you a wonderful piece of jewelry before breakfast, before lunch, and before dinner, each getting more and more beautiful and more and more valuable. That gold ring last night was the first gift. Now, shall I tell him you're sorry?"

"Sorry!" I yelled. "Tell him he can take the whole damned lot and stick it up his ass!"

"Well, I'll say you're upset."

"Upset!" My dignity had been insulted and my voice was loud. "Tell him I never want to see him again as long as I live. Do you know what he did? I was humiliated . . . I was frightened . . . I was . . ."

What else had he done? I couldn't think.

"All he did was knock a silly newspaper out of your hand." Bappie was plainly on his side. "Is that so dreadful when he was about to tell you of the wonderful surprise he had in store for you? Think about it. I'll go back and talk to him. He's upset, even if you're not."

Out she trotted across the drawing room, down the corridor and round to Howard's tiny garret. As far as I was concerned that was the only line of communication open between me and the enemy. And this went on not for minutes but for hours. Poor Bappie was acting as a Western Union messenger, shuttling between bedroom, drawing room, corridor, Howard's garret, and back again. Howard surrendered. He was willing to compromise, apologize, start over again as if nothing had happened. Let the magic week continue—and the gifts be showered. According to

Bappie's breathless testimony, there were twenty-eight pieces of glorious jewelry in that box. "God almighty, Ava, I've just held a gold bracelet in my hand studded with diamonds that weighs a ton. Not three pieces a day . . . four! One before breakfast, lunch, and dinner and 'one before she goes to sleep.' Isn't that sweet? 'One before she goes to sleep.'"

"With him around I'll never go to sleep. I've had no sleep all night. I've been laughed at, hurt, and humiliated. You weren't there when he came in in that goddamn ice-cream suit. Go in and tell him that. No, not about the suit, about the humiliation."

Poor Bappie, she must have made twenty journeys. Like most normal, well-adjusted women, she loved jewelry, and most women would have given their souls for some of that stuff. I admit it would have kept me for the rest of my life. But at that moment, with my temper aroused, I just didn't care. I knew exactly what I wanted and what I didn't, and what I did not want was Howard. My final ultimatum was: "And if he thinks I'm going back in that lousy train, he's got another think coming. If he can spend a fortune flying you here in a private plane, he can spend another fortune flying us back again."

And he did.

All I wanted to do was go home. I didn't want any of those gems or any part of Howard, and I didn't want any more of San Francisco, no matter how romantic it might be. Maybe I was a fool, but never mind, that was the way I was. I wanted to be in love, not bought for a damn box of jewelry.

Howard, however, saw things differently. I used to say that he met every train, plane, and bus that passed through L.A., picked out the prettiest ladies, put them under contract, and squirreled them away in a house somewhere. Even MGM wasn't as single-minded as Howard. He generally had five women at a time stashed away in various corners of the city. As it turned out, many of these girls never even met Howard—they were just part of the general turnover. After all, even Casanova or the Sultan of Zanzibar might have found keeping five women happy a tiring occupation. And Howard was a very busy man besides, producing movies and airplanes and who knows what else. So I think a lot of his affairs took place primarily in his mind: his sexual ambitions were always greater than his prowess.

It was through Charlie Guest that I found out so much about

Howard's women. He was one of Howard's "associates" for years, the man in charge of the housing situation for the young ladies. Charlie had a quiet voice, a lined face, a wry twist to his lips, and rather tired blue eyes. He was divorced and he drank too much; life had defeated him and he managed to live with that knowledge. Bappie met him and fell in love—after the antics of Larry Tarr, he must have been a rest cure. Bappie and I had moved into our first house, a small but pretty place we rented in Nichols Canyon, and Charlie moved in with us. And he played a part in an evening with Howard that set new standards, even for us.

It started late one afternoon when the phone rang. It was Johnny Meyer, Howard's aide-de-camp.

"Hi, Ava," he said cheerfully. "Howard's flying back to Los Angeles this evening, and he wants you and me to go out to the airport and meet him."

Now I had a date with Mickey that night. And I felt that Howard just couldn't call up and expect me to run out to the airport because he felt lonely on the tarmac.

"Sorry, Johnny," I answered. "I can't do that. I'm busy."

Johnny was much too clever to say, "Busy doing what?" He said only, "Howard will be a bit upset."

"Well," I said, "he'll just have to be a bit upset." Though Howard wasn't keeping me, he *was* always taking me out to dinner and dancing, not to mention paying for lessons in golf, tennis, even skeet shooting. Given all that, I realized I wasn't being very pleasant. He was playing a long waiting game for a pretty Southern belle, a fact that I understood and appreciated. But I was at no man's beck and call.

Anyway, I went out and had dinner with Mickey. He had an early call, and I was a working girl, too, so we said good night and I went home early to Nichols Canyon. I had a quick drink with Bappie and Charlie and then went upstairs to bed.

It was quite late when I was awakened by the light being switched on and there was Howard, standing in my bedroom. Bappie and Charlie must have let him in. He came to the bed and stood over me, and I could see he was very, very angry. With natural female intuition, I knew that he'd arrived silently like this, without even bothering to knock, because he thought he would catch me in bed with Mickey. No doubt Howard's network of spies had informed him that I was seeing Mickey again. And why not? I was divorced. I was a free woman. I did not belong to Howard Hughes. And now, his suspicions revealed, he was at a disadvantage and looking rather foolish. I smiled at him and said, "Why . . . Howard. Why don't you go downstairs? I'll put on a robe and join you there."

So off he went, very red-faced, and a few minutes later I joined him in the little bar. There were a couple of heavy hardwood chairs in the room, a few odds and ends on the bar, and Howard hanging around and looking as if he'd just been told he'd contracted a severe form of leprosy.

And I was still smiling a superior smile, because I hate being spied upon. Howard knew he was in the wrong, and suddenly, he completely lost his temper, pushed me back into one of the wooden chairs, held me down with one arm, and started hitting me across the face with his open hand. Baby, I saw stars. And it hurt—badly—and I could feel my face swelling and my eye closing. But most of all I felt anger, violent anger. I'd never been hit like that before in my entire life—and all because of his goddamn pride and jealousy. He walked away from me across the room, and let me tell you, I was not going to hit back, I was going to kill the bastard—stone dead! I groped around the bar for something to throw at him, the lamp, anything, and my hand closed around the handle of a large heavy bronze bell—the sort town criers use in England—and I threw it at him with all my strength. He had just half-turned back toward me when it hit him, bang, between the temple and cheek. He went over backward, with the blood pouring out. And I was right after him. He wasn't dead yet, and I was going to kill him. I grabbed a big hardwood chair—God knows how I lifted it—and lurched over to smash him to death.

All this must have made a lot of noise and alerted our elderly black maid as well as Bappie and Charlie. Because as I was poised with the chair above my head, ready to smash it down on Howard, the maid banged open the door, saw me there, and yelled, "Ava! Ava! Drop it! Drop it!" Her loud voice and the fact that she called me "Ava" instead of "Miss Gardner" stopped me dead in my tracks, and I stood back, trembling as my violent anger began to ebb away. If she hadn't rushed in, God knows what I might have done. I put the chair down and all hell broke loose. Not over me—over poor Howard lying on the floor and bleeding everywhere.

"Quick, Charlie," Bappie said. "Get an ambulance, get a doctor. Poor Howard, poor Howard!"

I said, "Fuck poor Howard," and went off to the bathroom to examine the bruises on my face, and my huge black eye. I was furious with Bappie and Charlie Guest. So Howard was Charlie's boss? I couldn't have cared less. In my terms he was just a goddamn woman beater.

Bappie outlined his injuries later. I had split his face open from temple to mouth, knocked out two of his teeth, and loosened others. I felt no remorse. In the hospital he had about five expensive doctors sewing him up and putting him back together again. All I had was our nice old black maid who fished a piece of raw steak out of the icebox and placed it over my black eye to help with the swelling.

One would have thought, one might even have been forgiven for hoping, that after that debacle Howard's interest in me would not only have waned, it would have disappeared altogether. But oh, no. In Howard's terms, he'd just lost a round, and within three or four weeks he was back in circulation, calling me up as if nothing unusual had ever happened. It was hard for Howard to take no for an answer, even when it was delivered in the shape of a heavy bronze bell to the temple. What Howard wanted, Howard was going to get. He hoped. The saga of him and me was going to be one hell of a long running serial.

NINE

I met Seymour Nebenzal one night in 1946 when I was dancing at the Mocambo Club. Dim lights and soft music. Smoke in the air and smart-looking people. My companion was Frances Heflin, Van Heflin's wife, a gorgeous redheaded Texan with a beautiful body and what they call a great lust for life. Like me, she loved late nights, clubs, and anyplace you could dance. Frances would have loved to be in movies but nobody asked her and she didn't push.

Seymour Nebenzal was a smart German producer working for United Artists. He told us that in the first breath, not that it was any big deal. Hell, in those days Hollywood was awash with smart European film men who'd escaped from Nazi Europe with the hope that our streets were paved with gold.

Short, dark, and intense, albeit a bit pudgy, with thick horn-rimmed glasses that magnified his dark eyes, Nebenzal was a convincing talker. He told me he'd purchased the rights to a best-selling novel called *Whistle Stop* by Maritta Wolff. Because it dealt with prostitution, not to mention brother-sister incest, *Whistle Stop* had been quite a hot item a few years back, even making it onto a list the Hays office kept of books that absolutely positively could not be filmed.

But Nebenzal had a way around that. He'd keep the title, and the notoriety that went with it, but he'd hired a man named Philip Yordan to totally rewrite the story so that any relation between it and the original book was purely coincidental. Mary, the female lead, still returns to a small Midwestern town after two years in Chicago swathed in mink, but the furs are now vaguely described as (ha-ha) "presents" and the lady no longer has a brother.

For some reason I could never figure out, Mary is in love with Kenny, a loutish type who considers drinking, card playing, and womanizing a full-time career, and is eager to turn him into an honest character. George Raft, who no one had ever accused of serious acting, was to play Kenny in his usual cigar-store Indian style, and Nebenzal wanted me to play the lady with the shady past.

In truth, Nebenzal was just being polite in talking to me at all. Or maybe he wanted to do his own personal screen test. Because the facts were that MGM told me what roles I played and when and where I played them. And what Nebenzal didn't tell me was that he'd already sounded out Metro, who, not surprisingly, were not unhappy with idea of renting out their now two-hundred-dollar-a-week starlet for the far larger lump sum of five thousand dollars.

A Frenchman, Leonide Moguy, whose command of English was negligible, directed the film. He was a dear man whom I liked very much, and although everybody in the film business rated it as a piece of rubbish—a verdict I had to agree with—I enjoyed it mainly because George Raft, great actor or not, was such fun.

I had seen George Raft, with his lovely, slinky hair, playing dark, debonair, and dangerous film roles since I was about eight years old. In my terms he had now matured into a father figure. In George's terms, not so. He was my lover in the film, and naturally he thought it would be a good idea if he continued that role outside the studio. I think George was always teasing a bit, too. We went dancing on a couple of occasions—and George danced like a dream—and though there was always a small wrestling match when he dropped me off, our relationship remained stable.

"Ava, you're a grown woman now, and this should be our great romantic love affair."

"George, we're in your front seat, not on the set. You don't drink, you don't smoke, you're a serious Catholic, and married! Plus you're old enough to be my father!"

"My thoughts aren't very fatherly."

"You've made that clear, George, but all I can say is I love dancing with you, and I hope you take me dancing again very soon."

A quick peck on the cheek, and as I was a very agile girl, I was out of the car. George took it all with a smile, and we stayed wonderful, laughing friends. I've read all that stuff in the papers about how George was supposed to be fronting for a Mafia gang. I've heard that sort of nonsense about a lot of people in my time. In my terms, the only way you *know* people is the way *you* know them. And I know that in those days, George was one of the sweetest, nicest men I've ever met. And he made *Whistle Stop* worthwhile.

Despite its numerous shortcomings, including a bogus happy ending that one critic accurately noted was "so patently phony and out of keeping with the melodrama that has gone before, it probably will send audiences out on a laugh," *Whistle Stop* was my first leading role and as such finally did get me noticed. After years as an MGM china doll, I had now broken the mold and, though I didn't know it, I was about to form a new one.

The postwar boom was at its height in 1946, and both the movie business in general and MGM in particular marked that as the most profitable year in their entire history. Nobody dreamed that they'd never see profits like that again, and when I was loaned out again later that year, this time to Universal for something called *The Killers,* I didn't dream either that that picture would forever change my career in movies.

The Killers was the first of three pictures I made based on Ernest Hemingway's writings, a happy situation that eventually led to Papa and I becoming good chums. He always considered *The Killers* the best of all the many films his work inspired, and after Mark Hellinger, the producer, gave him a print of his own, he'd invariably pull out a projector and show it to guests at Finca Vigía, his place in Cuba. Of course, he'd usually fall asleep after the first reel, which made sense, because that first reel was the only part of the movie that was really taken from what he wrote.

Like *The Snows of Kilimanjaro* years later, *The Killers* came from one of Papa's short stories. It was a *very* short story about two big lugs, Max and Al, who come into a small-town lunchroom and announce that as a favor to a friend they're going to kill a Swede named Ole Andreson as soon as he comes in for dinner. The Swede never shows, the killers leave, and Nick Adams (Papa as a boy) goes to warn the Swede. He, however, says he's tired of running and refuses to leave town. End of story.

Which left the filmmakers with a number of problems. Even if they filmed the story as written, which they pretty much did, even using a lot of Papa's dialogue just the way he wrote it, they still had about an hour and a half of screen time to fill and a lot of problems to solve. First of all, they had to get the Swede killed, something the story neglected to do, and then they had to figure out the reason why someone had wanted him killed, the reason why he'd refused to run, and a way for the audience to find all those reasons out.

The screenwriters—Anthony Veiller, credited, and John Huston, uncredited—were up to the job. They created the role of Riordan, a tough insurance investigator, who digs into the murdered man's past and uncovers his story, which the audience sees through a series of flashbacks. Turns out that the Swede was once a promising boxer until he caught a glimpse of a swell-looking babe named Kitty Collins wearing a drop-dead black dress and singing "The More I Know of Love, the Less I Know" in a husky, inviting voice.

Intoxicated by Kitty's beauty, the Swede takes a rap for her, goes to prison and, still smitten when he comes out, joins her in a gang plotting a payroll robbery. Thinking Kitty loves him, he doublecrosses the gang, but Kitty has a triplecross up her sleeve. By the time she says, "I'm poison to myself and everyone around me," there's practically no one left alive to give her an argument.

Mark Hellinger had cast Edmond O'Brien as Riordan, and for the Swede he went with an actor who'd never been on screen before, a young man named Burt Lancaster. And having seen *Whistle Stop*, he wanted me to play the deadly Kitty. I was very excited at the opportunity. I liked the odd but interesting twists of Kitty's character, the lack of emotional security she felt in her early years, and the way this contributed to what she turned into later. But there was a problem. Hellinger's deal was with Universal, and it looked for a while that Metro would refuse to lend me out for the picture.

Which quite frankly surprised me, because, given Mr. Mayer's idea that it was family-oriented, happily-ever-after Lassie and Andy Hardy movies that attracted customers to the box office, the studio's interest in my movie career had been minimal. And, sure enough, once enough money had been waved in Metro's face, I got the job.

I liked Mark Hellinger at once, because I could tell he saw me as an actress, not a sexpot. He trusted me from the beginning and I trusted him. He even talked me into relaxing enough so I could sing that sensual song in my own voice. And he gave me a feeling of responsibility about being a movie star that I'd never for a moment felt before. Until I played Kitty Collins, I'd never worked very hard in pictures, never taken my career very seriously. I felt no burning ambition to become a real actress. I was just a girl who was lucky enough to have a job in pictures. Playing Kitty changed that, showed me what it meant to try to act, and made me feel that I might have a little talent in that area after all.

Director Robert Siodmak was equally helpful, but in a different way. A German-born director who was giving Alfred Hitchcock a run for his money with suspenseful films like *Phantom Lady* and *The Spiral Staircase,* he was an expert at this kind of dark drama, filling the screen with deep, troubling shadows and knowing just how he wanted me to look.

One day early in the filming, I saw him and his cameraman looking at me very carefully. "What is that stuff all over your face, please?" he said in his typically fractured English.

"Regulation MGM makeup."

"This is not MGM. Will you please go away and wash it all off, please."

I did as I was told, and quite happily, in fact. My regulation face was gone for good.

Siodmak also helped me with my toughest scene, the one at the end of the movie where I scream, "Tell them I don't know anything. Save me," over and over again to my dying partner in crime. Siodmak made me play that scene so many times that I truly became hysterical and gave a more convincing performance than I thought I had in me.

One thing I especially liked about filming *The Killers* was that Burt and Eddie and the rest of us were in the early stages of our careers, fresh kids enjoying life. Burt had all the confidence in the world. He'd never been in a movie before, but he seemed competent enough to take the whole thing over, and if Robert hadn't been such a strong director, he might have.

The publicity department set up a few beach scenes as gimmicks to promote the movie, and I'll never forget giving Burt piggybacks on *my* back instead of the other way around. But he was such a marvelous athlete he seemed able to make himself pounds lighter. Or maybe it was all those screams of laughter that made everything seem so easy. All I know is that whenever I hear the "dum-de-dum-dum" *Dragnet* theme, which was originally part of the score Miklos Rosza wrote for *The Killers,* it's those moments I remember.

Although some critics sniffed and one called *The Killers* "merely sensational, designed for no other purpose than to jangle emotions and nerves," most of the reviews were excellent, and for the first time in my life, I got some especially good notices as well. A lot of people have told me through the years that it was *The Killers* that set me on the road to stardom, that defined my image as the slinky sexpot in the low-cut dress, leaning against a piano and setting the world on fire. Maybe it did, maybe it didn't, but at the time it was all happening, I couldn't have cared less. And the reason was simple: I'd fallen in love.

TEN

"**A**va," Frances Heflin said in her quiet, dreamy way, "this is Artie Shaw. He's just come back from the war. You've heard of Artie and his music. I thought you two might get along."

I caught the edge of mischief in her smile. I guessed that she and Artie had had a little flirt going, but what the hell—that was in the past. And here was Artie, grinning down at me. Oh, my God, I thought, what a beautiful man! Artie was handsome, bronzed, very sure of himself, and he never stopped talking. It was a way of life with him. Artie could go on about every subject in the world, and for that matter, a few that were outside it as well. But he was full of such warmth and charm that I fell in love with him, just like *that*. That's the way it always is with me, immediate or never.

I suppose Artie was the first intelligent, intellectual male I'd ever met, and he bowled me over. He was born in New York in 1910, the child of immigrants, and grew up in the city's crowded tenements without the benefit of much formal education. He didn't have much money either, but he did have a compelling determination to succeed, not only as a musician but as an intelligent, creative, pugnacious human being. In every area of knowledge, Artie was thoroughly—and relentlessly—self-educated.

As a musician, Artie was a genius, brilliant at everything he touched—playing, composing, conducting. He was always experimenting, always looking at new forms of musical expression. At age fifteen, he was a professional. Ten years later, at a New York swing concert, he was playing one of his own compositions accompanied by a string quartet, the first time that had been done in jazz. By 1937, he'd formed his own big band, and in 1938 he became internationally famous with his version of Cole Porter's "Begin the Beguine." And though it sounds almost unbelievable, he was the first jazz orchestra leader to include black musicians and black vocalists (including Billie Holiday) in his band.

I'd grown up in the big-band era, adoring every sound the great ones made, but Artie, strangely enough, never seemed to care very much for his own profession. He was always giving it up to spend months in Mexico or go into "retreat" somewhere. But when he was on the job he was a great organizer and disciplinarian. No musician in his band could arrive late, or half-pissed, or smoking pot. They had to play, and play right. His recording sessions were absolute perfection, and they had to be. In those days of 78s, there was no way of splitting notes and doing all the funny things they do now with tape. It had to be three minutes of perfection: piano, percussion, violins, trumpets, saxes, trombones, clarinets—and, oh, God, Artie was such an artist on a clarinet.

Anyhow, Artie and I started going out from that very first night of our meeting. Not occasionally. Every night. I remember that first time he took me to Lucy's, a little Italian restaurant across from RKO studios. Small, intimate, piped in music, candlelight, and wine, that sort of place. I was in a great glow about the whole thing, and Artie looked across at me, and said, "Ava, I think that physically, emotionally, and mentally you are the most perfect woman I've ever met." His eyes never moved from mine as he went on, "And what's more, I'd marry you tonight, except for the fact that I've married too many wives already."

I mean, I do love the man, but that moment was pure Artie. He didn't dream of saying, or implying, that he was asking *me* to marry *him*. Artie took it for granted that everyone was panting to marry Artie Shaw. And I guess that set the tone of our scenario from then onward. We spent our first eight months or so dining, dancing, and talking our heads off. No funny business. Hands off. Then we decided that if we were going to have an affair we'd better make it a real one, so I moved to Artie's huge mock-Tudor house on Bedford Drive in Beverly Hills. He had very good taste, and had filled it with expensive Chippendale and Sheraton furniture. He'd never gotten around to furnishing the dining room, though: his last divorce had cropped up just as he was thinking about it.

I adored my time with Artie before we got married. We traveled all over California and went to Chicago and New York, with Artie's band playing one-night stands while I sat backstage, sipping bourbon, listening to the music, and having a ball. It was during this period, however, that Artie's penchant for self-improvement—*mine,* not his—first surfaced and nearly frightened me to death.

"Avala," he said one day, tacking his usual endearing Yiddish tag onto my name, "I want you to sing with the band." Now I've already described how my heart was half-broken at age sixteen by that band leader who I never heard from again. This should have been my great opportunity for triumph and revenge. But I didn't see it that way. I was just too frightened.

"No need for that," Artie said, confident as ever. "We'll rehearse as long as you want. I'll get you a singing coach, and a backup group that's so good nobody will even hear you. Your voice is good, you can learn, and you'll look absolutely gorgeous, the most beautiful songbird in the business."

"Artie," I said, putting my foot down, "you're wrong. I'll make mistakes because I'm scared." And I absolutely refused to go on with it. Which was a pity. It would have been the thrill of my life, but I just could not do it.

Artie and I were married on October 17, 1945, he for the third time, me for the second. Frances Heflin, of course, was my bridesmaid and Art Craft, one of Artie's oldest friends, was the best man. I wore a blue tailored suit and a corsage of orchids, not that different from the outfit I wore when I'd married Mickey not so long before.

Artie and I honeymooned at Lake Tahoe for a week. We had terrible fights but also a lot of romance. Because one thing is certain: Artie and I never had any quarrels in bed. If only everything else about the marriage had been as wonderful and easy as that.

Marriage, if anything, increased Artie's determination to improve me, something he had been set on doing from the first moment we met. I didn't mind at first, but unfortunately Artie had no intention of being subtle about the business. He had gotten his education the hard way and, worse luck for me, he thought the hard way was the only one worth pursuing.

The world Artie introduced me to, the world of music, art, books, politics, and psychology, was more than a bit beyond my experience, and unfortunately it showed. I'll never forget the time I was sitting at his knee on the floor, a position, I might add, Artie thought all women should adopt. "You know, Ava," he said to me in a quiet, considerate voice, "I don't think I would ever have fallen in love with you if you weren't so beautiful." Though he had the good sense not to add, "Too bad I didn't know you were just a dumb broad," that implication was clear to me, and it wasn't the sort of remark guaranteed to instill confidence in a young lady.

If I could ever be born again, an education is what I'd want. My life would have been so different if I'd had one. You don't know what it's like to be as young as I was then and know you're uneducated, to be afraid to talk to people because you're afraid even the questions you ask will be stupid. My shame at my ignorance had even caused me to lie to Artie about my age when we first met. I thought if I shaved a year off, it would make it easier for him to accept me as I was.

When Artie and I began going together, *Gone With the Wind* was still the only book I'd ever read. Artie vowed to change all that, deluging me with works by Sinclair Lewis, Dostoyevsky, Thomas Mann. I read them all, or tried to. I'll never forget *The Magic Mountain;* I thought I'd never finish that damn book. Once, when we were in Chicago, *Forever Amber* had just come out, so I bought a copy. He saw me with it and said, "If I'm in charge of your education, you're not going to read rubbish like that," and threw it across the room.

Artie had been released early from the navy after an illness in which exhaustion from a tour through the Pacific theater had combined with depression with devastating results. Psychoanalysis had helped him enormously, so much so that when I listened to Artie's soliloquies on the subject, he practically convinced me that he'd invented the damn system himself. Understanding himself, self-exploration, was the basic drive in Artie's life, and he seemed to live only for his sessions with May Romm, his analyst. In fact, Freud's *The Interpretation of Dreams* was the first book he ever gave me—pretty tough going for the average Atlantic Christian College student.

May Romm struck me only as a rather skinny old lady, but since she was high on Artie's list of priorities, I made her high on mine. We even went to one of her Christmas parties, which was filled almost entirely with psychiatrists, which I thought rather strange given that Freud had said that doctors and patients shouldn't mix socially. I felt about as much at home at that party as a chicken at a fox convention. Artie was immediately off somewhere else holding the floor on some minor topic that would revolutionize the solar system, so I crept into a corner and got into conversation with a nice little man who seemed to be able to put up with me.

He was quietly dressed, a studious sort of character, looking more like a stockbroker. But, naturally, he was a psychiatrist, and, naturally, if I was to get even remotely into a discussion with him, the only thing I could discuss was my own symptoms.

"You know," I said, "ever since I was a child, when I am faced with any sort of emotional problem I seem to get this sort of stomach cramp."

Now I know that this is not your standard cocktail party chatter. But my new conversationalist brightened immediately.

"Really," he said. "What sort of childhood did you have?"

I gave him a short sharp fifty seconds on life in the tobacco fields. It didn't sound half good enough to me. No brutal father. No black dreams. No screams in the night. I thought he'd say, "How interesting," and go in search of another dry martini. But he didn't. He looked thoughtful and said, "Perhaps you'd better come and see me in my professional capacity." His office was on Bedford Drive, only a short distance from where we lived. I said I would make an appointment, and I did. What the good doctor didn't know was that I had my own secret and special reason for making that appointment, something I'd been considering for quite a long time, certainly ever since I met Artie.

In the quiet, reassuring confines of his office, I took a deep breath and said, "Doctor, I think I should have an IQ test."

There was a long pause and he said, "You don't need an IQ test."

I didn't pause. I said, "Oh, yes, I do."

He said, "You are so sure now that things aren't quite right that you will without a doubt unconsciously score a low mark."

I said, "Doctor, I *would* like a test."

He said, "I don't think it's a wise idea."

I thought: He's got the same doubts that I do; and I repeated, "Doctor, I *would* like a test."

So, finally, he set up an appointment with another doctor who did this sort of thing. It took a hell of a long time, hours, because once I got started I had to have every damn test known to man.

I was summoned to his consulting room for the big news.

"Well," he began. "You have an extremely high IQ." And then he went on to explain that I had never really used, stretched, or extended the brain that God, plus Mama, Papa and a healthy upbringing, had endowed me with. I had never needed to use the millions of brain cells that most human beings normally possess, quite a common occurrence. That not only reassured me; it gave me a certain impetus.

So now I was into analysis and I found it a great help. I still do. When I get depressed or into a situation that is difficult, I can reason myself out of it, make sense of it, know what the hell's going on in my life at a particular juncture. I can get *through* a depression, not fall into it and never come out.

With the confidence of that IQ test behind me, I decided to do something about Artie's constant carping about my lack of education: I looked into taking classes at my local institution of higher learning, UCLA.

I had to be careful about this. Enrolling and physically attending classes might have put a strain on Metro's publicity implications that all its starlets were ladies of the highest intelligence and accomplishments. So I took extension courses at home, signing up for English literature and economics.

Artie grunted noncommittally, but I really studied and did well. I can still remember showing my report card to everyone on the set of *The Killers* and bragging about my B-pluses. The company didn't know whether to laugh or cry. I guess most people making pictures are more satisfied with their level of education, no matter what it is, than I was.

And then, of course, there was chess. Artie liked the game, and one day he said to me, "Avala, why don't you learn to play chess? We could have a game occasionally."

I said I'd be happy to try, and he offered to find someone to give me lessons. But Artie, being Artie, didn't arrange for any old teacher; he got hold of a Russian grandmaster to introduce me to the game. Stepan Vronsky was, I guess, in his sixties, with thick gray hair and blue eyes. He'd come to the house three or four times a week, we'd sit together at a little chessboard in the living room and he'd show me what it was all about. After I learned the basics, we'd play games together, and he'd show me all kinds of moves and countermoves. Sometimes he'd throw in a trick move to see if I could block it, and then explain how I should have counterattacked. Vronsky chuckled a lot, and seemed to enjoy the process.

Finally the day came when Artie casually asked, "How about a game?"

"Of course, Artie," I replied.

We sat down at the little table. We played for perhaps fifteen or twenty minutes. We exchanged several pieces. Then, very quietly, I said, "Checkmate." I'd won.

Artie never played chess with me again.

Now I can look back and understand that I was not Artie's wife in any real sense of the word, only one of his pretty possessions. I was charming as a girlfriend, but as a wife I became a hindrance. Artie's natural tendency to be impatient and irascible was intensified where I was concerned, and the increasingly hostile way he put me down both at home and at parties wore my nerves to shreds.

If I was quiet when friends were around he would say, "Why don't you say something? Don't you have anything to add to the conversation?" And if I did open my mouth he'd just say, "Shut up." His open contempt in front of our friends was particularly painful. He disregarded my smallest wish and humiliated me every chance he got, until I was barely able to hold back my tears. I worshiped the man, but that period was one of the worst I ever endured.

It all came to a head very late one night. Artie and I had been drinking old-fashioneds made with Wild Turkey bourbon, a fairly potent drink. He began needling me and I just couldn't take it anymore; I was at the point of hysteria. So I ran out of the house, leapt into the car, and headed off into the night.

I went out of our driveway peeling rubber so loudly that any cop could have heard it a mile away. And, sure enough, I was spotted by a police patrol before I'd covered three hundred yards. That didn't bother me in the slightest, because I knew where I was going, and I knew no one was going to stop me. I was going to the Van Heflins', where I knew I would be sane and safe and to hell with the cops.

It wasn't a reasonable way of thinking, but then I wasn't in a reasonable mood.

So there I was cutting corners and weaving across roads in that expensive neighborhood, engine roaring, police car on my tail, lights flashing and siren screaming, like a maniac from one of Hollywood's early thrillers. I was gonna reach the Van Heflins' or die in the attempt—which didn't seem that unlikely.

I screeched to a halt outside the house. I grabbed the door handle to make my escape, but I wasn't quick enough. Two young cops, each with a big revolver in his hand, appeared on either side. One pushed the barrel within four inches of my head and growled, "Now where d'you think you're going in such a hurry?" Which was reasonable, because I must have been a drug addict or a lunatic as far as he was concerned. And I went on behaving like one.

I pushed the gun barrel aside as if I were flicking away a fly, and snapped, "How dare you!" Which was a silly thing to do because he might have blown my head off, but maybe he was young and romantic. I pushed past him and made a rush for Heflins' door, with the other cop yelling, "Hey, Miss, you've got to walk a straight line," but he was too late. Van must have heard the noise of my arrival because he opened the door, and I was through it and slamming it shut behind me before he could utter a sound.

"God," I gasped, "the police are after me outside!" It was almost morning by now, Van was fully dressed and I saw he was drinking that awful stuff that I hate—Fernet Branca—which is suppose to cure hangovers. I must say he reacted like a champ. He shoved the full glass into my hand and said, "For Christ's sake, drink that." As it went down he popped a sweet-tasting pill into my mouth, grinned, and said, "Now, let's go outside and face them."

The two young cops hadn't even had time to knock, but they were still there, looking very grim-faced.

I'm sure it was Van who spoke first, saying something like, "Why, officers, I'm sure we can work this thing out. My young friend here was just in a hurry to pay us a visit."

The two young cops were certainly aware of that; they must have had at least a dozen traffic violations to bring me in on, not to mention "resisting arrest" and interfering with an officer in the line of duty—which could have been shooting me! But one thought was uppermost in their minds: I was drunk. In those days there were no breathalyzers; you walked a straight line. I really don't know why they just didn't handcuff me and take me straight to jail. But they didn't. They just went on looking grim and saying, "Now, Miss, will you please walk a straight line."

"Of course," I said, and I hope I gave them a sweet smile.

One thing about me, and it's been a gift straight from heaven, or maybe it's from the other place, is that no matter how drunk I get, I never stumble, never weave, and I never slur my speech, qualities I put down to a good Irish-Scottish capacity to hold strong drink. This time, however, with the dawn breaking and the Fernet Branca in my stomach, I was as sober as one of the little birds chirping in the palm fronds. And I guarantee I walked the straightest line possible, far better than the two cops could have done. And by this time I wasn't very nice to them either, accusing them of "frightening me to death and making me go faster than usual with all those lights flashing and sirens sounding. I could have had a heart attack."

I think Van was more placatory, whispering things about "young actress, naturally highly strung, having trouble with her husband, confused at this time in the morning, certainly never touches alcohol—ever. No harm done, is there, officer? . . . grateful for your cooperation."

The young officers were still grim-faced but they touched their hats and drove off. I went in and had a large something with Van, who abandoned Fernet Branca for the real thing and listened in fatherly fashion to my hesitant confession about life with Artie.

I should have had my first clue that Artie was thinking about ending our marriage when he suddenly decided he would sell the palatial Bedford Drive house and move us to a much inferior place in the San Fernando Valley. The thought of having to divide the property between us, as California law mandated, must have sent cold shivers down his back. I didn't like the house in the Valley; I thought it was cheap and ratty. I was so upset with all of this that I couldn't eat; I was just skin and bones; so I decided to literally save my life as well as my peace of mind by finding somewhere else to live.

I moved in with Minna Wallis, sister of Hal Wallis, the producer, and I was living there when I got a call from Artie. He said he was in his office in Beverly Hills and asked if I could come over as he had something important to tell me. Chivalry was not in Artie's makeup, and the thought that it might have been more gentlemanly for him to come to me did not cross his mind. But to hell with all that. I was thrilled by the message. Maybe this was the beginning of a reconciliation. Because in spite of all the troubles and traumas, I still loved Artie dearly. Maybe we could make it all work again.

So I dressed up real pretty, and went across to his office and sat down in a chair that, naturally, Artie did not pull out for me. And I waited while he smiled and looked across at me with his dark eyes and did not even think of saying how nice I looked. He just quietly went about knocking the bottom out of my world when he said, "Would you object if I went off to Mexico and got a quick divorce?"

There were all my hopes piled on the floor, as I heard my voice coming out my mouth saying.

"Sure . . . fine."

So that was it. He got our divorce for us, and married, of all people, Kathleen Winsor, the woman who'd written *Forever Amber*. I paid for my California divorce and asked for nothing in settlement. We'd been married for one year and one week.

One thing I will say, given all the problems we ended up having, was thank God we didn't have a child as I'd wanted to. But I have to admit I still have thoughts about that, because I know we could have produced a fabulous baby.

Still and all, Artie was one of the deep hurts of my life. I was so much in love with the man, I adored and worshiped him, and I don't think he ever really understood the damage he did by putting me down all the time. On the other hand, Artie was not the apologizing kind. To him I was sort of a pretty little pupil who was just hanging around. I was never an equal, I was never given the dignity of being a wife. Just like with Mickey, our interests were poles apart. I thought at the time that love could cure anything. I found out the hard way that it can't. You have to have more in common than mad love for a marriage to work.

Yet Artie and I remained close for years, and I can't say anything against him. He taught me to study, to think, to read. Thanks to Artie, I read *Death in the Afternoon,* which meant I had a little something to talk to Hemingway about, not to mention having a leg up on the bullfighters who entered my life. Of my three husbands, I had the most admiration for Artie. He's impossible to live with, sometimes even to be friends with, but he is a worthwhile human being, an extraordinary man.

I remember, for instance, a night in 1944. I was with Artie and his band for a one-night stand in San Diego. The audience was packed in and waiting but, for some reason, Roy Eldridge, Artie's marvelous black trumpet player, didn't show up.

Artie was furious, so much so that he was still steaming when we went out the stage door after the first set to enjoy a cigarette. And there was Roy Eldridge, sitting in the gutter, holding his trumpet and crying, the tears pouring down his cheeks. He hadn't been allowed in the building. He'd been told: "A nigger playing in a white man's band? Don't give us that crap. Get out of here, nigger, if you know what's good for you."

Artie was often testy. This time he was not testy, he was volcanic with anger. The result: Roy Eldridge was allowed into the building.

At that next set, Roy Eldridge blew his horn until the notes shimmered off the rooftops. He played a tune called "Little Jazz"—maybe Artie wrote it. In those days, when the kids really liked a number, they stopped dancing and clustered around the bandstand. This time they hemmed it in to listen to Roy's fantastic rendering. I'll never forget that occasion. Roy stood there blowing his heart out, tears streaming down his face. It was heartbreaking. I wept with him.

Dear Artie. Wherever you are I wish you well, and thanks for all the memories and the guidance. And I'll make one little wager to myself. I bet you're still in analysis up to your eyebrows.

ELEVEN

I was twenty-four years old. It is not an age when you pause to take a long and careful look at yourself. There are too many other things going on. But in passing I did do a little check.

I had now been through two marriages, each of which, in terms of actual time elapsed, had lasted barely more than a year.

I had left Mickey. Artie Shaw had discarded me. I was working hard, MGM saw to that. I was dating quite a few men but jumping into bed with none of them. I was not drinking seriously— just a few in the evening. But I guess as a twice-divorced starlet, there were a few predators around.

That's how I first met John Huston. I knew John's name because *The Killers* had been adapted from Hemingway's short story by John along with Anthony Veiller. I'd also become friends with Jules Buck, the film's assistant producer, and his wife Joyce. They knew John well and they said to me, "Poor John. He's sitting around alone and miserable in that big house out there in the San Fernando Valley. Let's go and have drinks and dinner with him. He'd love that."

Lonely and miserable my eye!

But as soon as I met John I liked what I saw. He was tall, thin, and gangly. He had a long Irish face, a quick smile, a soft voice, and a line of talk that could charm cows in from the pasture or ducks off the pond. No doubt at all where his ancestors came from.

John's place was about an hour's drive from Beverly Hills. Quite lonely. A big ranch-style house on huge grounds with a swimming pool into which you could dive from a board fixed on a veranda about twelve feet above. We had a swim and drinks around the pool; then we had a marvelous dinner and more drinks, and then we went on drinking because John was more than a great boozer, he was in the world heavyweight championship class of boozers. And you've got to remember that the standard greeting of this period, from the end of the Second World War to well into the fifties, was "Let's have a drink." No one talked about anything as tacky as alcoholism. Booze was *the* essential part of the social scene.

During this drinking session, John said, "Tell you what, fellas, what about if I try and hypnotize you lovely people? One at a time—okay?"

What no one knew at the time was that naughty John knew an awful lot about hypnotism. At the end of the war he'd been assigned by the army to make a documentary called *Let There Be Light* in some hospital on the East Coast. Through it passed hundreds of ex-soldiers still suffering from traumatic breakdowns due to their combat experiences. The doctors, psychiatrists, psychologist, and therapists found hypnosis a very useful aid. John filmed it all, and in the process he learned a lot about that unique, complex, and unusual remedial aid. He said, "What about you, Jules, for a start? Gentleman first?"

They were old friends. Army friends. They'd been together in a photographic unit in the Pacific war zone, and seen a lot of action. But Jules didn't know what John had learned in that hospital on the East Coast.

"Okay," he said, fortified by dry martinis, wine, and a lot of cognac. "How are you going to start? Shine a light in my eyes, or wave a watch on a chain . . ."

"No film tricks. No rituals—those are for charlatans. You are not under the power of the hypnotist. You cannot be forced to do things against your will. The power of hypnosis lies in the interpersonal cooperation between the patient and the hypnotist."

It was all slightly chilling. Jules was apparently an easy subject. John took him back to those days in the Pacific, the cries of wounded men in battle, the piles of casualties, the dead. Jules remembered it with clarity and related it all in a state close to hysteria, his mind unburdening itself of those memories. It was then I realized that John had a bit of a cruel streak in him, for he seemed to enjoying his mastery over Jules.

He looked at me and smiled. "Your turn?"

"You won't put me under. I'll resist."

John grinned and said, "Ava, darlin', it's not a contest. It's supposed to be a collaboration between hypnotist and hypnotized."

His voice was tranquillizing and relaxing. But I was *not* going to reveal myself as Jules had been revealed.

John smiled happily and said, "Ava, love, let's all have another drink."

(I thought I'd won. But, given how splendidly we got along through the years, I'm not sure. I strongly suspect that that crafty young man had hypnotized me after all.)

It was now getting very late—about two or three in the morning—and Jules and Joyce said, "It's too late to drive home now, and John's got plenty of spare bedrooms. You can put us up for the night, can't you, John? We'll all drive home in the morning."

"Sure," says John. "Take your choice."

So Jules and Joyce settled for a double room, and I took a smaller room some distance away. I had just removed my shoes and was thinking of undressing when—without word or knock or even a gentle tap—the door opened and John was standing there beaming at me. The situation was obvious to any lady over the age of seventeen. John was about to make a pass. But I was just as fast on my feet as he was. And as John approached, a quick twist and sidestep put me through the door and down the stairs heading for the open countryside. I'm barefoot, as usual, so he would have to run pretty fast to catch me. And by God, he really was after me! And just as fast and just as fit as I was! At top speed I circled the pool and headed out through the bushes, then started to zigzag between the trees, then came back again and headed off on a second circuit. And then, as we headed back toward the pool, I realized I had only one chance of a ladylike escape. From the first floor of the house that diving board stretched out over the pool. If I could take a header off that, John would have to realize that I was a very reluctant seductee. And a very wet one, too! I raced up the stairs, swung along the balcony, out to the board, and splosh—down I went, fully clothed and head first, into the pool.

Soaked to the skin, I scrambled out looking like a drowned something, with John roaring with laughter. But I was furious. I was not talking to him. I was getting Jules and Joyce out of their bed and into their car and we were going home—now! I think John had gone back to the bar to freshen his drink. At any rate he was standing on the veranda holding it and waving us an alcoholic good-bye as we drove into the sunrise—I must have seen more sunrises than any other actress in the history of Hollywood—with Joyce still murmuring, "Poor John. He really is very lonely, you know."

Lonely my ass! Within twenty-four hours all the Los Angeles papers carried the story of how John Huston had just rushed off to marry the actress Evelyn Keyes (who was later to become Artie Shaw's eighth wife). I guess chasing me was just his way of keeping in training.

I'd decided after the breakup with Artie to leave Bappie and Charlie Guest to their privacy and move into my own small apartment on Olympic Boulevard. And I had acquired a new friend. Mearene Jordan (everyone called her Reenie) was supposed to be my maid, but she was also as good a friend as I've ever had. She was petite and pretty, with an infectious laugh and a wonderful ability to cope with all of life's storms. We hit it off from the start and we've spent more years as close companions than I care to think about.

After my successes with both *Whistle Stop* and *The Killers,* Metro finally woke up to the fact that there might be something to be gained from my emerging as a sexy nightclub girl and cast me opposite Clark Gable as Jean Ogilvie, a (what else but) sultry singer, in *The Hucksters.* Having been in love with the man since I was that little girl in North Carolina, I was thrilled, and the icing on the cake was that Clark, who'd pushed for me for the part, actually came to our modest apartment to talk to me, a little nobody, about the role. But that was Clark: down-to-earth, informal, liking people, helping them, and all done with style. He was very sweet, and very big and masculine with lots of personality. You can say he wasn't the greatest of actors, but my God, he was more than that. He was a star.

Clark didn't really have to encourage me to play Jean Ogilvie. MGM had already marked me for it and MGM owned me body and soul. I had to get permission from Mr. Louis B. Mayer for everything I did; sometimes I felt I might have to get permission to go to the bathroom. And since *The Hucksters* was a project the studio was strongly committed to, even if I'd hated the idea I would have had to go along.

The Hucksters started life as a novel by Frederic Wakeman. A scathing attack on radio advertising, a kind of pretelevision *Network,* it spent nearly a year on the top of the national best-seller list, fully justifying the two hundred thousand dollars Metro paid for it in a prepublication sale. When Gable read the novel, he called it "filthy and not entertaining," but the studio cleaned up the sex for the screenplay, making his lady love (played by Deborah Kerr in her American debut) a war widow instead of an unfaithful wife. As for my character, she was an old flame of Clark's, sort of a bad smell if you know what I mean. I did have an amusing scene, however, when my search for romantic mood music for a home-cooked dinner with Clark was constantly interrupted by the blare of mindless commercials. Sounds familiar, doesn't it?

The man who must have had the most fun in the picture, however, was Sydney Greenstreet. He played Evan Llewellyn Evans, the tyrannical manufacturer of Beautee Soap (a character apparently based on George Washington Hill, the Lucky Strike king) who wants his product to get attention and doesn't care how it's done. "Repetition" is what he insists on in one of his juicy tirades. "By repetition, by God, I mean until the public is so irritated with it, they'll buy your brand because they bloody well can't forget it."

Sydney, however, didn't get involved in love scenes with Mr. Gable. And sometimes, I have to admit, kissing Clark with twenty-five people looking on was not the answer to a school-girl's dream. Not to mention that I'd have to be thinking about whether my lipstick would smear, how long to hold the kiss to conform to the Hays office guidelines, how I should act when I came out of the clutch, whether I was holding my head right for the camera, as well as trying to remember my dialogue. But, in truth, there were those other times, when I would be playing a scene with Clark, in his arms, perhaps, and suddenly the thought would hit me, This is Clark Gable. *This is Clark Gable!*

And my mind would be completely blown. Every line, every word, every little nuance suggested by director Jack Conway, it would all go right out of my head. But in some magical Gable way Clark would understand that, bless him. He'd lean in a bit, all those crow's feet at the corners of his eyes crinkling, his face beaming, and he'd whisper, "Hey, kid, where are we? You stuck? Let me give you a lead." He was always trying to calm me down, always telling me, "You don't see yourself as an actress and I don't see myself as an actor. That makes us even." Right.

This was a big movie for Clark in more ways than one. Not only was he in every scene but one, which meant he had to be on the set every day, but it was also his first film in eighteen months, a long break for MGM's king, which meant our set was a mecca for a horde of visitors, everyone from Henry Ford II and Sinclair Lewis to the president of the Canadian National Railways. But when it came to doing the right thing, Clark was never too busy.

Take, for instance, the nightclub scene where I stand at the piano and croon my love song, "Don't Tell Me." Even though the version the audience was going to hear had already been pre-recorded by someone else, to make the scene work I had to sing my heart out and pretend it was the real thing.

Unfortunately, when the time came to film this sequence, it was past five o'clock. All the stars had gone home, as well as all the extras who'd previously filled the nightclub tables. And Clark, I knew, walked off the set every day promptly at five. Boom!—he was gone.

So there I was, standing in an empty nightclub with a full orchestra behind me, wearing a slinky black dress and trying to be the hottest torch singer in the business, but with absolutely no one to sing to except some prop man. If there's anything more depressing than attempting to sing to an empty cabaret room, I don't know what it is.

Then, just as we were ready to start, I saw this handsome man carrying an old wooden kitchen chair onto the dance floor. He placed the chair right in front of me, reversed it and sat down with his arms folded across the back. It was Clark Gable, grinning at me to begin.

For God's sake, how could I help but adore the man? There was never anything between us—ever. He'd lost his heart, and almost the sense in his life, when Carole Lombard was killed in that plane crash. I never met Carole, but Clark told me that at times her language had the same—shall I say—forthrightness as mine. And she loved playing practical jokes, though her last one proved unexpectedly tragic. I had dinner with Clark occasionally during that time, and he told me the whole story.

As she set out on her war bond tour, Carole decided to leave a little surprise behind for Clark. So with the help of the studio makeup and costume departments, as well as a convenient tailor's dummy, she smuggled an exact replica of herself into their bedroom. Carole never came back to that bedroom, but Clark did, beside himself with grief when he heard of her death. Can you imagine his shock when he thought he saw Carole in their bed? That first agonized moment almost destroyed him. Poor Carole's joke had misfired.

When *The Hucksters* finally came out, I received some of the best notices of my career, with *Newsweek* insisting that "Ava Gardner walks off with a good portion of the footage." And *Esquire,* claiming I'd been "tough enough to be 'Miss Pig Iron of 1946' in *The Killers,*" noted that in this picture I was "refined enough to be 'Miss Stainless Steel of 1947.'" Furthermore, my performance seemed "so serene and worldly-wise that it is hard to recall her as a wife of Mickey Rooney. But maybe that's one of the quickest ways to get worldly wisdom." I wasn't about to argue with that.

In that period of my life, however, both men in my life were named Howard: Howard Hughes and Howard Duff. But the difference between them was immeasurable, and the difference in my relationship with each of was equally immense. Hughes, naturally, was on the phone to me the minute he knew that Artie and I were splitting up. With his very own security and spy system, he knew about it practically before I did. But that was Howard for you: he could be cruel and ruthless, although with me he was always gentle and concerned. His objective by now was clearly marriage, and on a couple of occasions I gave that offer a lot of careful thought. But I never loved Howard Hughes, and after two failed marriages, I wasn't going to try again until I was sure.

The other Howard was young, handsome, and athletic, with a

wonderful rich voice which he put to good use in his films and on radio. And as one of my girlfriends said about him, "Howard Duff's the kind of guy you could take home to mother and she would adore him and say how lucky her daughter was."

I met Howard in Hollywood, at a party or a nightclub, I can't remember which, and we hit it off at once. He was warm and generous, fun to be with, and it wasn't long before we were sharing the same bed. Not on a regular basis, but often enough. I didn't find out until much later that Yvonne De Carlo, a lovely girl, was his steady date at the time.

To tell the truth, though Howard said he was infatuated with me, there were things about me that drove him around the bend. Changing my mind every ten minutes, going one place and immediately deciding I wanted to be somewhere else, that was not his style. We were both night people, but Howard was very professional, and we went to bed early and *not* together when we had to work the next morning. The idea of marriage? It came up mainly from Howard. I loved him, but not deeply enough to start down that route. Let's have fun, I said. And we sure did.

MGM, trying to capitalize on whatever fame I had, used to send me off on publicity trips to various parts of the country. I would be taken to the local radio station, where in addition to the broadcast there would be reporters and photographers ready to spread the gospel of the studio's future attractions. Howard Duff came with me on several of these trips, including a particularly memorable one to San Francisco, where I'd been interviewed on radio by someone known locally as "the Walter Winchell of San Francisco."

He took Howard and me to dinner at a superb restaurant, and the conversation got around to the good—or bad—old days of San Francisco, when the gold miners and the sailors from the three-masted ships hit what was known as the Barbary Coast, storming ashore looking for—hmm—well, looking.

Immediately I wanted to know where all the fun was today. What about showing me some of it? Here I was with Howard as my escort, ready and willing to swing the night away. Get movin', fellas!

The local Walter Winchell cocked a knowing eye and said, "Well, there are some interesting places still around."

I said, "Let's go."

The local Winchell said, "Well, we could start off at undoubtedly the classiest bordello on the West Coast."

I had some idea what a bordello was, and I felt it was about time my education was improved, so I spoke right up and said, "Let's give it a try."

Who could refuse an offer like that? We all piled into a taxi and headed up toward Nob Hill, which everyone knew was one of the posh areas of the city. Our leader explained that the house in question had once belonged to a famous actress of the twenties whose hobby had been to relax in her enormous marble bath filled with warm milk.

The house was very imposing. Nothing garish or cheap about the heavy stone facade, and nothing to reveal that it concealed a brothel. The doorman was in livery, and wore a top hat. His eyebrows didn't move as he plainly recognized our local guide, and he opened the stout oak door leading onto a long corridor. The carpet was as deep and soft as a well-kept lawn, the mirrors and antique furnishings were exquisite. But the most astonishing thing about the place was that a series of corridors separated by heavy doors ran on like a maze. Each door was attended by a granite-faced flunky dressed in brilliant livery which would have been envied by any royal court in Europe, and was opened only by a special knock that passed you through to the next section.

Finally we reached the main salon. The door opened into one of the most beautiful rooms I have ever seen: a huge marble fireplace and a roaring fire, fine wallpaper, carpets, furniture, and mirrors—oh, lots of mirrors.

And the madam—well, you could hardly call her that, she was so elegant and welcoming, as if she were meeting her country-house guests for an intimate weekend. She was beautifully gowned, her coiffeured hair just touched with gray. Her voice was upper-class English, and she took such a fancy to me that I thought she might be trying to recruit me as one of her flock. And she knew my name.

"Ah, Miss Gardner," she said as she steered me across to a high-backed chair, "I want you to sit in this particular chair so that you may see *everything* that is happening. . . ."

I did a slight inward cough as I realized I had been placed opposite a see-through mirror. Now *what* was I going to see?

Slightly relieved, I saw that the only view was of a beautiful well-stocked bar with a handsome barman, and nobody else in sight. I realized that at a ritzy joint like this there would be no goings-on on the carpet.

Meanwhile the housemother was filling me in on the details, "My girls are all dressed by Dior," she whispered, and I wondered if Mr. Dior knew he had been quite so privileged. I also wondered with all this total security how a gentleman and his lady managed to get into each other's clutches. Plainly things had altered from the old gold-rush days when the guy marched in, hitting the spittoon and yelling, "Now where's my harpy for the night?"

The housemother was also whispering, "In my house no two gentlemen are ever allowed to meet each other; you could *imagine* the complications that might cause." I really couldn't, but my attention was now occupied by the beautiful young woman—gowned magnificently, as advertised, by Dior—who swayed into the bar without a trace of indelicacy. She stood there looking like a million dollars and I was wondering why Mr. L. B. Mayer hadn't got her under contract when an equally elegant gentleman joined her. The housemother smiled at me to show that I would understand that the preliminaries were now starting. He shook hands politely. They both sat down. The barman poured champagne from an expensive-looking bottle. It was also plain that the conversation was polite, without any of those old gold-rush realities of: "For Christ's sake—twenty dollars! You must think I've hit the mother lode!"

The housemother went on whispering, "You see, when the gentleman takes his leave he goes out through another exit so that no one ever sees him come in or leave this building."

"Would you like to see the marble bath and the rest of the house?" she asked. And off we went on another little tour. The bath was impressive: a huge white marble piece with downward flowing steps. It was now empty, so I knew that nothing very interesting went on there. I gave the housemother another one of my inquiring looks, which made her say, "Oh, I expect you'd like to see the rooms where the girls, er—"

I smiled back encouragingly, and off we went down another corridor.

And there the dream ended.

A room not much larger than a cubicle. No bathroom, just a

basin in one corner. I've seen better rooms in second-class motels. And the bed . . . for God's sake, one would have expected a huge four-poster with creamy sheets and lush bedspreads. What did they get? A low, king-size square covered with a red drape. So this was where lust was satisfied. If I'd been an old-time miner I'd have asked for my gold nugget back.

ARLENE DAHL

I first met Ava in 1948, when I was assigned a dressing room right across from hers at Metro. Sydney Guillaroff was a mutual friend of both of ours—he would do our hair regularly when we were working—and he said to me, "She really needs friends. She has men friends, but she doesn't have many women friends." She was too beautiful; she was considered a threat by the so-called glamour girls at Metro.

Ava was not working at the time, but she usually preferred to have her lunch brought into her dressing room because she was really painfully shy. It was not a cover, not a pretense—she was timid, she was afraid. So either I'd come to her dressing room or she would come to mine. She told me she was very nervous about entering a room, even the commissary. "I would just as soon crawl under the carpet until I get to my seat," she said, "because I hate to have people look at me."

"But, Ava, this is crazy," I said. "You are just fantastic-looking. What happens when you're on the screen?"

"When I'm on the screen, I'm playing a role, I'm playing a part," she said. "I am somebody else. I'm not me."

Yet she never thought of herself as a good actress; she just did not believe in herself. Acting for her was like a child playing in the garden or with her dolls. It was make-believe. It didn't have any substance, and she was looking for substance in her life. Or someone to share it with or give it to her.

At that time, I was also writing a beauty column for the Chicago *Tribune*/New York *Daily News* syndicate, and she was the very first person I wanted to interview. "Ava," I said, "you are, if not *the* most, one of the most beautiful women I have ever seen in my life."

"Oh, come on, Arlene," she said. "You don't have to say that to make me feel good. Why don't you interview Elizabeth Taylor?"

I said I was determined to begin with her and added, "If you put pâté de foie gras under your eyes, my editor is going to love it."

"No, I do nothing at all," she said. "I try to take my makeup off when I come home from the studio. Sometimes I succeed, sometimes I don't."

Gee, I thought, this is not going to be a very successful column if I can't come up with anything. But Ava didn't have to wear makeup. She had naturally beautiful skin, and great color to her lips. She dressed very casually; she was never so happy as when she wore slacks and a blouse. But the slacks were well tailored, she was never sloppy, and she was very clean. She would wash her hands at least three times during lunch. And there was no one who could touch that posture, the way she walked and presented herself. She was a sexy woman without trying. All she had to do was walk into the room.

Metro in those days was just like being part of a very rich family; you had everything at your disposal. If you went from Stage 1 to Stage 9, you didn't walk, you took the limousine. If you had to go to the dressing room, or to the loo, you took the limousine. I mean you never walked anywhere. If you were going out to a premiere or something, you could go to wardrobe and take any clothes that would fit and sign them out for the evening. It was just a fascinating life. You were pampered and spoiled. Some actresses thought they deserved it, but I think because Ava had been poor, she didn't know how long it was going to last. She thought: One day, it's not going to be this way.

And L. B. Mayer was the emperor. He'd call you to his office either before, during, or after you were cast in a film, and he'd want you to sit on his lap in front of a mirror while he taught you how to act. It was really the Loretta Young School of Acting. We'd complain to Lillian Burns, the dramatic coach, and she'd say, "Well, Uncle Louie is Uncle Louie. Just put it in the back of your mind and don't pay any attention to it." Ava also thought it was ridiculous, but she played that game. "You know," she said, "there are certain games in life you have to play."

One thing she hated, though, was PR. She thought it was phony and false, and she was against anything that was phony and false. Not only was she a Capricorn, an earth sign, she was really down to earth as well. But she did what she had to do in order to make the money she wanted to make, and in order to please Mayer and the powers that be. She would kick and scream but finally, when it came right down to it, she did it. But she did it with taste.

One game she did *not* play was the couch game. She never had to and she never did. She was *not* promiscuous, she was true—true blue. When she was married, she was married. She didn't fool around; there was never any scandal about her. She was exactly the opposite of the roles she played. She looked like a femme fatale and she wasn't. She was really sweet and dear and lovely, and, at the time that I knew her, she wanted a baby, a child, more than anything in the world.

We often talked about the kind of man that we'd like to marry, that would make us happy. "Oh, God," she said, "the thing I dream about is having someone really love me for myself, for what's inside of me, and not who I am on the screen or what they think I am. The *happiest* time in my life would be finding the right person and marrying him."

Ava was always looking for a father figure, I think. One of her favorite songs, something she used to hum to herself, was "I'm a little lamb who's lost in the wood, I know I could always be good, to one who'll watch over me." And she had that quality of bringing out a person's protectiveness. Men would like to protect her. Sometimes they protected her too much.

Mickey Rooney was a protector up to a point. He was cocky. Big star. *Big* talent. He could do anything—he could sing, he could compose, he could play the piano, the drums. And he was a fine actor. I don't think there was anything he couldn't do. But he was cocky. And he rubbed people the wrong way. He had a wicked sense of humor, you know. He could take you down with one line.

But he never did that with Ava. He was very protective. In a funny way, Mickey also had an inferiority complex. He wasn't tall, he wasn't handsome, he did not think too much of himself. So they had a lot in common, these two, and they gravitated toward each other because of that. Together, they were strong. And she never complained about him. I mean, he was boastful, he was this and he was that, but she'd just say, "Well, you know Mickey." And he was always a good friend to her.

As for Howard Hughes, the main thing that threw her off, and me, too, was his body odor. Howard never bathed, he never used a deodorant. And I'm sure he never cleaned his clothes. They were always dirty, and he never bothered to change. I remember standing next to him at Ciro's one night, and I smelled him before I knew who it was. I turned around and saw his shirt, he had dirt on his collar and around his neck, and I had to excuse myself.

And here was Ava, washing her hands three times during the course of lunch, very insistent on cleanliness. She told me Howard was besieging her with calls and setting up traps for her, and it was always a challenge to get out of those assignations. She couldn't get past the body odor, and neither could I. We laughed about that.

When Ava's marriages to Mickey and Artie Shaw didn't work out, she said, "You know, I don't trust love anymore. It's led me astray. If a man knows you love him, then he'll take advantage of you and treat you badly." But part of her still believed that the greatest day of her life would be when she could leave it all behind and just live her life as she wanted to with someone that she loved. That she was never allowed to do that was one of the great tragedies of her life. And the fact that she didn't have the children that she really wanted was a tragedy as well. She was beautiful and famous and idolized and still was one of the most unhappy women. She was an unfulfilled flower.

TWELVE

R ita Hayworth once said the problem with her life was that the men in it fell in love with Gilda, her most glamorous role, and woke up the next morning with her. That's a sentiment I can fully identify with. I've always felt a prisoner of my image, felt that people preferred the myths and didn't want to hear about the real me at all. Because I was promoted as a sort of a siren and played all those sexy broads, people made the mistake of thinking I was like that off the screen. They couldn't have been more wrong. Although no one believes it, I came to Hollywood almost pathologically shy, a country girl with a country girl's simple, ordinary values.

Hollywood, however, saw a lot of money in promoting me as a goddess, and that process moved into high gear with *One Touch of Venus*. Here I played literally the ancient goddess of love, a naturally amorous type who comes to earth imprisoned in a statue of the Anatolian Venus purchased by an art-loving department store owner. But when "a little old good-for-nothing window trimmer" named Eddie Hatch, played by Robert Walker, kisses me on the lips in a fit of inebriated passion, I climb down off the pedestal and make everyone's life a comedic hell by falling madly in love with him.

Venus started as a stage musical written by S. J. Perelman and Ogden Nash, with music by the great Kurt Weill, but only two of the original songs made it into the film. One of those, "Speak Low," was nominally a duet between me and Dick Haymes, who played Eddie Hatch's best pal. But, as usual, another voice was dubbed in instead of mine.

Before shooting could begin, however, a statue of me as the Anatolian Venus had to be created. Sparing no expense, Universal commissioned sculptor Joseph Nicolosi to do the job. And that's where the crises began. Most Venuses I'd seen in art books were nude or had a magically clinging drape low on the hips, and Mr. Nicolosi clearly had the same idea. Because when I took off my clothes behind a screen and appeared modestly clothed in a two-piece bathing suit, he looked at me rather severely and gave a sigh that could have been heard as far away as the Acropolis.

Nude? Me? Not even MGM had *that* in their contract. Bare my breasts? What would Mama have thought? Jesus, I had a hard enough time with two husbands and one boyfriend. No one darted into bed faster than I did. I had a fine time with sex, but the thought of exposing my body was something else again. I guess my mother's puritanical zeal had left some marks on me after all. Besides, it was February, and cold, and the sculptor's wife had to supply a steady stream of hot drinks just to keep us functioning.

The artist, however, prevailed. First he got me to change into a more shapely bra, because the suit top had the unfortunate effect of flattening the true line. But that didn't stop his numerous sighs and hesitations, and after several more hot drinks, I knew I'd have to make the supreme sacrifice.

"Would you like the bra off?" I asked cautiously.

Nicolosi smiled and nodded. "Your body is beautiful. It will make all the difference." And do you know what? He was right. Immodest as it may sound, I have to say that the final statue looked very nice indeed. It was carted off to the studio, with filming scheduled to begin in little more than a week.

Then came the explosion. A *nude* statue! Who said anything about nudity? Tits! Didn't anyone tell you that tits aren't allowed in a Hollywood film? It doesn't matter how beautiful they are, it's immoral and indecent. Plus, the goddamn statue has to come to life on screen. Do you want us to be accused of corrupting the whole of America?

As the owner of the offending objects, I sat back and did not say a word. After all, I'd done my bit for the arts. But the poor sculptor, who'd poured his soul into this clay, was shattered. No one had told him they'd wanted a Venus dressed up like Queen Victoria. Finally, another statue was made, this one with me wearing the belted-at-the-waist off-the-shoulder gown that Orry Kelly had designed for Venus, and America's morals survived to fight another day.

One Touch of Venus ended with the inevitable Hollywood fadeout, with everyone paired up with just the perfect person. It's often struck me as sad that the actors and actresses involved in these fantasies can't arrange the same kind of rapture for themselves. Because if anyone needed or deserved a happy ending, poor Bob Walker certainly did.

While we were filming Venus, the rumor-mongering movie magazines were all claiming that Bob and I were engaged in the inevitable ecstatic affair that's supposed to go hand-in-hand with moviemaking. And, I admit, sometimes it does. But not this time.

Bob Walker had been married to the beautiful Jennifer Jones. Whether he was then into booze to the point of being an alcoholic, I don't know. He sure was when I knew him. And his agony was compounded by the fact that *Gone With the Wind*'s David O. Selznick was also intoxicated with Jennifer, and had pursued her as only a determined producer can. When a girl is young and beautiful and an ambitious actress, it's very hard to resist that kind of attention.

The non-Hollywood ending to this story was that Jennifer divorced Bob, David divorced his wife Irene, and the two of them wed. Irene went to New York to become a very successful stage producer, and only Bob was left to grieve. And grieve. And grieve.

Poor baby. He tired so hard to stay off the drink. He actually lived at Universal, in his dressing room, a sort of bungalow, with a man who did exercises with him and was supposed to make sure he didn't touch the stuff. No parties. No interruptions. No hangovers.

It worked for the first part of the movie; then Bob's cronies and hangers-on discovered what he was doing. They soon found ways of sneaking into his company with the age-old come-on: "One little drink won't do us any harm."

One night Bob rang me up and asked me out to a restaurant. But by the time we had finished dinner, and Bob had finished drowning his sorrows, he was in no state to go anywhere. I decided I would drive and said casually, "Bob, let's go home and we can have a nightcap at my place—okay?"

By the time we got back to my apartment and Bob had had his nightcap, Reenie and I were exchanging glances. Bob had as much chance of reaching his bed by car as he had of swimming across the Pacific.

He was quite agreeable when I said, "Bob, why don't you spend the night here? I can move in with Reenie. Then we can both arrive early at the studio tomorrow morning." Bob thought that was a splendid idea. He staggered off to the bathroom, and when he returned we poured him into bed. There were two single beds in Reenie's room—evasion insurance against nights like this. I went to sleep. Reenie, however, was kept awake for hours. As she told me the next morning, "It was really pitiful listening to Mr. Walker weeping all night long. Really sobbing and moaning, moaning, 'Jenny, where are you, Jenny? Why don't you come back to me, Jenny?' Honest to God, Miss G., he never stopped. I've never known a man in such a state."

Reenie had gotten up early to get the coffee and get us off to the studio. She went into the bathroom where she kept the cleaning materials, and opened the cupboard door. And what was on the floor—a sort of harness. At first she didn't know what it could be, and then she worked it out. Poor little Bob wore it under his suit. A padded harness that gave him bigger shoulders, bigger arms, bigger muscles, a bigger chest. Reenie didn't touch it. Bob visited the bathroom and came out ready to go. And we drove out to Universal to get on with *One Touch of Venus*. I don't know if Bob ever got over his booze problem. I do know he died at far too young an age: thirty-two—more I think from a broken heart than from the alcohol he drank.

The next year, 1949, saw me costarring in *The Bribe* with another Robert—Robert Taylor—with far more satisfying romantic results. Not that the plot was much help. Set on some fictitious island off the coast of Central America, which looked suspiciously like Mexico on MGM's all-purpose back lot, *The Bribe* had me tangentially connected to a nasty plot to smuggle surplus American aircraft engines into South America. I was excused from my usual slinky black dress and put into Mexican huaraches and fetching native blouses to match the climate. And though I seemed to be happy singing and dancing at the local cantina, my main job was to take one quick look at Mr. Taylor, a federal agent dead set on catching those smugglers, and fall into his arms. This time, it not only happened on screen, it happened for real.

There's no rhyme or reason about a love affair. In those days, I was in constant proximity to some of the most handsome, romantic figures on earth, and they didn't move me the slightest bit. Not that I didn't adore men. I did. I liked their strength, their laughter, their vulnerability, and I liked them in bed! But I was a one-man woman. I did not want a string of lovers. I had to like a man one hell of a lot to let him disturb my sleep. But since Howard Duff and I had split by that time, I was available. And Bob Taylor surely fit the bill for me, and I did the same for Bob.

Bob was married to Barbara Stanwyck at the time, but the marriage had been on the rocks for a long time and was soon to end in divorce. For one thing, Bob had not endeared himself to Barbara when he'd been surprised by a photographer outside a whorehouse in Rome with a young lady who looked suspiciously like one of its employees. Poor Bob, he never had much luck. The story hit most of the papers back home, and Barbara was not amused. What wife would be?

Bob thought *The Bribe* was one of the worst movies he'd ever made, but then he always hated the parts that Metro inflicted on him. It all started with *Camille,* the movie where he played Greta Garbo's beautiful romantic lover and became a star. Women all over the world swooned, and Bob was done for, typecast forever. Metro had discovered a new romantic hero, the male equivalent of that love goddess I'd just played, and the studio didn't like to tamper with money in the bank, no matter what anyone's personal preferences were.

And Bob couldn't stand those parts. Sure, he made enough money to buy a huge ranch, and the studio loaned him a plane and a copilot to keep him happy, but he thought the parts he played demeaned his manhood, and that ate away at his self-respect. Because Bob wasn't some effeminate type trying to hide reality under a macho exterior; he *was* an outdoor man. Bob lived and worked on a ranch because he loved it. He rode, worked horses, and handled cattle as well as any cowboy. He hunted, fished, shot, and roamed the wild country as well as any ranger. And he wanted parts that mirrored his real life. He wanted to be out there fighting against the toughies and shooting the baddies. But his good looks mitigated against him: he was always going to be slotted into the matinee-idol category. I think that created a sense of disappointment in him, almost a sense of failure.

I knew him as a warm, generous, intelligent human being. I especially remember that though I smoked cigarettes in those days, Bob Taylor left me miles behind. He was completely addicted: fifty to seventy a day before the cocktail hour, and God knows how many after that. And he carried around this big thermos of black coffee, even keeping it in his car. Cigarettes and black coffee kept him going all day long.

Our love affair lasted three, maybe four months. A magical little interlude. We hurt no one because no one knew—only Reenie on my side, and no one on his. I've never forgotten those few hidden months. I made two more films with Bob, *Ride, Vaquero!* and *Knights of the Round Table,* where he played Sir Lancelot (of course!), but we never renewed our romance. And Bob, despite all his efforts, couldn't break the mold of the beautiful lover. The film world remembers him that way, and I have to say that I do, too.

Yet another Bob, Bob Mitchum, came into my professional life a couple of years later, and he was a different sort of character altogether. And let me make a frank admission: if I *could* have gotten him into bed, I *would* have. I think that every girl who ever worked with Bob fell in love with him, and I was no exception.

The film in question, yet another loan-out, was called *My Forbidden Past.* Someone once called it "a steamy tale of adultery, notorious antecedents, a mysterious inheritance, and an impecunious aristocratic family embroiled in strange goings-on beside the bayous of New Orleans," which I guess is as good a description of that melodramatic mishmash as we're going to get. Although I do not immediately ride off into the sunset with Bob at the close, there is little doubt that I'm already saddling the horses.

Bob had recently gotten out of jail after being set up for marijuana possession. He and another actor on *My Forbidden Past* smoked pot, and one day Bob said to me, "Honey, have you ever tried this stuff?"

Actually I had. It started when I was in a jazz club in down-town L.A. with Artie Shaw, listening to Count Basie and his or-chestra. I knew musicians were supposed to smoke pot, and I whispered to Artie, "Why don't I try it?" And Artie said very severely, "You're not going to try it. I'm dead against drugs and you are going to be against them, too." But I went on coaxing him and complaining I was missing out on a vital experience. So he broke down and got these four little funny-looking sticks of the stuff and we took them home with us. Then I lost my nerve and decided I didn't want to become a drug addict after all, so Artie hid them so well I thought he'd thrown them away.

Then, months later, I was cleaning out the dressing room and I came across these four little things lying there. So I called one of my best girlfriends, Peggy Malley, who was into everything, and I said in my most conspiratorial whisper, "Peggy, come on over. We're going to smoke some pot."

So Peggy came over and we sat there very soberly and began to puff on these little sticks, and I said, "I think you're supposed to inhale very deeply." So we tried that, and we smoked all fucking four of them, waiting for the skies to open, the roof to fall in, waiting for something marvelous to happen. It didn't. I remem-bered that music is supposed to enhance the high, so we put some on. "Doesn't sound any different to me," I said. "Doesn't sound any different to me either," Peggy said. And that was it. Nothing happened, except that we wondered if Artie had been conned into buying something that wasn't the real thing.

When I told all this to Bob, he said, as they always do, "Well, maybe you didn't get the good stuff." So he got some of what he considered "the good stuff" and both of us, his hairdresser and that other actor climbed into his trailer and started puffing away for all we were worth. And, Jesus, I still didn't feel anything at all.

So on the way back home we stopped at a bar and I ordered a martini. I was sitting on the stool and about to reach out for the glass when everything started to feel sort of funny, in an unsta-ble, uncomfortable sort of way. I almost lost my balance. I couldn't even tell if I was really on that stool or not. The hell with this, I thought. I like to know where I'm sitting and what I'm reaching for and what it all feels like.

That one experience put me off pot for the rest of my life. It sure wasn't worth all the hassle. I just stuck to my normal drug, alcohol. Booze was more reliable. And a lot easier to get. And the truth is, I never considered myself to be the great boozer the press made me out to be. I was never one of those solid, silent, day-in-and-day-out drinkers. I did love parties and staying up late, and I occasionally pretended to have a lot more than I actually did. And when I did drink, it was only for the effect. As many drinks as I've had, I can't remember enjoying one. The only reason I drank was to get over my shyness.

But drunk or sober, I wasn't kidding when I said I really fell for Bob Mitchum. A lot of girls did. I remember once chatting with Shirley MacLaine, another member in good standing, about this, and we both reached the same conclusion about Bob's evasive tactics. As soon as he felt another woman's vibes reaching out to entangle him, he'd look around with those soulful Irish eyes of his and make a beeline for the phone. "Help," he'd yell, and Dorothy, one of the most understanding wives I've ever met, would be on the scene. Dear Bob. A lovely, lovely character. I never pursued him. Didn't have the time. Frank Sinatra had now entered my life.

THIRTEEN

The first time I met Frank Sinatra, I was still married to Mickey Rooney. We were out at some Sunset Strip club, probably Mocambo, and Frank was there. He knew Mickey pretty well—who didn't?—and he stepped across to meet the new wife. And being Frank he did the big grin and said, "Hey, why didn't I meet you before Mickey? Then I could have married you myself."

That caught me off guard. I guess I smiled back uncertainly, but I don't think I said a word. Because in those early days, I was always feeling out of my depth. Even to meet Frank Sinatra was exciting enough. To have him say a thing like that left me dumbfounded.

But Frank was always like that, always the engaging flirt. I remember being on my way to Metro's famous twenty-fifth-anniversary group portrait about five years later, an event that Red Skelton broke up by walking in, raising both hands in the air, and saying, "Okay, kids, the part's taken, you can go home now." As I drove to the studio, a car sped past me, swung in front, and slowed down so much I had to pass it myself. The car overtook me again and repeated the process. Having done this about three times, the car finally pulled alongside me, the grinning driver raised his hat and sped away to that same photo session. That was Frank. He could even flirt in a car.

I, however, was not about to flirt back that first night. Mr. Frank Sinatra was a married man. Not a particularly faithful married man, according to Hollywood gossip. But a married man—*with children*! And I, a faithful, virtuous nineteen-year-old bride, definitely did not flirt with married men. What would Mama say?

This is not to say that I did not think, even then, that Frank was one of the greatest singers of this century. He had a thing in his voice I've only heard in two other people—Judy Garland and Maria Callas. A quality that makes me want to cry for happiness, like a beautiful sunset or a boys' choir singing Christmas carols.

And not only, like hundreds of other girls my age, was I intoxicated by the distinctive sound of the big swing bands, but I've always loved musicians. I'm absolutely intoxicated with them. All I have to do is stand in front of a bandstand and I'm in love with the whole band. It's not only the beautiful swell of music that emerges from the group, it's the instruments, and the whole ensemble look—I think it's sexy as hell. Some women fall for writers, some for sailors, some for fighters. I'm hooked on bands.

Despite this, it was quite some time before Frank and I hooked up together. My next contact came when he maintained a bachelor pad at the Sunset Towers, a structure that literally towered over the apartment house where Reenie and I shared a small place. Frank knew I was there, and occasionally, when he and his buddies were having a few drinks, we'd hear their boozy voices shouting, "Ava, can you hear me, Ava? Ava Gardner, we know you're down there. Hello, Ava, hello." It wasn't the most charming way to get acquainted, but Reenie and I always politely nodded and smiled back.

Finally, after a few casual meetings outside our apartment houses, Frank stopped me and said, "Ava, let's be friends. Why don't we have drinks and dinner tonight?"

I looked at him. I damn well knew he was married, though the gossip columns always had him leaving Nancy for good, and married men were definitely not high on my hit parade. But he *was* handsome, with his thin, boyish face, the bright blue eyes, and this incredible grin. And he was so enthusiastic and invigorated, clearly pleased with life in general, himself in particular, and, at that moment, *me*.

"Okay," I said. "Sure." He sure was attractive. Very attractive. What else could I do?

We drank quite a bit that night, had dinner, and ended up at some place Frank owned, or had borrowed. It certainly wasn't the Sunset Towers, but it was very chic. I suppose you could say it was perfect place for seduction. And yes, we kissed, and not just like good friends. But even if I had been the most willing girl in the world, which I wasn't, I felt it was all wrong. Somehow cheap and wrong. I was increasingly attracted to Frank, but this just didn't feel like the time or the place to do something about it. So I went home alone and, though it had in truth barely began, I thought the chapter on Mr. Sinatra in my life had closed.

Then, sometime early in 1949, Bappie and I rented a house in Palm Springs, a desert town that had become a favored holiday retreat for Hollywood types. People were always giving parties there, and Bappie and I were usually invited. These weren't necessarily the most scintillating affairs, and at one of them Bappie got so bored that she left after an hour. She took our car, knowing that I could easily get a ride home from one of the guests.

And who should arrive at my elbow, dry martini in hand, but one of those guests. The blue eyes were inquisitive, the smile still bright and audacious, the whole face even friendly and more expressive than I remembered. Oh, God, Frank Sinatra could be the sweetest, most charming man in the world when he was in the mood.

"Good to see you again," he said. "It's been a long time."

"Sure has," I answered, feeling better already.

"I suppose we were rushing things a little the last time we met."

"*You* were rushing things a little."

"Let's start again," said Frank. "What are you doing now?"

"Making pictures as usual. How about you?"

"Trying to pick myself up off my ass."

I knew what that was all about. Everyone knew that Frank was at one of the lowest points in his career. His golden voice was letting him down, hitting the more than occasional clinker; his marvelous phrasing was losing its smoothness. After years on top, he'd fallen to number five on the *Downbeat* vocalist poll, had gone quite a while without a bestselling record, and suffered the humiliation of having Metro switch his billing from No. 1 to No. 2 when *On the Town* with Gene Kelly was released.

But though I knew all about Frank's problems, I wasn't about to ask him about them that night. And, honey, I didn't bring up Nancy either. This night was too special for that. A lot of silly stories have been written about what happened to us in Palm Springs, but the truth is both more and less exciting. We drank, we laughed, we talked, and we fell in love. Frank gave me a lift back to our rented house. We did not kiss or make dates, but we knew, and I think it must have frightened both of us. I went in to wake Bappie up, which didn't appeal to her much, but I had to tell someone how much I liked Frank Sinatra. I just wasn't prepared to say that what I really meant by like was love.

Back in Hollywood, Frank called me up. We met for dinner at a quiet place, and we didn't do much drinking. This time I did ask him about Nancy. He said he'd left her physically, emotionally, and geographically years before, and there was no way he was going back. The kids, however, were something else; he was committed to them forever. I was to learn that that kind of deep loyalty—not faithfulness, but loyalty—was a critical part of his nature.

We didn't say much more. Love is a wordless communion between two people. That night we went back to that little yellow house in Nichols Canyon and made love. And, oh, God, it was magic. We became lovers forever—eternally. Big words, I know. But I truly felt that no matter what happened we would always be in love. And God almighty, things did happen.

Frank and I didn't hide ourselves away, but we kept, as they say, a fairly low profile. Still, one or two people tried to warn me about him. Lana Turner was one. She had been one of Artie Shaw's wives, and she'd had a very serious affair with Frank a couple of years before me. We met in the ladies' room during a party, and she told me her story. She had been deeply in love with Frank and, so she thought, Frank with her. Though he was shuttling backward and forward between her bedroom and Nancy's, trying to equate obedience to Catholic doctrines with indulgence in his natural inclinations, divorce plans were all set up and wedding plans had been made.

Then Lana woke up one morning, picked up the newspaper, and read that Frank had changed his mind and gone back to Nancy for good. It was the old Catholic arrangement: wife and family come first. Nancy had almost made a theme song out of it: "Frank always comes back to me."

I really liked Lana. She was a nice girl, and she felt neither malice nor anger toward Frank and me. She just thought I ought to know. I told Lana gently that Frank and I were in love, and that this time he really was going to leave Nancy for good. If I'm in love, I want to get married: that's my fundamentalist Protestant background. If he wanted me, there could be no compromise on that issue.

As much in love as we were, Frank and I didn't really care if, sooner or later, people found out about us. But we thought it was basically our private business, something between two people. And those feelings led me, early in 1950, to make a very fundamental mistake.

One of Texas's gaudiest millionaires, the model in fact, for the James Dean character in *Giant,* had built the enormous Shamrock Hotel in Houston, and Frank had accepted a singing engagement there. So I called Dick Jones, one of his best friends, and said, "Let's go to Houston and surprise Frank."

I can still hear the doubt that crept into Dick's voice as he said, "Ava, I don't think that's such a good idea."

That's all I needed to hear to make me even more determined to go. "Of course it's a good idea to go," I insisted. "Frank will love it. You're not going to back out on me, are you?"

So we went, and Frank did welcome me with appropriate hugs and kisses. The trouble started when the mayor of Houston invited us to dinner at one of the city's best Italian restaurants. In the middle of the meal, a photographer from the Houston *Post* arrived to commemorate the occasion with a bunch of pictures. Frank reacted as if he'd found a live cobra in his salad. No punches were exchanged, only a few angry words, before owner Tony Vallone calmed everybody down.

No harm seemed to be done, but within twenty-four hours the news that Frank Sinatra *and* Ava Gardner were honoring the new Shamrock Hotel with their presence made headlines all over the world. A press storm of major proportions broke over our heads, dooming forever the "just good friends" line we'd been successful with so far. Now, nearly forty years later, I can be fairly rational about this, even smile ruefully at all the fuss. Then, however, I was deeply hurt and upset. All I had done was fall in love. It was, unfortunately, with a married Catholic man.

If the Shamrock mess had one positive result, it convinced Nancy that this time Frank was for real. She picked Valentine's Day 1950 to tell the world they'd separated. "Unfortunately, my married life with Frank has become most unhappy and almost unbearable," her statement read. "We have therefore separated. I have requested my attorney to attempt to work out a property settlement, but I do not contemplate divorce proceedings in the foreseeable future."

Now the shit really hit the fan. In the next few weeks, I was receiving scores of letters accusing me of being a scarlet woman, a home wrecker, and worse. One correspondent addressed me as "Bitch-Jezebel-Gardner," the Legion of Decency threatened to ban my movies, and Catholic priests found the time to write me accusatory letters. I even read where the Sisters of Mary and Joseph asked their students at St. Paul the Apostle School in Los Angeles to pray for Frank's poor wife.

I didn't understand then and, frankly, I still don't understand now why there should be this prurient mass hysteria about a male and female climbing into bed and doing what comes naturally. It's blessed in weddings, celebrated in honeymoons, but out of wedlock it's condemned as the worst of sins. Maybe people are paying too much attention to the "lock" part of wedlock. And maybe, just maybe, there's a touch of jealousy somewhere.

As if all this press attention, the idea the world had that it was entitled to know all about every minute of our lives, wasn't enough to put strains on our love, neither one of us had exactly what you could call a tranquil temperament. Both Frank and I were high-strung people, possessive and jealous and liable to explode fast. When I lose my temper, honey, you can't find it anyplace. I've just got to let off steam, and he's the same way.

But, despite the different directions our careers seemed to be moving in, we never fought about professional matters. It was another sort of jealousy that ate into our bones. Primitive, passionate, bitter, acrimonious, elemental, red-fanged romantic jealousy was our poison. Accusations and counteraccusations, that's what our quarrels were all about.

Frank hated two men in my life—one past, one still present. Artie Shaw and Howard Hughes. Artie Shaw he could just about stomach because we had been respectably married and that was all over. Howard Hughes he saw red about. He refused to understand or believe that I had never slept with or even had a necking session with the man.

Howard Hughes was not helping things along either. His spies had me watched from the very first time he met me. Spying was one of Howard's continual preoccupations. He spied on and learned things about people. That gave him power to exert leverage. At times, as I was to find out, Howard Hughes was not a very nice man.

I never gave a hoot about his spies. I did my own thing. If he found out—and I'm sure he did—that I was sleeping with Mickey Rooney after our divorce, as well as making love with the likes of Howard Duff, Robert Taylor, and Frank Sinatra, and he didn't like it, he could go and jump in a cold shower.

But he went on about Frank over and over again. Maybe Howard had thought that after two failed marriages the coast was clear for him to press his case, and now this *singer* was getting in the way. He first raised the subject at dinner one night.

"Ava," he said, "you should not be getting mixed up with this man."

"Mixed up with what man?"

"Frank Sinatra."

"What the hell's it got to do with you?"

"He's married. He'll never get a divorce. His constant affairs with women are notorious. He's not good enough for you."

"Who *is* good enough for me? You?"

"He has woman after woman. You can't keep up with them."

Howard had forgotten that through Bappie and Charlie Guest I knew all about the houses and the stashed-away babes. I began to laugh. Howard didn't like that either. He began to fuss. I told him to forget it. It was all over between us, even though I don't think Frank ever believed it was.

In March of 1950, Frank was opening a new show at the Copacabana in New York, a show that we both hoped would end his career skid. Naturally, I wanted to be there with him, and since the next film I'd be doing, *Pandora and the Flying Dutchman,* was about to begin shooting in Europe, stopping off in New York on the way made perfect sense.

Frank was nervous before he went on, which was unlike him, but he sang like an angel, especially "Nancy with the Laughing Face," a song written about his daughter, not his wife. I've always thought it was a beautiful song, and contrary to what everyone seems to believe, it was never the reason for a single quarrel between us. Unfortunately, we never had any trouble inventing other reasons to be at each other's throats.

One evening, we escaped from our friends and went alone to a restaurant. Restaurants were frequently where our quarrels began, and I have to confess I started a lot of them, sometimes before the appetizer arrived. A pretty girl would pass and recognize Frank. She'd smile. He'd nod and smile back. It would happen again. Frank would feel the temperature rising across the table and try to escape with a sort of sickly look. I'd say something sweet and ladylike, such as, "I suppose you're sleeping with all these broads," and we'd be off to the races.

The quarrel started on those lines that night. The claws of my jealousy were showing. But had I known what the outcome of that night would be, I would have stayed for the coffee, the check, and the taxi ride home.

As it was, one second I was there and the next I'd scooped up my handbag and was outside the door and hailing a taxi.

I was angry. I was angry with Frank, myself, and the whole wide world.

In the Hampshire House, where we were staying, the three of us occupied a large suite. There were two bedrooms, with Frank using one and Bappie and I the other, both divided by a large living room and kitchen.

Bappie was in our room asleep, so I sat in the living room feeling lonely and miserable. I knew I couldn't go to bed—I would have lain awake for hours.

So who could I talk to about my problems? I had to explain things to someone. Here I was going off to Europe for months, and Frank and I were having these constant dramas. Then another thought hit me. Artie Shaw was in town. He had a small apartment in New York. If he happened to be home he would talk. Artie solved other people's problems in a couple of sentences. I still met him occasionally, which, Frank being Frank, made him jealous.

I phoned Artie. He was at home and his current girlfriend was with him. I guess he could tell by my voice I was down, so he said, "Tell you what, Ava. We're going to bed pretty soon, but why don't you come by and have a nightcap before you turn in?"

I thought that was a good idea. And off I went leaving my address book open to the page with Artie's phone number. I try and tell myself I didn't do that deliberately, but it was a pretty classic slip-up if I do say so myself.

Artie and his girlfriend were sitting there in their dressing gowns when I arrived, but they said they were in no hurry to go to bed. I was there maybe twenty minutes to half an hour before the doorbell rang. Artie answered it, "Why, hello, Frank. Come on in. Good to see you. Yeah, Ava's here. Do you know my girlfriend?" A real smooth customer, Artie, and maybe he had to be at that particular moment.

Frank came in. He had his buddy Hank Sanicola with him, and Hank hung back a little embarrassed. Frank looked a bit gray and haunted. I could see how he felt, sense his distress. We were living together. I was his girl. We were in love. He had followed the clue left open in my address book and he was ready to do battle if necessary. Now I had made a fool of him. There we were sitting around sipping drinks, Artie and his girlfriend in their robes, a domestic idyll if ever there was one.

Artie knew the score and did his best to act as if this visit was the most natural of social events.

"Frank, sit down and have a drink. You, too, Hank."

Frank shook his head. He turned, his head a bit low, his shoulders hunched. He and Hank walked out the door together and closed it behind them. There was not much we could say either. I sipped at my drink and Artie went on making casual conversation. After a few more minutes, I thanked them for the drink and made my way back to the Hampshire House.

By now, it was pretty late at night. I don't know how long I'd been back in the suite when the phone rang. It was Frank, and I'll never forget his voice. He said, "I can't stand it any longer. I'm going to kill myself—now!"

Then there was this tremendous bang in my ear, and I knew it was a revolver shot. My whole mind sort of exploded in a great wave of panic, terror, and shocked disbelief. Oh, God! Oh, God! I threw the phone down and raced across the living room and into Frank's room. I didn't know what I expected to find—a body? And there was a body lying on the bed. Oh, God, was he dead? I threw myself on it saying, "Frank, Frank . . ." And the face, with a rather pale little smile, turned toward me, and the voice said, "Oh, hello."

The goddamn revolver was still smoking in his hand. He had fired a single shot through a pillow and into the mattress. He'd thought that a pillow and a mattress would muffle the sound of the shot, and I would be the only one startled by its noise. He hadn't realized that half of New York had been sitting up, pencils poised, waiting to include this moment in their memoirs. I remember my feelings very well. They were not of anger or frustration, they were of overwhelming relief. He was alive, thank God, he was alive. I held him tightly to me. What would I have done if he was dead? My mind could not comprehend that thought.

I didn't ask him why he'd done it. I knew that without asking. But now reason had to take over. It had been one hell of a bang and people would be asking questions. Frank got up and put on his robe. The phone rang. It was the desk clerk. "Mr. Sinatra, have you heard a gunshot from anywhere near your room?"

Gunshot? What gunshot? Frank's innocence could have won him an Oscar nomination. But now we had to get rid of the evidence. We called Hank Sanicola, who was down several floors below us, and he was in the room within seconds. The hot gun was stowed under Bappie's pillow—didn't all virtuous North Carolina girls sleep with a gun under their heads? Hank took a quick look outside at the empty corridor, grabbed the mattress and made a run for the back stairs leading to his room. No one who stayed at the Hampshire House would have been seen dead on a back stairs.

I sat there in a chair, the shock now taking over, and trembled. There was another knock at the door—one that we were expecting—and two police officers introduced themselves. Frank invited them into the living room. I was there fully dressed, Frank was in his robe. "Sorry to disturb you, Mr. Sinatra, but there seems to have been a gunshot fired around this part of the hotel. We're trying to find out what happened." Frank's innocence was very convincing. Although I was trembling like jelly inside I was probably convincing, too. The policemen left very politely, and Frank and I never mentioned the incident again. Postmortems were not our style, at least partly because we knew that if we started going back over old arguments we'd probably end up repeating them. Besides, there were plenty of others waiting for us in the future.

FOURTEEN

O f all the damn films I made, *Pandora and the Flying Dutchman* would probably rank as one of the most obscure. Yet almost nothing I've done before or since had as much of an effect on me. In fact, it wouldn't be an exaggeration to say making it changed my life forever. Because *Pandora* got me outside these United States for the first time and introduced me to the two countries, England and Spain, where I was to spend much of the rest of my life. One trip abroad, honey, and I almost never looked back.

With the crumbling of the studio system and the strength of the dollar, it came to make more and more financial sense to shoot films outside of Hollywood, especially since a lot of American film money was frozen overseas. *Pandora,* to be filmed in Spain, was part of that trend. But England, where we had to stop to fit costumes and take care of preproduction stuff, was actually the first country outside the United States I ever saw. And strangely enough, England proved to be very much like North Carolina. The English use expressions I've never heard anyplace else but back home, so I felt comfortable with them right away. If Spain hadn't gotten in the way, I might have moved there first.

While I was in London, though, the minions of Metro wouldn't rest until they involved me in one of their silly publicity stunts. The bearskin-wearing Grenadier guardsmen who stand watch over Buckingham Palace are known for their stone-faced reaction to any kind of tourist provocation. So naturally, I was dispatched, with a photographer conveniently in tow, to make one of them *smile*.

Well, the man in the red tunic would not grin no matter what I did. The British press were not amused, one man writing rather witheringly that "This is the kind of conduct we have to expect of gawking tourists, but not of an important actress working in and enjoying our country." And to tell you the truth, I thought it was rather cheap myself and for a long time I was somewhat ashamed of having harassed the poor man.

Many years later, however, I was passing through London's Heathrow Airport when a girl at the airline desk smiled, asked for my autograph, and said, "Miss Gardner, do you remember how you tried to make that guardsman on sentry duty smile?"

"Of course I do," I said. "And I'm still ashamed of it."

"That was my grandfather—" she began.

"Well, apologize to him for me, will you?" I cut in. "It was the silliest thing I've ever done."

Then I saw that she was laughing.

"Apologize—why? Miss Gardner, that was the most exciting thing that ever happened to him, and he's boasted about it ever since. He'll go on telling that story down at the pub until the day he dies."

I was pleased about that.

Much as I loved London, I was also dying to visit Paris, just hours away. I had studied French in high school, my teacher was adorable, and I'd loved her. "Do you understand . . . *Paris!*" I just about screamed at Bappie, who had come over on the trip with me. "I can use my *French!*"

Metro did have its uses in those days. They arranged for a first-class trip to Paris and put Bappie and me up at the Hôtel Georges V, one of the classiest in town. And we were all set for a classy dinner at the Tour d'Argent, the kind of restaurant that made Paris Paris.

But was I satisfied? No, I was not. "Darling," I said to Bappie, "I do *not* intend to go around Paris in a Metro-Goldwyn-Mayer Rolls-Royce with a uniformed chauffeur. I want to really experience this town. I want to speak *French*." It did cross my mind that my Tobacco Road pronunciation might be a little difficult to understand. But to hell with that. I knew about three sentences in French, and I figured that should get us anywhere.

In the ladies' room at the Tour, I gave Bappie the word. "This is the breakaway point. We get rid of the Rolls, ditch the chauffeur and the Metro man who's looking after us, and off we go."

Bappie gave me one of those grim North Carolina looks, so pained I might as well be offering her a tour of the Bronx. "There's a very good bar at the hotel," she said. "Are you sure this is a *good* idea?"

"Of course it's a good idea. This Tour d'Argent stuff is strictly for tourists. I can speak French. What's to be afraid of?"

So, safely outside the restaurant, we stopped a *real* Paris taxi driver. He was not likely to understand any language, especially his own, coming out of the mouths of a couple of North Carolina broads . . . but one thing he did understand was money, and we were American so we *had* to have money.

So we start our tour with my French and his determination not to understand it. I was trying to make it clear that as *American ladies* we would like to see both Paris and real Parisians, and he was "Je ne comprend pas"ing and waving his arms, while Bappie was using her undertaker's voice to repeat, "Oh, for Christ's sake let's go back to the Georges Cinq and have a drink." So we drove around Paris for about forty-five minutes with me going on about two women without a male escort wanting to see the real Paris, and then suddenly something under that cloth cap clicked. A ray of light penetrated. Two ladies alone . . . "Ah, Mademoiselle . . . je comprend . . . oui." I sat back triumphant, saying, "You see, Bappie, all it takes is a little patience," and Bappie was still going on about the bar at the Georges Cinq.

So we drove up in front of this little joint that looked very elegant. Lights above a striped red canopy, and neat little stairs leading down to what looked like an underground cellar. All done up in scarlet. Very chic. Very colorful. Very French. And I could hear music!

"Who the hell wants to go back to the Georges Cinq when we can find a real swinging place like this?" I hissed in Bappie's ear. "We're gonna hear some wonderful jazz here, I can feel it in my bones." Even the doorman in his uniform was a good-looking guy. We walked in, and it was all extremely chic, with little tables round the walls and a sprinkling of couples sitting at them, violin players in full white tie and tails sawing away at violins, all the waiters resplendent in tuxedoes. The headwaiter, another good-looking guy, smiled and showed us to a discreet little table. I thought maybe he recognized me, but I couldn't have cared less, because within seconds a magnum—not a bottle, mind you, a magnum—of champagne had arrived and the maître d' bent low and whispered, "On the house, compliments of the management, no charge," which was rather sweet music to start the night off with.

The five violinists were now converging on us like a flock of friendly vultures, all bright smiles and sawing violin bows. I'm whispering triumphantly to Bappie, "What did I tell you? What's the Georges Cinq bar got to compare with this? This is the real Paris!"

At that moment Bappie seemed more interested in the champagne than in my little gloat, though I did notice that her bright eyes were scrutinizing the joint with their usual sharpness. Then I heard her say something, but I wasn't paying attention to anything except the special attention we were getting. Then I caught it.

"D'you notice, honey, there are no *girls* in this place?"

I didn't bother to look round. "So what?" I said. "Isn't that lovely?"

Then I realized that was not what Bappie meant. So I put down my glass and refocused my eyes just as I heard her say, "Funny thing, none of these musicians need a shave."

I took a long peek.

"No, they don't need a shave. They're darling."

"Not a mustache or a beard among them," Bappie went on in an increasingly sinister voice.

I got the essence of her conversation and had another look at the smooth chins tucked under the singing violins. They were as polished as peeled hard-boiled eggs. The maître d' arrived back at the same moment to do a little more pouring and establish that there was a lot left in the magnum, and I looked straight into his beautiful soulful eyes. Jesus! No! *Her* beautiful, soulful eyes.

I did a quick scrutiny of all the tables. They were all men. No, they were not. They were all women dressed as men. The customers, the orchestra, the maître d' . . . I expect even the goddamn doorman outside was a *girl*!

"Ava," Bappie said in her dark-brown North Carolina Baptist Belt voice that fortunately nobody understood except me, "we are in a *House of Lesbians!*" But she was kind enough not to add, "So this is where your so-called command of the French language has brought us."

I swallow my champagne very carefully, and smile as the maître d' gives me a refill. I am twenty-seven years old, and I know what lesbians are. I am not certain I know what they do, but I am a big, five-foot-six healthy girl, and I am sure I can defend us if necessary. Then common sense comes to my rescue. All the girls have been welcoming, and charming. We will conduct ourselves like a couple of equally nice Southern ladies, equally well behaved. After all, they may think we'll be back tomorrow night to join the gang.

We do not stay much longer. We get up, we smile, we shake hands, we say good-bye. There is no mention of a bill. Outside there is a taxi, and the driver understands my hissed "Hôtel Georges Cinq" very easily.

Bappie only felt safe when we were inside its doors.

After an outing like that, Bappie and I were none too unhappy to be leaving for Spain, where filming was to begin in the spring of 1950. A car took us from the Barcelona airport on the bumpy road north toward France and the Pyrenees, passing through pine-clad green hills as we turned down toward the Mediterranean and the ancient town of Tossa del Mar. The port slid into view around a golden curve, an ancient castle dominating its entrance.

The streets of Tossa were narrow, opening into pleasant, shady public squares, many with bubbling fountains. The markets seemed everywhere, full of bright vegetables and gleaming wet fish. There were few cars and even fewer gasoline pumps, and package tours had not even been invented yet. Every night the sky was filled with stars and the cellars and bars were filled with flamenco songs and Gypsy dancing. Goddammit, the whole of the Costa Brava was one long, continuous film set in those days.

I have to admit, I was fascinated by Spain from the first. I felt a kinship with the flamenco; it was alive then, and pure. The bullfights made for beautiful, exciting pageants, as did the fiestas, when everyone dressed up in those wonderful costumes. It was all wonderful, and it went on all day and all night. I loved it.

I wasn't in Spain just to gawk, of course; I had a picture to make, and one with a quite unusual plot. I played Pandora Reynolds, a 1930s playgirl, loved by many but never touched by love herself, driving men to distraction but a perfect stranger to personal happiness. During the course of the film, three very different men fall in love with her: a celebrated bullfighter; the world's fastest racing car driver (who Pandora, in a typical whim, refuses to consider marrying until he pushes the vehicle in question off a goddamn cliff!); and a mysterious yachtsman, Hendrick van der Zee (played by James Mason), who Pandora stumbles upon during a nude midnight swim in the bay.

That yachtsman, it turns out, is the celebrated Flying Dutchman, a sixteenth-century sea captain who got himself in big trouble with the powers that be by first murdering his wife for unfaithfulness without giving her so much as a chance to prove her innocence, and then blaspheming against God for making women so fair and so treacherous.

As punishment, he was doomed to live a ghostly existence, sailing alone on the seas of the world. Every seven years he was permitted to live among men for a short period of time, and if he was able to find a woman who loved him enough to give up her life for him, his punishment would end and he would be permitted to die. Can the carefree Pandora Reynolds fall in love and become unselfish enough to fill that rather tall order? Honey, do you even have to ask?

The man who concocted this supernatural romance was one of Hollywood's more curious writer-directors, Albert Lewin. An executive at Metro who'd been very close to wonder-boy production chief Irving Thalberg, Lewin had directed a pair of fairly arty films for the studio, *The Picture of Dorian Gray* and *The Moon and Sixpence*. He knew that this particular tale was much too noncommercial for MGM, so he left the studio to do it, asking that they loan me out to him as settlement of his contract. Metro being Metro, they didn't hesitate for a minute.

Al was famous, if that is the right word, for asking for an ungodly number of retakes. One story had it that on *Dorian Gray* he asked for one hundred and ten retakes and ended up using number four. He used the same technique on this picture, and one day I had to say to him, "Al, do you think I could go to the bathroom after the eighty-first take?"

Painstaking as he was, Al caused nowhere near the problems for me that toreador-turned-actor Mario Cabre did. Mario played Juan Montalvo, my bullfighter lover, in the picture, and his ambition was to continue the role in real life. Unfortunately, Mario got carried away confusing his onstage and offstage roles. In every country in the world, you find men who are pains in the ass. Mario was a Spanish pain in the ass, better at self-promotion than either bullfighting or love.

Yes, Mario was handsome, and macho as only a Latin knows how to be, but he was also brash, conceited, noisy, and totally convinced that he was the only man in the world for me. Now, everyone else in the world seemed to know that I was totally in love with Frank Sinatra and no one else but Frank Sinatra. We suffered agonies trying to tell each other how much we loved one another during the first weeks of filming, what with the hours it sometimes took for our transatlantic calls to come through, and the faraway voice at the bottom of the bathtub once the connection was made. But Frank supplemented his affection with daily letters and telegrams, and we had arranged before I left that he would travel to Tossa for a two- or three-day visit.

This all sounds very reasonable, but reason didn't always rule my actions in those days. I made a single mistake, and it turned into a blunder of major proportions. Because after one of those romantic, star-filled, dance-filled, booze-filled Spanish nights, I woke up to find myself in bed with Mario Cabre.

That was the one and only time. Not that it mattered. Because Mario was ready, willing, and all too able to broadcast his good fortune to the entire free world. Someone had passed on to him the concept that there is no such thing as bad publicity: if you want to be famous you've got to get into the headlines. And what greater opportunity could he have than an attempt to replace Frank in my affections? His motivation was cynical self-interest. His declamatory rhetoric about this *great* passion in his life, his love for me and mine for him, made headlines in Spain, America, all over the world, and that's all he cared about. He gave interviews saying I was "the woman I love with all the strength in my soul," wrote the most idiotic love poems imaginable, and then marched off to recite them at the American embassy in Madrid.

Initially, I suppose I thought this was vaguely amusing, and since we played lovers in the same film, no one was exactly encouraging me to come out and publicly say he was a nuisance and a jerk. But when he started to involve Frank in his shenanigans, saying he would not leave Spain alive if he came on that visit, Mario became a major pest.

As the guy hardly ever left my side and was constantly warning me of his intentions, I took Mario's threat seriously. To him, my feelings were of little consequence. He was sure a woman would naturally fly into the arms of the stronger, dominant male, and that he could believe that sort of crap was typical of the man. Still, I think poor Al Lewin was a little nervous, too. Because when Frank did fly in to see me in early May, Al saw to it that Mario was involved in some second-unit shooting many miles away in Gerona.

Though we were hounded as usual by the press, Frank and I enjoyed our two days of romance in Tossa del Mar, and I looked forward to more when I would be in London for exteriors on *Pandora* and Frank would be in concert for a week or so at the Palladium. But Mario had scenes in London, too, and he and his cuadrilla, the four members of his ex-bullfighting team who were part of his inevitable macho entourage, arrived soon after I did.

By this time, perhaps because he feared his fame might plummet as quickly as it had risen, Mario's demand for publicity had ballooned beyond all reason. He went so far as refusing to go out to the MGM studios for his scenes unless I was with him. I sputtered to Al Lewin, "But he wants me to go in the damn car with him even on days when I'm not *working*!"

Al nodded, sighed, and patted my arm.

"Be a good girl, Ava. Go with him. Humor him. Let's get the goddamn movie finished and then we can get rid of the son of a bitch. Do it for me, Ava."

I did it for Al. And Mario was finally getting the message. His English was negligible, and London did not smile on phony love-sick matadors. He left London and, thank God, I never saw him again. When I headed back to Hollywood, whatever regrets I had about leaving Europe behind had absolutely nothing to do with him.

FIFTEEN

The year 1950 was not a banner one as far as Hollywood was concerned. On the one hand, the Joe McCarthy–inspired blacklist was beginning to wreck people's lives and careers, and on the other, the emergence of TV as a powerful entertainment medium attacked the box office like a plague. Figures are not my strong point, but I've read that from a high of ninety million in 1948, movie theater admissions plummeted to seventy million in 1949 and dropped even further to sixty million in 1950, with the bottom still nowhere in sight.

Not only was MGM, all those damn stars notwithstanding, vulnerable to this slide, it suffered most of all in this period, going through its worst years since the Depression. The studio had only one film among the top twenty hits of the 1940s and early 1950s, and that was the expensive costume drama *Quo Vadis*. Partly as a result, the old lion himself, Mr. Louis B. Mayer, resigned in 1951 in a dispute with the studio's new chief of production, Dore Schary.

If there was a bright light for Metro during those days, it was in the glorious Technicolor musicals turned out by the studio's Arthur Freed unit. So when I was told that I was to have a key part in producer Freed's latest opus, *Show Boat,* to begin shooting in mid-November 1950, I was certainly pleased. After all, even I knew that this story of women who love well but not wisely was one of the great musicals of the century.

Show Boat started out as an Edna Ferber novel dealing with three generations of the Hawks family, from Captain Andy to daughter Magnolia to granddaughter Kim, all of whose lives revolve around a showboat cruising up and down the Mississippi in the late nineteenth century. It was the great Flo Ziegfeld himself who saw the theatrical possibilities in the book, and who convinced Oscar Hammerstein II and Jerome Kern (whose daughter Elizabeth was an earlier wife of Artie Shaw's!) to do the words and music.

The show opened on Broadway in late December 1927, and with songs like "Bill," "Can't Help Loving That Man" and, of course, "Ol' Man River," proved a real Christmas present for New Yorkers. It also established Helen Morgan as a star with her performance as Julie Laverne, the singer with a touch of black blood whose attempt to pass for white has the kind of tragic consequences the poor South was famous for.

Even then, it didn't take Hollywood long to see the movie possibilities in this story. Universal did a version in 1929, but unfortunately, with the film practically completed, sound came in and gave everyone fits. The result was a half-sound, half-silent hybrid that made nobody particularly happy.

Then, in 1936, James Whale, who'd made his reputation by turning Boris Karloff into Frankenstein, surprised everyone, perhaps even himself, by doing a very creditable version that gave the peerless Paul Robeson a chance to sing an unforgettable "Ol' Man River."

By the time MGM got hold of the property, they thought the show's central story, a star-crossed love affair between Captain Andy's daughter Magnolia and gambler/turned actor/turned gambler Gaylord Ravenal, would be perfect for Nelson Eddy and Jeanette MacDonald. That never worked out, however; the project got postponed, and Freed and director George Sidney ended up with Kathryn Grayson and Howard Keel in those roles. As for Joe, the man who gets to sing "Ol' Man River," they cast William Warfield, someone who'd rarely attempted anything but classical music before.

Freed, Sidney, and screenwriter John Lee Mahin also determined that a restructuring of the show's plot was in order. No longer would Gaylord and Magnolia be separated for over twenty years—movie audiences were deemed too impatient to stand for that. And Julie Laverne, the beautiful half-caste, would

141

not only become a running character, helping to unify the sprawling time frame, but also be instrumental in reuniting the parted lovers.

All of which meant that the part of songstress Julie Laverne, "the little sweetheart of the South," was going to be quite a plum. Judy Garland, Metro's musical star, would have been everyone's first choice, but Judy's increasing health problems had led the studio to scrap her contract. Dore Schary wanted Dinah Shore, of all people, to play the role, while my own personal choice would have been Lena Horne. I've always thought that she, along with Greta Garbo and Katharine Hepburn, was one of the three most beautiful women in the world. She was really born for this part. She would have been perfect for it, and not only that, she was a close friend and neighbor of mine in tree-shaded Nichols Canyon.

George Sidney, however, wanted me. He'd been the MGM executive who'd viewed my first test and approved my being shipped out from New York, and he saw qualities in me, including the chance to use someone who was *really* from the South and understood Julie's situation, that made me seem right for the part. Not to mention the fact that I was getting increasingly popular. By the end of 1950, MGM's publicity department was sending out black-and-white photos of me to the tune of three thousand requests per week, a figure that only Esther Williams bettered.

But if you think everybody jumped up and down at the chance to use me this way, you'd better think again. The studio brass, the gossip columnists, everyone thought giving me this kind of a plum role was a mistake. However, George was determined, and I got the part, which turned out to be one of the few I rather liked.

Having cast me, George turned me over to his wife, Lillian Burns, Metro's chief drama coach. A very important post because you didn't have to know much more about acting than you did about differential calculus to become a star at MGM. As I've said before, you came under Lillian's purview only when you reached the level of speaking parts, and as your roles grew more important, so did your time with her.

Lillian was slender and dark and volatile. She loved teaching and she loved talking about everything from actors and acting to jewelry to the whole business of moviemaking. And, Jesus, in those days, I thought Lillian could play any part ten times better than I could. She said she was struck by my beauty, and she's said that it was "like a piece of Dresden, so fine and pure, it struck you right in the heart." But to play Julie, more than beauty was going to be needed.

While Lillian was working with me, Metro's ace production people were seeing to the construction of the stern-wheeler *Cotton Blossom,* which, at a cost of over one hundred thousand dollars, was for quite a while the most expensive single prop ever made. Originally, the film's exteriors were going to be shot on location around Natchez and Vicksburg, but once it turned out that the weather would be wrong, Metro opted to use its own durable back lot instead. The ten-million-gallon Tarzan Jungle Lake was drained and this enormous triple-decked, one-hundred-seventy-one-foot-long, fifty-seven-foot-high boat was built on top of metal pontoons, so it could actually float up and down the back-lot version of the Mississippi.

During the shooting, Kathryn Grayson, Howard Keel, and I got along with each other extremely well. After each day's shooting we would meet in one of the dressing rooms and, ignoring one of Metro's cardinal rules, smuggle in enough tequila to send us back home in the best of humor. Howard was young, handsome, and full of laughter. He had that wonderful rich voice, and Kathryn matched him note for note. When it came to my own singing, however, the studio ran me so ragged that I never did forgive them.

Now, I *can* sing. I do not expect to be taken for Maria Callas, Ella Fitzgerald, or Lena Horne, but I can carry a tune well enough for the likes of Artie Shaw to feel safe offering to put me in front of his orchestra. But since Julie's two songs, "Bill" and "Can't Help Loving That Man," are so beloved by everyone, I decided to work as hard as I could to fit the bill. I even found this marvelous teacher, who'd worked with both Lena and Dorothy Dandridge, and we slaved away for several weeks and produced a test record of those two songs.

Then, rather nervously, I took my life into my hands and gave the record to Arthur Freed himself, God Almighty of musical productions. I don't think the son of a bitch ever even listened to it. He just put it on a shelf and delivered the usual studio ultimatum: "Now, listen, Ava, you can't sing and you're among professional singers." So that settled that one.

Or did it? Because the singer they'd chosen to dub my singing had a high, rather tiny voice, totally inappropriate when it was paired with my own speaking voice. The studio spent thousands and thousands of dollars and used the full MGM orchestra trying to get this poor girl *right*. I mean, there was nothing *wrong* with her in the first place, except for the obvious fact that she wasn't me.

Finally, they got Annette Warren, this gal who used to do a lot of my singing off-screen, and they substituted her voice for mine. So my Southern twang suddenly stops talking and her soprano starts singing—hell, what a mess.

When it came to the album version of the movie, things got even worse. Being a great fan of Lena's, I had copied her phrasing, note for note, on my test record. So they took my record imitating Lena and put earphones on her so she could sing the songs copying me copying her.

But Metro soon found out that they couldn't legally release the album with my name and image, as they called it, without my voice being part of the package. So then I used earphones to try to record my voice over her voice, which had been recorded over my voice imitating her. I did it note for note, they wiped Lena's voice off the album, and the record was a success. That's the way they worked in those days. And I still get goddamn royalties on the thing!

Considering all of this, my reviews on *Show Boat* were excellent, really better than I expected, except for a busybody from *The New Yorker* who said that I was "subjected to such close scrutiny by the camera that [my] handsome face often takes on the attributes of a relief map of Yugoslavia." But the success aside, my anger about how callously Metro had treated me intensified the fury I'd been feeling toward them throughout my career.

Frankly, MGM was never the right studio for me. When I'd done *The Bribe*, it was my first starring role in seven years there. The studio never bothered to package me. They never bought a property for me. In fact, they had so little interest in me they just about *never* wanted me around. The idea was, "Toss her out, lend her out, and give her away!"

And, except for Lillian Burns from time to time, I only remember a single example of someone caring about the quality of my work. In the breaks during the filming of *The Bribe,* Charles Laughton, one of my costars, used to take me aside and read me passages out of the Bible, then make me read them back with the right cadences and stresses. He was a brilliant classical actor absorbed by his craft and loving it. And he was the only one in all my film years who took the time and went out of his way to try and make an actress out of me.

In fact, if Metro did anything, it was to stand in the way of my learning anything. I remember Greg Peck asking me if I wanted to do a part in a play they were doing in La Jolla, just to work out, to learn. "Okay," I said, "if I can start with something very small."

But before I could commit I had to ask Metro. "Small part? Not the lead? Of course you can't do that," I was told. "You either play the lead or nothing."

"But I can't possibly play the lead," I said. Little did they care. And that was the last time I allowed myself to even think about learning on the stage.

But it was those loan-outs to other studios that infuriated me the most about my position at MGM. Even as my salary was rising (I was getting around fifty thousand dollars a year at this time, and it was to creep up higher) they lent me to other companies at salaries five and six times better than I was getting— and a percentage of the gross on top of that. They got well paid for giving me to those other studios, but I wasn't allowed to share in the wealth.

Plus the atmosphere at Metro was stifling, killing. When I appeared for Henry Wallace when he ran for president in 1948, Mr. Mayer called me in and told me I had to stop. He told me that Katharine Hepburn had ruined her career doing things like that. They liked to terrify you, to threaten that if you didn't do what they said, they would ruin your career, too. And they could do it. No one ever thanked me during all those years when I was the good girl on the lot. I felt like I was in slavery. They may have found me, but I came to feel I owed them, and the business they represented, nothing at all.

LENA HORNE

Ava was like my younger sister; she and I were spiritually akin. The main thing is that she was Southern. Though I was born in the East, I was sent South when I was five years old and I lived around the kind of people that she lived around. Ava was not one of those la-di-da Southern ladies. She was of a breed that, when they're wonderful, really are. She didn't feel she was born to rule. She felt that life was crappy and that a lot of people got mistreated for weird reasons, and she liked to see people like each other. She was a real good dame.

Ava and I also liked the same men, musicians mostly, black and white. We often had been hit on, or had hit the same guys. We'd show up at parties on the other side of town, very crowded, a lot of musicians and showgirls, not any MGM people. At one of them, where we really got down to it, we both wound up under the piano. We didn't talk about the business; we talked about men. Like Artie Shaw and his mental domination, which drove us both crazy. We laughed because he liked his women to read a lot of books. And he'd pick the books, but she wasn't ready for them. It's kind of like a child of nature being shut up in a room to study.

We lived near each other in Nichols Canyon, and one day we had a very long discussion about men. She was seeing someone, and seeing someone else. And the someone else was a guy who had a marvelous voice, Howard Duff. And the point being that Howard was a fantastic lover. And though she liked the other person, we were both regretful that frequently the finest lovers were not the ones you really *loved*.

People would say, "Oh, she drank so much whiskey." I don't know about that. I think she drank as some women do. I think she drank because she was bored with people often. I think it upset her that men that she *did* like were not as strong as they *could* have been. And she liked the ones who were not too intimidated by her. She didn't emasculate anyone, but she was an equal partner. And many men at that time didn't like that.

Another big problem was that both of us had to like who we went to bed with. And when it came to the power people who could have perhaps done tremendous favors for us, we thought they were ugly and unlovable. She was just a wild, good-looking girl that they wanted to harness, and dominate. "Well, she's a kook," they said. "She's too dumb to know what she's missing." But she knew what she was missing.

Because of her looks, Ava was awe-inspiring to the outside world. She didn't consciously use herself, it was there. But it was intimidating to other women. And she was not a girlie-girlie, chummy, let's go house-hunting and decorating or have cocktails with the girls type. She was an unfeminine, very feminine woman.

And Ava had great inner warmth that, for instance, I never saw in Lana. Lana was a little more aware of being a star. I don't think Ava thought about it that way. She was *down*. She was *Ava*, not Ava Gardner the star. She never believed that the image that they saw was what she really was. And she resented that that image made people expect something, when she wanted to be herself.

But because of who she was, Ava could never get but so much freedom. When I met Hedy Lamarr after one of my shows she said, "Wasn't it wonderful at MGM? Our clothes were chosen, we didn't have to think for ourselves, Howard Strickling took care of everything we had to say." And I was sort of punchy from that remark, because *I* knew that it was half-horrible.

You want to be able to think for yourself, and Ava always did. She hated the fact that we were made to feel like we were being possessed by somebody, or that we were owned body and soul if we wanted to work. MGM created a certain name, but they didn't prepare you for *real* life. I mean, what do you say when

Howard Strickling wasn't around and you had to get an abortion?

We talked about the nonsense about *Show Boat*, the fact that she was going to do it and I wanted it. "I'm sick of these sessions," she'd say, "I don't know how to sing." The reasoning behind it made her angry, for my sake. "Forget it," I said. We knew, we understood why it happened. So there was no friction about it. We were both very logical. It was a big laugh.

If Ava came to you, you couldn't help but like her, because she wasn't competing with anybody. She walked a mile in everybody's shoes. She really did.

SIXTEEN

fter *Show Boat* was finished, it began to finally look like my own personal show was about to go into production. On May 29, 1951, Nancy Sinatra's attorneys made the announcement Frank and I had been waiting for: she'd agreed to a divorce. Hallelujah! Everything would be simple from here on in. Or so we were in love enough to think. I just never seemed to learn that nothing was ever going to be simple between Mr. Sinatra and myself.

Take the time I said to him, "Honey, if we're going to get married, don't you think it would be a good idea if I met your parents?"

The blue eyes flashed in my direction.

"No," said Frank.

"Why not?"

"Out of the question."

"Why the fuck not?" I said, my temper heating up. After all, I'd already taken Frank down to North Carolina to meet my family, and that had gone very well.

"Because I haven't spoken to them for two years, and I don't intend to start now."

"This is your own mother and father we're talking about?"

"Right."

Well, it didn't seem right to me.

The split between Frank and his parents had come about apparently over a matter of finances. I didn't go into it. It was none of my business. What was my business was meeting Marty and Dolly Sinatra. In North Carolina, when you were contemplating marriage, it was usual to meet the mother and father of the bridegroom. That was a pleasure I didn't intend to miss if I could help it. And naturally I thought I could.

I kept nibbling away at Frank, and the next time we were in New York together I said, "Well, if you're not going to call your parents, I am."

Frank didn't make a big protest so I called, and he said with a certain grudging interest, "What did she say?"

I said, "We're invited to an Italian dinner in Hoboken tonight. Okay?"

"Okay," said Frank.

Hoboken bears little resemblance to Beverly Hills. It sits on the western banks of the Hudson River, directly across from Manhattan's spectacular skyline. When the Dutch and the British showed up, it was nothing but Indians, green woods, and grass sloping into clear water. Then God knows how many millions of immigrants arrived, and the woods were turned into fine houses for the first German merchants and later into crowded tenements for the Irish and the Italians. It was a city of narrow streets, outdoor markets, small shops, and factories, a crowded, vigorous, bustling place. The prevailing local philosophy was: If you make the dough, get up and go.

Dolly Sinatra was a survivor. If you lived in Hoboken in the twenties and thirties, as she had, you knew what hard times meant. I took one look at Dolly and saw where Frank got it all from: the blue eyes, the fair hair, the smile, the essential charm, cockiness, and determination. She took one look and hugged me like her own daughter. She always said I'd brought her son back to her.

Frank had bought his parents a house; no one could call it pretty but it was nice enough and Dolly was very proud of it. Marty Sinatra, Frank's father, was quieter, withdrawn, with a nice smile. Dolly set the pace; Marty nodded and followed.

Dolly showed me the house, every inch of it, and was it clean? Oh, my God. I mean Frank was the cleanest man I ever knew, forever changing his clothes and underwear, always showering and washing. If I'd caught him washing the soap it wouldn't have suprised me, and he inherited it all from his ma. Every room had a cross or a resident Jesus Christ; there seemed to be a cross on everything, because Dolly was deeply into the Catholic faith. And of course Dolly had to tell me all about Frank, with Frank squirming at every word. First the photograph as a baby, naked, weighing fifteen pounds. His grandmother took him under her care when he was born, because the doctor thought Dolly was dying. Poor Frank had been dragged into the world with forceps and apparently was almost given up for dead. Grandma, dependable as the Tuscan earth, grabbed him, washed him under the tap, wrapped him in a blanket, and took care of him as only grandmothers know how.

Frank was getting more and more furious as Dolly dragged out album after album of cute pictures of Frank as a child, dressed up in all kinds of little outfits. Sweet little photos that mothers treasure and sons would like to stick up the chimney.

Both Dolly and Marty were great cooks, and one of the large beds was covered by this starched, brilliantly white sheet, which was covered in turn by dozens and dozens of these little pasta shells, uncooked, the ones you crinkle up with your fingers and put filling in. Dolly spoke about four or five Italian dialects, but you wouldn't even guess that because there was no hint of an accent in her voice. Frank, however, never spoke a word of Italian. In those days, Italian immigrants didn't want their children to speak any language except English.

It was all so welcoming, such a great warm Italian household with no holding back. They even had an old uncle, either her brother or Marty's, living with them. I knew Frank had been looking at me very carefully, trying to sense how it was going, whether I was approving or not, his face reflecting that slight worry you have when you want someone *you* love to love what *you* love. But he didn't have to worry about me, because my family was poor, too, and I could relate to his folks as if they were my own. And I could see that Frank was getting into it as well, relaxing and beginning to enjoy the intimacy created by people who loved, really loved, with nothing held back.

Back in Los Angeles, Frank and I divided our time between an apartment we had near the ocean in Pacific Palisades and Frank's house in Palm Springs. We also vacillated between happiness at our impending wedding and misery as Nancy took longer and longer to actually file for that damn divorce. And I was still reel-ing from my first immersion in no-holds-barred journalistic coverage. Nothing we did was too inconsequential for the everpresent swarm of reporters and photographers to feed on like bees at a honeypot. It's very easy to say that we should have accepted this as the price of fame, but that turns out to be a hell of a tall order to live up to when you practically can't go to the bathroom without finding yourself on page one.

By the end of August, Nancy still hadn't filed, and we were both nervous and on edge, desperately in need of a vacation. We decided to get away to Mexico, which in those days was hardly considered a prime holiday spot. We thought we could sneak in a little bit of peace and quiet. Not a chance.

The chaos started at the Los Angeles airport, when reporters and photographers filled the tarmac and even crowded onto the steps of the plane, treating our departure like a goddamn presidential visit. At El Paso, where we had a forty-five-minute stopover for refueling, reporters crowded onto the plane, bombarding us with questions. Things were quieter in Mexico City, but the press made the four days we spent at Acapulco not very pleasant. Nothing anyone in their right mind would have identified as peace and quiet.

A Mexican friend of Frank's, who'd made his money in American baseball, offered us the use of his private plane for the journey back to L.A. Since a car could be driven right onto the runway in those days, we hoped to be able to avoid the press and just drive home. Talk about naive!

It was dark when we arrived, but a horde of photographers were gathered anyway, eager to pounce, and flashbulbs were popping as we scrambled into the waiting car. Frank took the wheel and, given that there was a crowd, he drove quite slowly. Our windows were closed, and the chances of getting a decent shot through the glass were negligible. One of the photographers was quick-witted enough to realize that no photos meant no story, no nothing. And as we drove past him, he leaned across the fender and hood on my side, deliberately sliding along it and throwing himself off. I was so indignant I rolled down the window and shouted, "I saw that, buster."

I thought what I saw with my own eyes would make a difference, but it didn't. The story went around the world that Frank had driven straight for the photographers at high speed, taking special aim at my sliding friend. He, incidentally, was quoted as saying that all he was after was respect for the press. I love that line. It didn't seem to me that the press was doing a whole hell of a lot to earn respect where Frank and I were concerned.

Though I don't want to make those days seem worse than they were, there will always be an edge, a margin of unhappiness, associated with them in my mind. We were desperately in love and, what with drinks with friends and intimate dinners alone, we tried so hard to make each other happy. But Frank's deep depression at being at a career low, and the realization that people he'd once thought of as friends were pretty good at kicking him when he was down there, was not good for us. And we both had a terrible tendency to needle each other's weaknesses, a habit that led to fallings out, like one that Labor Day weekend, that often had melodramatic, not to say dangerous, consequences.

It all started innocently enough, with a phone call from Frank saying that because he had a pair of singing engagements in the area, he'd rented a house on Lake Tahoe, and why didn't I come by and check it out. Delighted at the opportunity to spend time with him in a secluded, romantic spot, I bundled Reenie into the car with me and roared off down the road.

I admit I'm not the world's most careful driver. Going fast just does something for me; and I'd already plowed through a snake and a rabbit before I swerved to avoid a deer on a lonesome stretch of road near Carson City. I hit something, maybe a boulder or a tree, but the windshield was smashed, the car wouldn't start, and since all I knew about cars was that if you put gasoline in them, they usually go, we were stuck there. It was dark, it was lonely, there wasn't a phone booth for miles, and I couldn't remember the last time I'd seen another car.

"We did overtake an old jalopy a couple of hours ago," Reenie reminded me.

"Let's hope they arrive here sooner or later," I said.

They did. Two hours later. They towed us into Carson City, where Hank Sanicola, Frank's man, came and picked us up and drove us, at a much safer speed, to Lake Tahoe. Now at twenty-two miles long and between eight and twelve miles wide, this was no small lake. Too big, you might have thought, for anyone to ever disturb its peace. And you would have been wrong.

That was the day we decided we would hire a boat and set off for picnicking on the still waters. The boat was beautiful, long and shining. Hank was deputized to handle the steering part of the trip, as Frank and I were far too busy opening more than our allotment of iced champagne and drinking it down. And before we knew it, Frank and I were in a shouting match.

The cause, as usual, was jealousy. Frank had always allowed thoughts of Howard Hughes and Artie Shaw to get to him, and just to make him more miserable, I'd recently confessed about my mindless night with Mario Cabre. Don't think I wanted to. I tried to evade the question, change the subject and brush it aside, but Frank suspected and he kept at me. There'd been too much gossip for him not to suspect, and his persistence was unnerving. Finally, he resorted to the oldest trick in the book. "Ava, honey," he said. "It doesn't really matter to me. We've all fallen into the wrong bed some time or other. Just tell me the truth and we'll forget all about it."

That's a laugh. So I told him and he never forgave me. Ever.

Then that day on the lake, with the sun hot on our faces, Frank decided to pick at me. "I suppose," he said with studied casualness, "you wish you were out here with Howard Hughes."

I swallowed a whole lot of champagne in one gulp. "Why the fuck should I wish I was out here with Howard Hughes?"

"I'll bet he's got a bigger boat than this, doesn't he? That guy's got enough bucks to buy ten boats the size of this one."

"I don't care if he owns the fucking *Queen Mary*. I'm not sorry I'm not with him. So shut up."

"Don't tell me to shut up."

"Then don't tell me I'm thinking about Howard Hughes when I'm not thinking about Howard Hughes."

Oh, boy, what a battle. Screams, shouts, threats. The fact that Reenie and Hank Sanicola were also on the boat didn't even slow us down. Unfortunately, our shenanigans distracted Hank, who probably wasn't much of a sailor in the first place, and he promptly ran us aground near the shore, tearing a sizable hole in the bottom of the boat in the process. Everyone immediately waded ashore except me. For some alcohol-induced reason— maybe I'd seen *Captains Courageous* one time too many—I'd decided it was my duty to stay on board and bale the goddamn thing out.

By this time, Frank's temper had reached its limits. "Get off that fucking boat while there's still time, you fucking fool," he roared, shaking his fist in exasperation.

"Go fuck yourself," I replied, always the lady. "I'm staying here."

It was about that time that I discovered that this fancy boat was stocked with a monstrous amount of toilet paper. Why in the name of God the owners had decided to store so much on one boat I'll never know. But all the champagne I'd drunk convinced me that this wealth must be shared with the world. So I unwrapped roll after roll and floated them all off in the general direction of Frank. His rage was now off the charts, and he screamed a variety of curses in my direction that even I found impressive, but nothing he said deterred me from my appointed rounds.

Eventually, the boat began to sink in earnest, and I carefully joined Frank on the shore, carrying with me, with perfect survivor's instincts, the last bottle of champagne and two glasses. We managed to get the bottle open and sat down to regard the scene. What was a little rumpus between lovers, anyway? We clinked glasses, laughed and made up.

But battles that fierce never really go away. And just a few nights later, when we both had drunk too much, Frank made an offhanded remark that hurt me so deeply that I didn't stop to argue or shout back, I just left. I ran out into the darkness, my bare feet heading toward the lake. The slope was steep down to the water and the trees were thick and solid. You've got to be very drunk, very lucky, or very quick on your feet to miss them all, and I was a combination of all three. Then I heard someone running behind me, trying to catch up. It was Reenie.

I stopped and we both sat there in the darkness. We didn't say anything. There was nothing to say. Finally, Reenie said in a quiet, resigned voice, "Come on, Miss G., knock it off. Why don't we just go home."

That was the best idea I'd heard in days. We climbed back up the hill, got our bags packed and into the newly repaired car, and set off for L.A. It was well after midnight, but we had a bottle of sipping bourbon to keep us warm along those dark, lonely roads. I'd been full of love and anticipation going up; now I was full of despair going back. I'd just left and probably lost the man I loved.

Dawn was breaking across the ocean as we reached the house in Pacific Palisades hours later. We were exhausted, hung over and miserable. We stumbled toward our respective bedrooms, hungry for sleep, when the telephone began to ring. I tottered back and picked it up. I could tell by the sound of Hank Sanicola's voice that this was for real. "Oh, my God, Ava. Hurry back. Frank's taken an overdose!"

God almighty! In the Hampshire House in New York, all I'd had to do was race through a couple of bedrooms. Now we faced hours of driving back over those tortuous roads.

"Reenie," I yelled. "You won't believe this. We've got to go back. Now!"

"We nearly killed ourselves driving there, and we did the same driving back," Reenie said. "Third time might be unlucky!"

That made sense. "I'll call the airport," I said. "We'll catch the next flight."

I have been exasperated with Francis Albert Sinatra many times through the years, but never more so than on that morning when I returned to his bedside at Lake Tahoe.

A car had rushed us to the L.A. airport. A car had rushed us from the Nevada airport to the house at Lake Tahoe. Hank Sanicola met me at the door. He looked as tired out and worn as I felt. I had difficulty speaking.

"How is he?" I said.

"He's okay," said Hank.

I thought, Thank God! I ran through into the bedroom. I looked down at Frank and he turned his sad blue eyes to look at me.

"I thought you'd gone," he said weakly.

I wanted to punch him, I really did. I wanted to punch him as much as I'd ever wanted to punch anybody. Frank had tricked both Reenie and me back to his bedside. He'd had a fine rest, doctors watching over him, feeling his pulse and all that sort of crap. And they didn't even have to pump his stomach—he hadn't taken enough phenobarbital tablets for that. Everybody had been up all night except Frank! Hank had been signaling for help from all over the U.S.A., Reenie and I had been charging back and forth across the mountains like demented pigeons. And Frank was just turning over, waking up, and saying, "Hi, kid."

The Larry Tarr photo that started my movie career.

My acting debut in the Brogden school's first-grade play, A Rose Dream.

This was taken a dozen years before I was born. Mama in the center is flanked by Daddy and his sister Ava. Left to right are my sisters Inez, Bappie (Beatrice) and Elsie Mae.

At age 16, with Bob Rose at his college prom.

One of my very first pinup photos.

Mickey's and my wedding. That's his mother.

This is posed but Mickey really did try to teach me to play.

After my operation for appendicitis.

*More dumb publicity shots. (Left)
Here I am on that block of ice.
(Below) With Gloria DeHaven
and some confused chickens.*

Publicity shots with Burt Lancaster for The Killers. Of course they had nothing to do with the story.

A rare photograph of Howard Hughes, since he hated publicity.

MGM/UA

With a dog Howard gave me.

Artie Shaw and me on our wedding day.

A scene from The Hucksters *with Clark Gable.*

Howard Duff visits me on my set—

—and I visit Lana Turner on hers.

Sculptor Joseph Nicolosi and the second, clothed statue he did of me.

Relaxing with Robert Walker as they set up a scene for One Touch of Venus.

Robert Taylor.

A visit back home in 1949. I'm looking at the window of the room I was born in.

My sisters Elsie Mae Creech (left) and Inez Grimes during the same visit.

Frank escorted me to the Show Boat *premiere.*

As Julie Laverne in Show Boat.

My marriage to Frank, November 7, 1951.

*Trying to make a Grenadier
guardsman smile, as a studio
publicity stunt.*

Bappie and me, 1951.

Gable and Grace Kelly on location in Africa for Mogambo.

Grace and me.

Our three-hundred-tent encampment for Mogambo.

*With Luis Miguel Dominguin
and Bappie at a Spanish
bullfight.*

Dancing the flamenco in
The Barefoot Contessa.

Strolling to work on Contessa *with Humphrey Bogart, Lauren Bacall, and David Hanna, the publicist on the film.*

My character Victoria Jones
sure had a hard time in
Bhowani Junction.
The rape scene is above.

It was my costars David Niven and Stewart Granger who had a tough time in The Little Hut. *That's Walter Chiari in the grass skirt.*

My fall in 1958.

With Gregory Peck in Australia for On the Beach.

© 1958, Ren. 1986 Titanus S.P.A.

With Anthony Franciosa in a scene from The Naked Maja.

At the Gala of Roses in Monaco as the guest of Princess Grace and Prince Rainier.

My portrait by the famous photographer Hoyningen-Huene for
55 Days at Peking.

With Richard Burton in
Night of the Iguana.

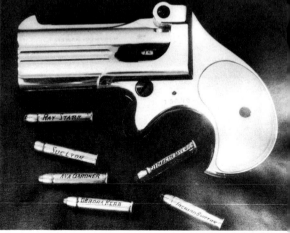

The notorious silver bullets John
Huston presented to members
of the company.

The Bible *with George C. Scott (above); directed by John Huston (below).*

I was the Empress Elizabeth and Omar Sharif played my son,
Prince Rudolf, in Mayerling.

Morgan and me, just before my stroke.

At home in London.

I could have killed him, but instead I forgave him in about twenty-five seconds. We had no time for these nerve-destroying incidents. I know now that Frank's mock suicidal dramas—his desperate love signals to get me back to his side—were, at root, cries for help. He was down, way down. His contracts were being canceled. His wife's lawyers were intent on screwing every possible dollar out of him, something that caused him to force a laugh and say, "Ava, I won't have enough bucks to buy you a pair of nylons once they're through with me." For Christ's sake, he was a human being like the rest of us. He'd been the idol of millions and now he was being taunted as a washed-up has-been. And Frank Sinatra was nothing if not a proud man.

Our love was deep and true, even though the fact that we couldn't live with each other any more than we couldn't live without each other sometimes made it hard for outsiders to understand. All I know is that if Frank had lost me or I'd lost him during those months, our worlds would have been shattered.

Finally, at the end of October 1951, Nancy's divorce was granted. She took her pound of flesh from him, and then some, but at the moment I didn't care. A week after the divorce, Frank and I were ready to stand at the altar. Then a shadow fell over our happiness. His name was—you guessed it—Howard Hughes.

SEVENTEEN

To say there was no love lost between Frank and Howard Hughes is like saying the North and the South didn't particularly care for each other during the War Between the States. The enmity was so thick you could cut it with a knife, and that knife cut both ways.

Frank, for his part, always flew off the handle every time Howard's name was so much as mentioned. Once, in one of my many ineffective attempts to prove my absolute devotion to Frank, I marched to a New York hotel room window, took off a gorgeous solid gold bracelet and a matching necklace, which, knowing Howard, probably cost a fortune and a half, and dramatically tossed the damned things right out the window. I hope whoever picked them up had better luck with them than I did.

And if you think Howard was an innocent bystander in all of this, you just don't know Howard. I'd made it crystal clear to him that when I fall in love with a man as I had with Frank, it's good-bye to everyone else, but Howard never took no for an answer. What can you expect from someone who shrugged off a brass bell tossed at the side of his head? Believe me, there was something scary about Howard's stop-at-nothing determination.

One of Howard's least charming traits was the way he insisted on scrutinizing everyone, putting a "watcher" on people he cared about so he would know what was going on with those he considered his property. This time, he put a detective on Mr. Si-natra. The idea? To discredit Frank in my eyes and prevent our marriage. I mean, Howard needed his head examined if he thought he could win my favor that way, but we already know that, don't we?

The first time Howard tried that ploy, Frank was working at the Copacabana in New York and I was staying at Frank's house in Palm Springs. And Howard showed up there one day with that sanctimonious look on his face which meant he thought he had the ammunition to wipe Frank off the face of the earth.

There was a chorus girl in New York, he said piously; he had her name, not to mention all the days and times and places where they met, the whole routine. I guess he'd have offered photo-graphic evidence if I'd been interested. And I hated him for it, I really hated him, because I loved Frank so.

I called Frank immediately, and he said, "Untrue, untrue." When I visited him in New York, he insisted on bringing this little chorus girl over to meet me, together with the guy who ran the joint, to convince me it wasn't true. Look at this poor girl, they said, she still has pimples on her face, she's still a virgin. "Virgin, my ass!" I said, right to her face. I was pretty rude. But I was angry and I was deeply hurt.

Finally, however, I let it ride, and when I let Howard know that this kind of shit cut no ice with me, I thought that would be the last I'd ever hear of it.

Then came the night before the wedding. Bappie and I shared one hotel suite, and nearby rooms held Frank and his entourage: Hank Sanicola, Dick Jones, a great piano player, and Manie Sachs, the former head of Frank's label, Columbia Records. There was a lot of visiting between rooms; the atmosphere could not have been more convivial and pleasant.

Until the letter arrived.

Apparently it had been given to the head bellman, and as it was handwritten and addressed personally to me, it was brought directly to our room. I opened it, I read it through, and I could hardly go on breathing. It was from a woman who admitted she was a whore and claimed she had been having an affair with Frank. It was filthy, it gave details that I found convincing, and I felt sick to my stomach. How could I go on with the wedding in the face of a letter like this?

Bappie saw the look on my face and knew that it was serious. "The wedding is off," I said. "Finished. Forget it!" I marched into my bedroom. Locked myself in. The wedding *was* off as far as I was concerned.

Now the bedlam began. Frank was going crazy. Bappie and Manie Sachs, Hank Sanicola, and Dick Jones were all rushing backward and forward between Frank's room and mine arguing, wheedling, yelling, protesting. They told me no one could cancel a wedding at this late date. It had all been prepared: the cars, the catering, the minister, the flowers, the elegant house. I said I was an important part of that wedding and I could damn well cancel it.

I think it took most of that night with a lot of back and forth before I agreed to change my mind. Thinking about it now, and wondering who could be so malevolent as to arrange for that letter to arrive at such a critical moment and drive me almost out of my mind, the finger points in only one direction—Howard Hughes. At the time, however, I didn't dream that Howard would try and pull a trick like that.

Manie Sachs' brother Lester had generously offered us his house in Philadelphia for the wedding, hoping against hope that reporters would not find their way there. Of course they did. Lester had to use a catering firm to arrange the reception and they were certainly not above gossiping to reporters.

Frank shouted insults down at them from the Sachses' bedroom window, and I tried to calm him down. My side of the family was represented by Bappie, Frank's by his mother and father and several of Frank's best friends: Hank Sanicola; Ben Barton, a partner of Frank's; his conductor, Axel Stordahl, and his wife; and Dick Jones, whose fingers were poised above the keyboard of a grand piano.

I glided down the stairs in my mauve marquisette cocktail dress, wearing a double strand of pearls, pearl and diamond earrings, my finger itching to receive the narrow platinum wedding ring that Frank and I had chosen. Dick Jones attempted to strike up Mendelssohn's familiar wedding march. Only this time it wasn't at all familiar. The piano hadn't been tuned for ages. Dick gave up on his recital and joined the champagne drinkers.

Lester Sachs had done a very good job. We stood at a specially erected altar and, on November 7, 1951, a judge named Sloane made us man and wife. Then we moved to the bar and went over plans for our escape.

Frank had hired a plane, a twin-engined Beechcraft, that he couldn't really afford. But what the hell, he said, it is *our* honeymoon. I'd changed into a blue traveling suit, and we hurried down the stairs kissing and hugging our good-byes. The front door was flung open and we sprinted through the photographers to the car. It was all a confusing whirl, and it wasn't until I was climbing the stairs into the plane to Miami that I realized that in the rush I'd left the suitcase holding my honeymoon trousseau behind. All I had with me was my handbag!

Well, there was no point in having a fit; it would rejoin me sometime or other. But hell, I didn't even have the beautiful little nightie I'd saved for our wedding night. I didn't have a bathing suit. I'd didn't have anything to go to the beach in—nothing! So I slept in Frank's pajamas, at least the top half of them, and the next day we walked along the empty beach, me in the bottom half of my travel suit and Frank's jacket. Naturally a photographer was lying in wait and snapped a shot of us, barefoot, holding hands. I've always thought it was a sad little photograph, a sad little commentary on our lives then. We were simply two young people so much in love, and the world wouldn't leave us alone for a second. It seemed that everyone and everything was against us, and all we asked for was a bit of peace and privacy.

We went on from Miami to Havana, where my luggage finally caught up with us. Havana in those Batista days was an American playground, complete with gambling houses, whorehouses, and brightly lit cafés, every other one boasting a live orchestra. Traffic, lights, bustle, cigar smoke, pretty girls, balmy air, stars in the sky, they all combined to form a Latin town that aimed to please.

We drank a lot of Cuba libres and went out to the nightclubs and the gambling joints. Fortunately, most of the paparazzi seemed to have other things to do, so we were pretty much left alone. I don't even know if I would have noticed if we weren't; I was finally on my honeymoon with the man I loved. On one of our last nights, I climbed up on one of the hotel's high archways, convincing Frank that I was going to throw myself off. But I was just being mischievous, swinging along on rum and

Coke with no intention of ending it all. I was having far too much fun.

Once we got back to the States, however, our battling picked up where we'd left off. Anything could get me going. I remember, though I wish I didn't, one of Frank's performances in New York when I somehow convinced myself he was singing especially for an old flame, Marilyn Maxwell, who happened to be in the audience. All these people there, and I believe that Frank is having a little flirt with Marilyn. I mean, the ability to flirt with the entire audience is one of Frank's primary gifts as a performer.

Naturally, a fight started back at the hotel after the performance. I ran out the door and into a pouring rain that was drenching the city's streets. It must have been two A.M. Everything was dark, deserted. There I was, dressed to kill (remember, I'd been at that concert), bareheaded, barefoot, and heartbroken, my tears mixing with the rain. I ran, God knows how far. When I spotted a subway entrance, I went down. I had no purse, but I did have enough loose change to buy a token.

I got on a train and I don't know how long I sat there. Maybe forty minutes, maybe an hour. I reached the end of the line. They told me there wouldn't be another train for a long time. I walked out of the station and found myself in a sleazy, dilapidated neighborhood on the fringes of the city. To this day, I have no idea exactly where I was. I didn't know a thing about New York.

It was still raining. A gray light was coming up behind the rooftops and it was cold. I walked around for perhaps fifteen minutes when a cruising taxi came along and I hailed it. The driver was very suspicious at first, especially when I said, "Hampshire House hotel, near Central Park." Then he caught on. At least he thought he caught on. Clearly, I was a prostitute out on a call! What else would a pretty, well-dressed young lady be doing walking around at this time in the morning, and asking to be taken to a posh New York hotel?

I caught his drift, but I wasn't going to argue for a single second. Just get me to the Hampshire House, that's all I cared about. Besides, how could I say, "No, I'm not a prostitute. I'm Mrs. Frank Sinatra out for an early-morning walk in the rain"?

So I went along with the idea.

And he was furious. Not at me. Prostitutes were part of every-day life for a New York cabbie. But how dare that goddamn jerk waiting in the Hampshire House get a nice girl like me out on the streets at this time in the morning in this sort of weather? These out-of-town pains-in-the-ass thought they could do whatever they damn pleased in New York. "Now listen here, hon," the cabbie said. "You make him pay for this. You hit him for plenty. If he wants you at this time in the morning, then he's gotta spend real bucks for the privilege. You got that, hon?"

"Hon," sitting in the back, got that loud and clear. I think with a little encouragement the driver might have come into the Hampshire House and punched my imaginary client in the nose. He had a real chivalrous nature, this guy did.

We slid to a stop outside the Hampshire House. It was daylight. New York was gently opening its eyes. The doorman hurried across to let me out. His face and his voice did not change but he recognized me immediately.

"Good morning, Mrs. Sinatra," he said politely.

Halfway through the door I glanced back at the taxi driver leaning across his seat toward me. He caught the name and the doorman's servility and his face became one of those frozen movie frames: the mouth open, the eyes fixed, the brain cells confused. Then he got his voice back and he was so apologetic that I felt awfully sorry for him after all the help he'd given me.

I stopped him in mid-confusion. "Please don't apologize. You got me out of a lot of trouble, and I'll always be grateful to you." I think a little smile may have strayed across my face. "And thanks a lot for the advice."

I tugged the doorman's sleeve and whispered in his ear. "Can you pay the fare and add on a ten-dollar tip?"

The doorman touched his hat and fished in his pocket. There were still some gentlemen left in New York City.

Frank was still up when I reached our suite. I could tell by his eyes that he was tired, but they lit up when I came through the door. Any young husband tends to get worried when his young wife goes tearing off into the wilds of New York in the middle of the night. "Egg sandwich?" he said. Frank can make an egg sand-wich like nobody else in the whole wide world. I can see him doing it now. I didn't say a word. I don't think he did either. I watched him heating up the olive oil in the pan, and then putting in the white bread—it's got to be white bread. Then he dropped the egg into the hot olive oil, added salt and pepper, and did the quick sandwich trick with the bread. He handed it to me and gave me a glass of milk. Then he said he was glad I'd got home in one piece.

I had my mouth full but I said I was, too.

EIGHTEEN

"Kilimanjaro is a snow-covered mountain 19,710 feet high, and is said to be the highest mountain in Africa. Its western summit is called the Masai 'Ngaje Ngai,' the House of God. Close to the western summit, there is the dried and frozen carcass of a leopard. No one has explained what the leopard was seeking at that altitude."

That paragraph, one of the most famous Papa Hemingway ever wrote, is also the first words you hear in the film version of his short story that I starred in in 1952, a film that really pushed me into international stardom. Yet if the filmmakers had been as faithful to the whole story as they were to those few words, there probably wouldn't have been enough of a part for me to play to get any kind of recognition at all.

Papa's short story, set on an African safari, appeared in 1936 and was eventually bought up for seventy-five thousand dollars by Darryl F. Zanuck, one of Hollywood's most powerful independent producers, who pretty much ran his own little kingdom at Twentieth Century–Fox. A big-game hunter himself, Zanuck was eager to see *Snows* filmed, and he gave the project to veteran screenwriter Casey Robinson to adapt.

Snows proved a tough nut to crack. First of all, like *The Killers* before it, it was only a short story, and one with a confusing stream-of-consciousness structure at that. It told of Harry, a successful writer who reviews his unsatisfactory life as he lies dying in the shadow of Africa's tallest mountain. Making things even harder was the fact that Papa, always the pessimist, has the writer die at the close, and Zanuck was adamant that this film have a happy ending.

Robinson came up with a solution that he called "one third Hemingway, one third Zanuck, and one third myself." For openers, he borrowed episodes so freely from Papa's novels that the poor man complained, "I sold Fox a single story, not my complete works. This movie has something from nearly every story that I ever wrote in it." He switches scenes from Africa to Michigan to Paris and Madrid until you think you're in a damn travelogue. Harry still talks about how "dying a failure leaves a bad taste in your mouth" and complains that, "I've lived, all right, but where has it gotten me?" But the movie version allows him to survive at the end, transformed by the love of his wealthy but loving second wife Helen, who chases away an ornery hyena and saves the day.

To fill out the story, Robinson also padded the stories of the earlier women in Harry's life. Harry was played by my old pal Greg Peck, and I was to play Cynthia, his first wife and true love, though you wouldn't know that from the ads, where I'm described as "a model from Montparnasse who lit a fire in him that could only be quenched by the eternal Snows of Kilimanjaro," whatever that means.

Harry runs into me during his early days as a struggling novelist in Paris, and he's immediately attracted, not only because I've got the kind of laugh strong men fight over but because, in a town full of earnest artists, I was easygoing enough to be "the only person in the whole darn place who's only trying to be happy." And when I look him right in the eyes and say, "I'm my own lady," I goddamn well make him and everyone in the theater believe it.

We get married, I offer moral support as Harry becomes increasingly successful as a writer, and I feel so happy "every bit of me said 'This is all of it.'" But then we go to Africa, on Harry's first safari, and I'm distressed at his wanderlust, not to mention his blood lust as he mows down assorted wildlife. I've also got a secret: I'm pregnant and I'm afraid to tell him.

Finally, fearing that a family would tie him down and ruin his career, I deliberately fall down a pretty fearsome set of stairs and miscarry. Then, to get me off his mind, I make him believe I've fallen for a fairly sappy flamenco dancer. He remarries. I don't reappear in his life until a decade later, when as an ambulance driver in the Spanish Civil War, I just about die in his strong arms.

Of all the parts I've played, Cynthia was probably the first one I understood and felt comfortable with, the first role I truly wanted to play. In fact, I did my biggest scene, the one in a Spanish nightclub where our marriage falls apart and I run away with Mr. Flamenco, in a single take without closeups. This wasn't at all like some of those other slinky-black-dress parts I'd had. This girl wasn't a tramp or a bitch or a real smart cookie. She was a good average girl with normal impulses. I didn't have to pretend. And if I hadn't proved that I was my own lady with the kind of life I'd led up to then, I hadn't proved anything at all.

My enthusiasm, however, apparently was not enough for Mr. Zanuck. There were rumors that he thought I might not be able to handle the role, though my work in *Show Boat* helped ease his mind. I've also heard stories that Arlene Francis was his original choice, but a key plot point is that Harry first meets second wife Helen by mistaking her for Cynthia in front of the Ritz Hotel in Paris, and I certainly fit that bill better than Arlene did.

One thing that turned out to be surprising about the film, once Metro lent me out and I got the part, was that though it was set in the four corners of the world, all the principal photography was done in Hollywood on the Fox lot. All of Stage 8, in fact, was turned into a massive African hunting camp courtesy of a three-hundred-fifty-by-forty-foot cyclorama painting of snowy Mt. Kilimanjaro itself. And some of the props they used, like an elephant-foot stool, came direct from Zanuck's office.

If I didn't have any problems with the role of Cynthia, I did have some difficulties with Frank. Shooting began just weeks after our wedding, and he was really up against it at that time. Unbeknownst to the public, he was having serious problems with his voice, and his agents were having difficulty booking him into top night spots. It seems hard to believe now, but he was having to play saloons and dates that were way beneath him. And feeling that way, it was really important to him that his wife be by his side in New York.

I talked to Zanuck, to Casey Robinson, and to director Henry King, and they rearranged the film's schedule so all my scenes could be shot in ten days. Frank agreed to let me go for that period of time. But on the last day of shooting, when we had hundreds of extras for one of our Spanish Civil War scenes, things took longer than we anticipated. Since it would have been too expensive to keep the extras late, it was decided that we'd finish shooting on the eleventh day. I knew Frank would give me holy hell about that, and he did.

A lot of silliness happened when the film was finally released, with exhibitors complaining that people wouldn't go to a picture whose name they can't pronounce, and Fox countersuggesting that theaters sponsor essay contests of a hundred words or less on what the hell the leopard *was* seeking at that altitude.

Though I got excellent reviews for my performance (*Variety* said I made Cynthia "a warm, appealing, alluring standout"), Papa was as unhappy with the film as Frank was. He took to calling it *The Snows of Zanuck* and kept threatening to oil up his old hunting rifle, return to the mountain, and go searching for the producer's soul. "Ava," he told me once, "the only two good things in it were you and the hyena." I never had the heart to tell him that the hyena on the sound track was an expert imitation provided by director King, an old Africa hand who everyone agreed sounded better than the real thing.

NINETEEN

Maybe it's the air, maybe it's the altitude, maybe it's just the place's goddamn karma, but Frank's establishment in Palm Springs, the only house we really could ever call our own, has seen some pretty amazing occurrences. It was the site of probably the most spectacular fight of our young married life, and honey, don't think I don't know that's really saying something. And even before that it provided me with a chance to spend some time with the most reclusive of Hollywood legends, Greta Garbo.

When Artie Shaw and I were married, Garbo had lived right next door on Bedford Drive in Beverly Hills, but in spite of peering over walls, through hedges, and over curtains I never caught so much as a glimpse of her. So now, when my old friend Minna Wallis called the house at Palm Springs and said she and Garbo would like to spend the weekend there and didn't care if Bappie and I stayed along for the ride, you better believe I was pleased at the opportunity.

"We'd love to have her," I said, the Scarlett O'Hara of hostesses. "When does she want to arrive?"

"In about five minutes."

"Oh, my God!"

It was midsummer in the desert, hot enough to fry an egg on the sidewalk, but Bappie and I rushed around, arranging flowers in Miss Garbo's bedroom and turning up the air-conditioning. We'd barely had time to do anything before a taxi pulled up and out she stepped, wearing not only the expected large sunglasses

and wide-brimmed hat but also, I swear to God, a wool tur-
tleneck sweater, this huge woolen scarf around her neck, and
quite a heavy coat on top of it all.

"Hello, Miss Garbo," I said, still the polite Southern miss.
"I'm Ava Gardner."

Did I get a hello back? A handshake? The slightest sign of
recognition? No, I did not. Instead there was this sweeping movement toward the house and a booming "Where is my roooom?",
the echoing vowels as broad as the great outdoors. And no
sooner were she and Minna settled in their rooms when word
came out that (a) Miss Garbo didn't like air-conditioning and (b)
if there was anything Miss Garbo liked less than air-conditioning,
it was flowers.

Bappie and I retreated to the pool, fortifying ourselves alco-
holically for what we were beginning to fear would be a grim
weekend. Then, about an hour later, Miss Garbo decided to join
us. She walked out to the pool and I really think she was the
most beautiful thing I have ever seen in my life. And I mean that
despite the fact that she wore a pair of men's baggy khaki shorts
that came down to her knees—and nothing else. Though she
must have been in her mid-forties, her breasts and shoulders were
glorious. Her face had just a touch of blue eye shadow, her lips a
trace of lipstick, and she had that wonderful hair that moved
from side to side as she turned her head. She was totally magnificent.

She was Greta now, all smiles, with the intention, she said, of
taking a little swim. She changed into a dress after that, accepted
our offer of vodka, and began a memorable weekend of drinking,
eating, laughing, and more eating. Because though she was involved with nutritionist Gaylord Hauser and had the stock of
health foods and vitamins to prove it, Miss Garbo definitely had
a robust Swedish appetite.

The only time she brought up health was when she made the
rather enigmatic comment that "it was the 'kneeses' under the
table that gives us diseases." After a few more vodkas, Greta
made her point clear. You sat down to dine, your "kneeses" carefully placed under the table. You had a plate in front of you. You
filled it, stuffed yourself, got fat, and contracted one of the many
diseases associated with that condition. True enough, those
"kneeses under the table" had brought you to an untimely end.

There were two other things I remember about Greta's conversation. At one point she admired a small, inexpensive bracelet that Frank had given me and said, rather sadly, "You know, I love jewelry, and yet men have never given any to me. I don't know why." And she also admitted that the only man she'd ever really loved was John Gilbert, her romantic costar, but that he'd "let me down" by having a surreptitious affair (is there any other kind?) with a little extra during their last film together. She had never forgiven him.

Brother, did I ever know about romantic battles. Or at least I thought I did, because soon after the filming of *The Snows of Kilimanjaro* was completed, Frank and I had a spectacular night of ridiculous boozy drama in Palm Springs that even French farce couldn't have competed with.

And the evening had started out so well. Frank and I had driven over the hill to the San Fernando Valley to have dinner with a couple of friends. Unfortunately, we drank quite a lot. I never much cared about what I was drinking, only about the effect it was having on me, and that night the effect wasn't very good. I took offense at some remark and all hell started to break loose. By the time we'd gotten home to Pacific Palisades, my mood had taken on an icy, remote, to-hell-with-all-men tinge. To emphasize the remoteness I felt, I retired to the solitude of my bathroom. So there I was, lying in my tub, soothing myself under the bubbles, when Frank came breezing in, picking up the argument where it had left off.

I was furious. I hate intrusions when I have my clothes off. It's a bred-in-the-bone shyness, some sort of deep insecurity which I guess comes from my childhood. As I've said, with each of my three husbands it took me several drinks and a lot of courage to appear disrobed in front of them.

I reacted instinctively. "Get out of here!" I yelled.

Naturally, that gave my husband the feeling that he was not truly loved.

Frank exploded. He yelled back, "For Christ's sake, aren't I married to you?"

That cut no ice with me. I was still outraged.

"Go away!" I screamed.

Which paved the way for what I have to admit was a truly memorable exit line. "Okay! Okay! If that's the way you want it.

I'm leaving. And if you want to know where I am, I'm in Palm Springs fucking Lana Turner."

The bathroom door slammed. The front door slammed. I heard the car roar away. My car. The only car!

So I got out of the bath. Thoughtfully. I got dressed and became all the more thoughtful about what Frank had said. At first it didn't bother me. But the more I thought about it the more it did bother me.

What does a young, recently married wife do in a situation like this? Hire a private detective? How the hell can I hire a private eye at this time of night? Better handle it myself. Catch 'em in the act! At that time Lana was staying at our Palm Springs house. Frank had lent it to Lana and her business manager, Ben Cole, for a few days. Ben was a nice guy. No romance between them.

I went to the telephone and called Bappie. Sometimes Bappie has a hard time forgetting that she's not my mother, but she is a good friend. It was past midnight and I could tell that, like me, Bappie'd had a little to drink.

"Bappie," I said, "I haven't got a car. I'm going to call a taxi and meet you in your car at the foot of Nichols Canyon. We're going to Palm Springs."

Bappie reacted as if she'd been stuck with an electric prod. "What?" she yelled. "Do you know what time it is?"

"Late," I said evasively. The hours after midnight had a habit of slipping away very quickly in those days. "But we've got to go to Palm Springs."

"What for?"

"Bappie, this is urgent. I've got to catch Frank in the act."

"Okay," she said grudgingly, "I'll be there."

We arrived at Frank's house in Palm Springs and I faced my first test. The gate was locked. I paused for thought. If I rang the bell, which sounded in the kitchen, someone would press a button and the gate would open. But that was no good. I had to remain invisible until the moment of discovery. "We'll drive around the back and get in that way," I said to Bappie.

"But that's all desert," Bappie wailed. "It's full of sidewinders—and they're deadly."

What's a sidewinder compared to the chance of surprising Frank Sinatra, I thought, and, headlights out, we headed for the back, where the pool that Greta Garbo had so loved was separated from the desert by nothing more than a six-foot chain link fence. Since climbing has never been a problem for me, I took off my shoes and scampered over, leaving Bappie behind me to fuss about those sidewinders.

I approached the house cautiously, and then realized I didn't have to bother. The curtains on all the damn windows were closed tight. That's something that never happens in detective movies. How are you supposed to catch 'em in the act if you can't see in?

I moved quietly from window to window, looking for even a sliver of light. Finally I found one at the kitchen window, and I'd just got my nose pressed against the glass when the back door right next to me opened, Ben Cole poked his head out and said, "Ava, is that you? Come on in, honey."

I went to rescue Bappie from the snakes and we went inside, where Lana was looking as lovely as ever. I knew that at one time she felt like she'd been on the verge of marrying Frank, which certainly gave some impetus to my suspicions, but we'd always been good, if not close, friends. And I'd always admired her as a great movie star. I remembered when I first arrived in Hollywood, a starlet green as a spring tobacco leaf. I'd glimpsed Lana on a set one day, and I'd thought, Now, there's the real thing. She had a canvas-backed chair inscribed with her name and a stool next to it holding her things. What struck me was that among them was a gleaming *gold* cigarette case and a gleaming *gold* lighter. Without envy I'd thought, Now that's what a *real* film star should look like. That's style.

What interested me at that moment, however, was that there was no sign of Frank.

Nothing daunted, the four of us settled down to have a party. The house had a big kitchen with a long bar and a row of stools. Lana had her bottle of iced vodka, and Ben was serving the rest of us drinks. I began to feel very happy, although I had a small regret that my career as a private eye hadn't lasted very long.

It turned out to be the calm before the storm. Lana, meanwhile, passed on one other item of news: she was expecting her current boyfriend down from Los Angeles, where he ran a club. Once it closed, he was driving across to Palm Springs to spend the night. Maybe, I thought, he'll arrive before Frank.

At that very moment the front door was thrown open. Frank

had arrived. Nothing subdued about that entrance. The door was behind us so we all swung round on our bar stools, caught in the middle of one of those inevitable pregnant pauses.

Then, aided by the booze, like a fool I tossed off one of those throwaway lines that would have been better thrown away. "Ah, Frank! I thought you were going to be down here fucking Lana."

That really got the blood flowing. Here I was mocking him and having a great time. Without him! In *his* house!

Frank, completely flustered, responded with the first thought that came into his mind and yelled, "I wouldn't touch that broad if you paid me."

It was a cruel remark but Frank was angry at me, not at Lana. She, however, immediately burst into tears and rushed away sobbing, "I'm leaving, I'm leaving!" And off she went to get her things. Ben Cole, who had been the complete gentleman throughout, raised his eyes to heaven and went off to help her pack.

"Out of my house," Frank was screaming. "Out, out, out! Everybody out!"

I felt that was very unreasonable. After all we'd been married for quite a few months and I thought it was my house, too. Also, an awful lot of my clothes, books, records, and God-knows-what shared the space with Frank's things.

I made that point clear. And though I *hadn't* had a whole lot of experience in playing empresses, queens, countesses, duchesses, or any other aristocratic ladies, I managed to be pretty damn regal and aloof at that moment.

"Okay," I said knowing that booze never affected my diction. "I will go. But in my own time. Taking my books and records and personal belongings with me."

To make a start, I got a ladder—who knows from where—and placed it against the highest bookshelf. Then I climbed to the very top and began carefully picking out books and records and dropping them all the way down on the carpet.

Frank seemed to approve of this idea. Furiously he scooped up everything I'd thrown on the floor and heaved it all out the still-open front door—he'd never bothered to close it—and onto the pitch-dark driveway. Not to be outdone, I stalked across to the bedroom and bathroom and started to pile my clothes, cosmetics, and every other goddamn odd and end I had in a heap on the floor. And Frank grabbed those as well, raced to the door, and tossed them out into the night to join the ever-growing mess in the driveway.

It was at least three in the morning when Lana and Ben, God bless them, departed to look for rooms somewhere, anywhere else. By this time, nothing was separating Frank and me. I was clinging to the nearest doorknob, holding on for dear life, and Frank, with both his hands around my waist, was trying to physically pry me off so he could throw me out of the house and onto the by now considerable pile in the driveway. Bappie, meanwhile, was watching all this in a sort of a trance, trying without much hope to make peace between us. "For God's sake, kids," she'd say. "Will you please knock it off? This is *disgraceful!*"

It sure was. But I wasn't giving up, and neither was Frank. Finally, having failed to pry me off my doorknob, he tried another tack. "The police," he yelled. "I'm going to call the police."

"Great idea," I said. "Call the police. Call the fucking police."

Frank rushed over to the phone. And right back into the middle of this, stepping gingerly over my personal effects, was poor Ben Cole. Could he reclaim, he asked apologetically, the cold chicken Lana had bought for a late supper between her, Ben, and the boyfriend, not to mention the bottle of ice-cold vodka that she had left behind? Would we mind if he took these things with him?

Nobody minded. Nobody cared. Take the chicken, the vodka, and the boyfriend out into the night and leave the ring free for the main event.

Right on schedule, the police arrived. Police chief Gus Kettman, who happened to be a friend of Frank's, was in charge. He had a worried frown on his face, but his manner was cool as you please. He could see he had a delicate situation on his hands. He struggled through our debris, came inside, and immediately figured out from his wide experience of life in Palm Springs that he had a classic drunken brawl to deal with.

Since this whole ruckus had taken place on private property, with no one hurt and nothing damaged except a few personal feelings, the chief really couldn't do anything except try and calm things down. He came closer and said, "Now listen, Frank. This is absurd. This had got to stop."

Then, looking reproachfully at me, he added, "Ava, why don't you calm down?"

"Calm down!" I replied with enviable dignity. "I am calm. Can't you see how calm I am? I'm simply leaving this house, but I'm taking my personal possessions with me."

Finally, the chief got Frank back to room temperature and Bappie and I stepped haughtily over the garage sale in the driveway and made our way back to wherever we'd left the car. As you might imagine, it took Frank and me a little time to make up after that escapade.

The man who helped make it happen was, of all people, Adlai Stevenson, the Democratic candidate for President. Both Frank and I were firm Democrats in those days, and when Adlai's office asked if we would turn up at a Hollywood for Stevenson rally at the Palladium in Los Angeles, we said yes. Not that my support was all that important. I just slid onto the stage in a strapless gown of black silk with the mink stole Frank had given me as an engagement present, and said, "Ladies and gentlemen, I can't do anything myself, but I can introduce a wonderful, wonderful man. I'm a great fan of his myself. My husband, Frank Sinatra."

Frank then sang "The Birth of the Blues" and "The House I Live In" and nearly brought the house down. That was the man I loved.

TWENTY

F rank Sinatra and I might well have had, as one Hollywood wag put it, the most on-again, off-again marriage of the century, but it always struck me as fascinating the way our lives seemed to double back and reconnect with each other. Just by chance, for instance, the summer of 1952 saw us both beginning to get involved in our most important film projects to date, me with *Mogambo* and Frank with *From Here to Eternity*.

Frank had been wildly excited about James Jones's tough best-selling novel about the dark side of army life in Hawaii on the eve of World War II ever since it had come out in 1951. He fell in love with the character of Angelo Maggio, the skinny Italian kid from New Jersey who wouldn't play the patsy for anyone. He knew that director Fred Zinnemann was planning a movie and he became obsessed with playing Maggio, so much so that he was prepared to do anything, even commit the ultimate Hollywood sin of working for practically nothing, to get the role. I found this strange, because Frank had never been that crazy about acting, but he knew he *was* Maggio and besides, he was dying to do a straight dramatic part and escape from the typecasting he'd been subjected to in musicals. Not to mention that his career didn't seem to be going anywhere else at that particular moment.

I decided to try and get into the act and influence the dread Harry Cohn, who was the head of Columbia, the movie company making *From Here to Eternity*. I knew Joan Cohn, Harry's wife, reasonably well: I'd been to their house for a few parties, and they lived quite close to us in Coldwater Canyon. We weren't bosom friends, but I knew I could talk to Joan, that she would be sympathetic. Through Joan I got to Harry, but he was dead set against the idea.

"Just test Frank," I pleaded. "Just give him a test."

"Why should I? The idea's ridiculous. Frank's a singer, not a dramatic actor."

"Frank can act, and he knows he can play this part better than anyone else."

"It's too late. I've already cast the role. Eli Wallach has got it and I'm happy with him."

I went away but I wasn't finished. I knew Joan was on my side; after all, all we were asking for was a test. So I niggled and niggled at Harry Cohn, and I even said, "For God's sake, Harry, I'll give you a free picture if you'll just test him."

Frank had made his own appeal, and offered to do the film for a giveaway salary of a thousand dollars a week. A lot of other people intervened, but director Fred Zinnemann wasn't convinced. Still, as long as Eli Wallach wasn't signed, I felt Frank had a chance.

Meanwhile, I was preparing to film *Mogambo,* a picture I felt a special attachment to. After all, I still remembered sneaking into the theater balcony in Smithfield, Virginia, in 1932 and swooning as my hero Clark Gable tried to decide between Jean Harlow and Mary Astor in *Red Dust.* And *Mogambo,* which, depending on who you asked, apparently meant either "passion" or "to speak" in Swahili, was nothing less than a bare-faced remake of *Red Dust,* with Gable repeating his gruff masculine role, Grace Kelly taking the old Mary Astor part, and me sitting in for poor Jean Harlow.

Instead of taking place, as *Red Dust* did, on a rubber plantation in the Malay Peninsula, *Mogambo* was set among the white hunters of Africa. And instead of being shot on the Metro back lot, it was truly going to be photographed where it was supposed to take place, or, as the ads later blared, "Actually filmed by MGM on safari in Africa amid authentic scenes of unrivaled savagery and awe-inspiring splendor." What that meant to me, however, was that I had to submit to a hellacious series of shots for smallpox, yellow fever, cholera, typhus, typhoid, and God knows what else.

Since nothing seemed to be happening with Frank's *From Here to Eternity* screen test, he decided he might as well go to Africa with me, shots and all. So we flew into Nairobi, Kenya, right around the time of our first wedding anniversary and joined up with the fifty-plus trucks that were going to take us to Uganda, the film's primary location, seven hundred miles away.

The whole damn trip was what the publicists liked to call the greatest safari of modern times, and I wasn't about to argue. Not only did it take eight genuine white hunters to get us in gear, but once we settled our encampment was three hundred tents strong. And if you think those were just for sleeping, think again. My God, we had tents for every little thing you could think of: dining tents, wardrobe tents with electric irons, a rec room tent with darts for the Brits and table tennis for the Yanks, even a hospital tent complete with X-ray machine, and a jail tent in case anybody got a tiny bit too rowdy.

I really shouldn't joke about security, because there were genuine worries for our safety in Africa. The movie company had its own thirty-man police force, and when we first got to what was then British East Africa we were under the protection of both the Lancashire Fusiliers and the Queen's African Rifles. The Mau Mau uprising was just getting started, and everyone in the cast was issued a weapon. Clark, an experienced hunter, got a high-powered hunting rifle, while they gave me a presumably more ladylike .38 police special revolver.

That was just like Metro, thinking of everything. They brought in three copies of everyone's costumes just in case and built an eighteen-hundred-yard air strip in the middle of the jungle in a whirlwind five days. Every day, supplies and mail were flown in from Nairobi on sturdy old DC3s, and exposed film stock, carefully packed in dry ice, would be flown out. The film's expense account even had a notation of five thousand African francs (fourteen dollars and change in those days) written off as "gratuities to witch doctors for favorable omens."

And, for once, as much attention had been paid to the John Lee Mahin script as to the logistics. I don't know if I'd describe the rivalry between Gracie and me quite the way the ads did— "They fought like sleek jungle cats! A flaming love feud! The jungle strips two civilized women of all but their most primeval instincts!"—but we sure had fun battling it out.

The film starts without either of us on the scene, as the movie introduces the virile white hunter Victor Marswell, played by Clark, who hunts animals for zoos and is man enough to deck insubordinates with one punch if they need that kind of treatment. Which, the movies being the movies, they inevitably do.

Irked that a prize black leopard has gotten away, Vic returns to the compound in a hell of a bad mood. His temper is not improved when he spots first my luggage, then my clothes, and finally my underwear strewn across his room. I'm out on the back porch, making good use of a makeshift shower. "Eloise Kelly," I say by way of introduction, "better known in the pleasure capitals of the world as Honey Bear."

Vic is less than impressed, and I am not any happier to learn that Bunny, the maharaja I've flown all the way from New York to accompany on safari, has had to make an emergency trip back home. "This is going to be the gayest week of the season," I say with Honey Bear's usual dose of sarcasm. And, truth be told, Vic is less than impressed with my kind of girl as well. "They cover the world like a paint advertisement," he tells one of his white hunter pals. "There's not an honest feeling from her kneecap to her neck."

Needless to say, despite my brave warning of "Look, buster, don't you get overstimulated with me," not much time is allowed to pass before Vic and Honey Bear fall into each other's arms. But though I start to get a little soft on the big lug, he is having no such thoughts about me, and by the time the boat out shows up, he insists that I be on it.

"Take it easy, Kelly," he says, patting my knee on the gangplank. "Drop me a line." Then he gives me money for plane fare home and says, "I'll brain you if you don't take it. Call it a ninety-nine-year loan." I snap back, just as romantically, "This is one loan I'll pay back if I have to live ninety-nine years to do it."

Getting off the boat just as I'm getting on are British anthropologist Donald Nordley, played by Donald Sinden, and his attractive young wife Linda, which is Gracie's part. Poor Donald passes out with some mysterious jungle fever practically the minute he steps ashore, which allows Vic to fall for Linda, a goody-goody type who is prone to saying things like, "At certain times, jokes are in very poor taste."

Then, like a bad penny, I show up again, courtesy of a boat

that won't float. "The Return of Frankenstein," I announce grandly at my reappearance. "Shipwrecked and me without a desert island to my name." Vic, naturally, is not happy about my arrival, and when he cautions me to have a little respect for Linda's delicate sensibilities, I snap back that "I'll act like your sister, down from Vassar for the holidays."

You can probably guess what happens from here on in. Vic and Linda dance around, not being quite able to decide how serious a play they should make for each other. Finally, when she shoots Vic in the arm in a jealous fit after finding him flirting with me, I reveal my true nobility by claiming she did it because he'd made what they used to call unwelcome advances. Her marriage is saved, good old Vic views me with new respect, and even though I've gone on the record as saying, "The only lions I want to see again are two in front of the Public Library," I end up staying on in Africa with my guy.

For someone with my naturally irreverent temperament, playing a sassy, tough-talking playgirl who whistles at men, drinks whiskey straight from the bottle, and says about wine, "Any year, any model, they all bring out my better nature" was a gift from the gods. I never felt looser or more comfortable in a part before or since, and I was even allowed to improvise some of my dialogue. Yet if you would have told me that I'd feel this way about a film directed by John Ford, I would have sent you straight to Artie Shaw's psychiatrist.

John Ford, familiarly known as Jack, was one of the crustiest sons of bitches ever to direct a film, and he directed plenty of them. On the job since 1917, he'd turned out classics like *The Informer, Stagecoach, The Grapes of Wrath,* and *How Green Was My Valley,* winning four Oscars in the process. He liked to say he was just a hard-nosed, hardworking, run-of-the-mill director, but a lot of people around Hollywood considered him the best in the business, and when he worked with actors like John Wayne, he could do no wrong. He could also be the meanest man on earth, thoroughly evil, but by the time the picture ended, I adored him.

It turned out that Ford hadn't wanted me at all. He wanted Maureen O'Hara, and he wasn't shy about letting that be known. He adored Gracie, but he was very cold to me. He called me in to see him before shooting began and he didn't even look at me. All he said was, "You're going to be overdressed." Just cold, and that was all.

So I went back to my room and talked it over with Frank. I told him, "I'm going to talk to Ford." Then I stomped in and I said, "I'm just as Irish and mean as you are. I'm not going to take this. I'm sorry if you don't like me—I'll go home."

He just looked up at me as if he didn't know what I was talking about and said, "I don't know what you mean. Who's been rude to you?"

And when it came to the first day of shooting, I can safely say that no picture in which I was ever involved got off to a worse start. One of the first scenes called for a leopard to casually walk through the flap of our tent while Clark and I were sitting on the bed, holding hands. Why this was one of the first scenes to be shot, I'll never know. Maybe the animal was on call somewhere else and had to return to the wild in a hurry. At any rate, he didn't seem to understand his cues. And the upshot was, the leopard goofed, Clark goofed, I goofed, and the scene was terrible.

To make things worse, just as Ford snapped, "Print the last take," the lighting man said apologetically, "I'm sorry, Mr. Ford, but the key light went out in the middle of it."

As I got off the bed I said, quite casually, I thought, "Oh, boy, that was a real fuckup. We goofed everything."

Not the most politic thing to say, especially on a Jack Ford set. Because Jack thought the remark was directed at him. He decided I had to be put firmly in my place.

"Oh, you're a director now," he said scornfully. "You know so fucking much about directing. You're a lousy actress, but now you're a director. Well, why don't you direct something? You go sit in my chair, and I'll go and play your scene."

All this was said in a loud voice in front of the cast and the crew and everybody. Every face was frozen, but nobody dared say a word. And Ford wouldn't stop: he went on ranting like a madman. The only thing that ended the whole charade was Mr. Clark Gable. He put his arm around me, gave me a squeeze, and walked off the set. And when Clark marched that was the end of the scene, because as a man and an actor he wasn't known as The King for nothing. His behavior on a set was always impeccable.

Now Jack Ford was in such a fury that he didn't know what to do. The fact that the key light was out meant the scene *had* to be reshot. So he closed down the whole set, and everybody left. I went back to my tent and sat there thinking, What the hell have I done wrong to incur this sort of fantastic fury? Then, about an hour later, the assistant director arrived with a message. "Mr. Ford says would you please come back on the set. They're ready for another shot."

I said, "Sure," and went quietly back to the set. It went like a dream. First take, no problems. Even the leopard behaved himself. He gave me a contemptuous look as he prowled through—probably thought I was too skinny to bite—and that was that.

Jack and I took a little longer to make up. I had a hard few days before he took me aside and said, "You're damn good. Just take it easy." From that moment on, we got along fine. I guess that's how he worked. He had to be top man—and why shouldn't he be? He just wanted to make sure I knew it. He was big. If he hated you, he let you know it and made you fight with him. The only people I didn't like were the nitty ones who never let you know. You could never fight with them.

It was great working with Clark again—he will always be my Sir Galahad. But as far as romance went, Clark's eyes were quite definitely on Gracie, and hers, for that matter, were on him. They were both single at the time, and it's very normal for any woman to be in love with Clark. But Gracie was a good Catholic girl, and she was having a hard time feeling the way she did about Clark. Not to mention that being in Africa, with exotic flora and fauna all over the place, and Clark, strong and smiling and completely at home, made her love him more.

I remember on Gracie's birthday we got a bottle of champagne from some bootlegger, and she and Clark and Jack Ford and I had a little party out in the tent. Later, we did the same thing for mine. And after that, no matter where in the world I was, every year a birthday present would arrive from Grace. She never forgot, and every year at Christmas she sent a handwritten card, not left for a secretary to do. She was a great lady, and also great fun, but she was never much of a drinker, though she tried hard. Her little nose would get pink, she'd get sick, and we'd have to rescue her. Or she'd get easily hurt and do my trick and run off into the darkness.

Clark would catch on after a few seconds and say to me,

"Sugar, where's she gone? This is Africa; she can't just run off in Africa." So I'd go off and find her and bring her back before the lions ate her.

Thank God, everyone in the cast got along famously, because filming in Africa was not exactly an experience I'd want to repeat. If nothing else there was the heat, so intense (anywhere from one hundred and ten to one hundred and thirty degrees) that the company used up literally gallons of cold cream to keep everyone's complexion from burning up. And when it wasn't hot, it rained, and in just a few hours everything turned to mud so deep it was impossible to move cameras, trucks, or people. And don't forget the wild animals. I had to hang a lantern in front of my tent to discourage the local lions, and one day a trio of rhinos ganged up on the camera car and nearly killed poor Bob Surtees, the cameraman.

When it came to crises, however, I was soon face to face with the most personal one of my life: I discovered I was pregnant. I was only a week or so late, but all the signs were there and I just knew. I also knew that if I was going to do anything about it, I had to do it *now*. Frank had gone back to Hollywood—the invitation to test for *From Here to Eternity* had finally come through. I hadn't told him and I wasn't going to tell him. He had enough troubles of his own. I sat in my tent and tried to think about it rationally. And it was hard.

I had the strongest feelings about bringing a child into the world. I felt that unless you were prepared to devote practically all your time to your child in its early years it was unfair to the baby. If a child is unwanted—and somehow they know that—it is handicapped from the time it is born.

Not to mention the fact that MGM had all sorts of penalty clauses about their stars having babies. If I had one, my salary would be cut off. So how would I make a living? Frank was absolutely broke and would probably continue to be (or so I thought) for a long time. My future movies were going to take me all over the world. I couldn't have a baby with that sort of thing going on. Even in *Mogambo,* the fact that I was pregnant would be showing quite plainly long before the picture was finished, so Jack Ford had to be told for starters. I felt the time just wasn't right for me to have a child. With that decision made, the most agonizing I'd ever had to face, I went to see my director.

Jack Ford tried quite desperately to talk me out of it.

"Ava," he said, "you are married to a Catholic, and this is going to hurt Frank tremendously when he finds out about it."

"He isn't going to find out about it, and if he does, it's my decision."

"Ava, you're giving yourself too hard a time. I'll protect you if the fact that you're having a baby starts to show. I'll arrange the scenes, I'll arrange the shots. We'll wrap your part up as quickly as we can. Nothing will show. Please go ahead and have the child."

I said, "No, this is not the time, and I'm not ready." So, reluctantly, John let me go to London in late November.

It was kept very hush-hush. I don't quite know who arranged it all but I expect that MGM, with an awful lot of money at stake, had a lot to do with it. One of the secretaries on the film whom I'd known for several years came with me, as well as one of MGM's publicity men. I went to this private clinic where they put me to sleep and took me to the operating room. I woke up in my room thinking that everything was all over, and the doctor walked in and said, "Yes, Mrs. Sinatra, you are pregnant."

I said, "For God's sake, I knew that."

So the doctor went away, looking very serious, and in came the psychiatrist. In those days, abortion was available in Britain but it had to be performed for what the male sex thought were the right reasons: their reasons. Even those very expensive London clinics had to be careful with their procedures. And they were not at all certain I was there for the right reasons.

Neither was the psychiatrist.

He began to lead me along the right lines, but I wasn't playing the game. He asked me if I would throw myself out of the window if I had to have this baby, and I said, "Certainly not," which floored him a bit. He kept on trying to lead me into confessing my so-called suicidal intentions, but I wasn't buying that. He insisted that I tell him that I would kill myself if I had to go through with having a child, and I wouldn't. I said, as simply as I could, "I don't think it's the sensible time for me to have a child. If you bring a child into the world, it's got to have a stable background, loving parents who can give it time and attention. At present my entire life is one mad whirl, and it is going to be like that for a few years to come."

They probably had to manipulate a few of my answers, but I got the operation and went back to Africa.

Frank came back to Africa in time for Christmas—and my thirtieth birthday—full of enthusiasm and joy. The test had been successful and the part of Maggio was his, partly because Eli Wallach simply looked too muscular for the role. Frank didn't know about my trip to London, and those few weeks we had together were easygoing and fun. He and one of the prop men built me a shower, the two of us fooled around in the river until a protective mother hippo chased us away, and he helped organize and conduct, despite local white supremacist sentiment, both a black and a white Christmas choir.

And then, of course, the silliest, stupidest, and most natural thing happened: I got pregnant again. Apparently, the reason that I hadn't gotten pregnant with my first two husbands was that something in the conception department was tilted the wrong way. Becoming pregnant the first time had tilted it the right way, and now I was highly fertile.

This time Frank did know, and he was delighted. I remember bumping across the African plain with him one day in a jeep, feeling sick as the devil. Right on the spot, for the first and only time in our relationship, Frank decided to sing to me. I know people must think that he did that sort of thing all the time, but the man was a professional and the voice was saved for the right occasions. This must have been one of them, because he sang to me, oh so beautifully, that lovely song, "When You Awake." It didn't stop me from feeling sick, but I've always remembered that moment.

Yet, despite Frank's feelings, I reached the same decision about my second pregnancy as I had about my first. As soon as we finished *Mogambo,* MGM had me slotted into another film to be made overseas, *Knights of the Round Table,* which meant that Frank and I would be separated again for month after month. And that situation brought to the surface all my old doubts about having no right to produce a child unless you had a sane, solid lifestyle in which he or she could be brought up. Frank and I had no such thing. We didn't even possess the ability to live together like any normal married couple. Frank would arrive home at about four A.M. after a singing engagement at a nightclub or concert. And I would have to leave the house at six-thirty A.M. or earlier to get to the studio on time. Not really much of a home life there.

I think Frank, in his heart, knew what I was going to do. But it was my decision, not his. I didn't think that that big expensive clinic was prepared for a second round of someone responding to their ever-so-correct questions with my incorrect answers, so I was checked into a small nursing home near Wimbledon where they didn't ask any questions at all. I knew Frank was coming across to London to start a singing tour through Europe, but I wasn't sure exactly when. But clearly someone told him about what I was doing, because as long as I live I'll never forget waking up after the operation and seeing Frank sitting next to the bed with tears in his eyes. But I think I was right. I still think I was right.

TWENTY-ONE

As far as my career as an actress went, *Mogambo* was probably as close to a pinnacle as anything I've done. I did get nominated for an Academy Award for best actress (though I was more relieved than upset when the Oscar eventually went to Audrey Hepburn in *Roman Holiday*) and I was told that I came within one vote of winning the New York Film Critics award, with even Bosley Crowther of the *Times,* who usually treated me like a bad smell, fighting gallantly in my defense.

If you sense a little ambivalence in my thoughts about my ability as an actress, you're right. On one level, all I wanted to be was an actress, and I often felt that if only I could act, everything about my life and career would have been different. But I was never an actress—none of us kids at Metro were. We were just good to look at.

Making things worse was that I really didn't have the correct emotional makeup for acting. If I'd had more drive, more interest, maybe I could have done better, but I disliked the exhibitionistic aspects of the business and the work was terribly frightening to me. My mouth would always dry up so completely when I was on the set that I had to keep lemon juice handy and take a sip from time to time. I remember a cutter once saying, "I'd like you to see what I have to take out of your scenes." He ran them through for me and there were all these audible clicks where my mouth had gone dry.

"I'm afraid there are two or three places where I just can't get the clicks out," he said. "We'll have to redub." I told him that even in redubbing I'd need a drop of Scotch or the clicks would still be there.

Given all this, why did I keep doing it? The answer I usually gave was, "For the loot, honey, always for the loot," and there was more truth than poetry in that remark. I had to do something and I didn't know how to do anything else. I once thought about becoming a nurse, but I knew I'd vomit every time a patient vomited and I wouldn't be much use. I could have been a secretary again, brushed up on my Atlantic Christian College dictation speed of a hundred and twenty words per minute. But I knew that would make me really crazy.

The truth is that the only time I'm happy is when I'm doing absolutely nothing. I don't understand people who like to work and talk about it like it was some sort of goddamn duty. Doing nothing feels like floating on warm water to me. Delightful, perfect.

My next film after *Mogambo, Knights of the Round Table,* did nothing to make me change my mind about working. It was a typical piece of historical foolishness, with folks in shining armor like my old beau Robert Taylor dashing across the screen and sticking each other in delicate places with horrible-looking pikes. Costume dramas were never my favorite vehicles, and besides, being married to Frank left little room in my life for drama of any other kind.

Frank had scheduled a singing tour of Europe—Naples, Rome, Milan, then Scandinavia—while I was in the early stages of filming *Knights* and I took a leave to accompany him. It was nothing that affected the shooting in any way: the director went right on filming the horses charging and the swords flashing. I knew MGM would look down their noses at this sort of behavior, and that suspension time would be added to my contract. If you did that often enough, you'd find yourself under contract to them for the rest of your life. But this was going to be another "try-again" situation for Frank and a second honeymoon. We never ever counted the "honeymoons" we had, but we had plenty.

This time, however, it would have been far better sticking to the battles coming from MGM's British studios, because our different sort of battles on that European journey were horrendous.

We started in Naples, Italy. The theater was packed with noisy patrons. Somehow, wherever we went, the rumor had been spread by an antagonistic press that Frank Sinatra was past his peak, and that these concerts were simply a patronizing gesture that insulted his fans. And Frank's constant clashes with press and photographers were held up as proof of this.

Frank arrived onstage to sing his first song. The applause was noisy but not necessarily polite. And, about halfway through it, by a deliberate piece of stage managing that nobody warned us about, a spotlight suddenly picked me out of the audience while Frank was in the middle of a song.

Immediately the audience was on its feet going wild and yelling, "Ava! Ava! Ava!" It was me they wanted, not Frank.

I don't think Frank has ever been more publicly humiliated in his life. The noise was so great he stopped singing. The orchestra stopped playing. Frank walked off. I got up, left the theater, and went back to the hotel. After a pause Frank came back onstage and finished the show.

Wherever Frank and I went, the press had a field day. They loved printing the picture of the movie queen and the man who a decade earlier had been the idol of screaming teenagers playing to half-empty halls and jeering fans. They were right about one thing: it was truly a sad situation.

And let me say right now that these episodes hurt and hurt and hurt. Don't think for a minute that bad publicity and endless criticism don't leave their claw marks on everyone concerned. Your friends try to cheer you up by saying lightly, "I suppose you get used to it, and ignore it." You try. You try damned hard. But you never get used to it. It always wounds and hurts.

We came back to London under a terrible cloud. I had to finish the picture and Frank returned to the States. As soon as I was done, I moved heaven and earth to rejoin him. I'll always remember Clark Gable watching me pack and saying, "Ava, honey, you do know what you're doing, don't you? You're packing up and throwing away a hundred and fifty thousand dollars in those suitcases." That's how much I was going to lose if I didn't stay out of the country long enough to conform to those damn tax codes. I couldn't have cared less. And besides, I now had a new contract at Metro that gave me a hundred and thirty thousand dollars per picture. Still not the top of the heap, and still less than the studio got from loaning me out, but enough so that I didn't hesitate when I felt that returning home would help save our marriage.

What a joke. Our marriage was past saving. Not even the great success Frank had in *From Here to Eternity,* the part that eventually won him an Oscar and totally revived his career, could help put us together again. Once things start to eat away at the facade of the marriage—things like overhearing a hotel elevator boy tell your husband, "Oh, Mr. Sinatra, last time you were here it was with Miss X"—once you lose your faith in what the man you love is telling you, there is nothing left to save.

I don't think I ever sat down and made a conscious decision about leaving Frank; as usual I simply acted on impulse and allowed events to sweep me along. But I remember exactly when I made the decision to seek a divorce. It was the day the phone rang and Frank was on the other end, announcing that he was in bed with another woman. And he made it plain that if he was going to be constantly accused of infidelity when he was innocent, there had to come a time when he'd decide he might as well be guilty. But for me, it was a chilling moment. I was deeply hurt. I knew then that we had reached a crossroads. Not because we had fallen out of love, but because our love had so battered and bruised us that we couldn't stand it anymore.

When you have to face up to the fact that marriage to the man you love is really over, that's very tough, sheer agony. In that kind of harrowing situation, I always go away and cut myself off from the world. Also, I sober up immediately when there is genuine bad news in my life; I never face it with alcohol in my brain. I rented a house in Palm Springs and sat there and just suffered for a couple of weeks. I suffered there until I was strong enough to face it.

I'm pretty sure it was Howard Strickling, Metro's legendary publicity director, who on October 29, 1953, issued what I thought was the most honest and sincere explanation for our impending divorce: "Ava Gardner and Frank Sinatra stated today that having reluctantly exhausted every effort to reconcile their differences, they could find no mutual basis on which to continue their marriage. Both expressed deep regret and great respect for each other. Their separation is final and Miss Gardner will seek a divorce."

I guess that about covered it.

I'm not proud of my three matrimonial failures. What woman would be? I know I loved each of my husbands sincerely and deeply, but things like career crises, the nagging Hollywood spotlight, all the criticism we took every time we turned around, got in the way of our genuine feelings.

I suffered, I really suffered, with all three of my husbands. And I tried damn hard with all three, starting each marriage certain that it was going to last until the end of my life. Yet none of them lasted more than a year or two.

I think the main reason my marriages failed is that I always loved too well but never wisely. I'm terribly possessive about the people I love and I probably smother them with love. I'm jealous of every minute they spend away from me. I want to be with them, to see them, to be able to touch them. Then, and only then, am I happy. For instance, when I couldn't get Frank on the telephone immediately, I wanted to kill myself. It was stupid, I suppose, but it was me.

I knew that the men I married were very attractive to the opposite sex: the twenty marriages they had between them proves that, if nothing else does. And I knew they had to face situations where the ladies concerned were practically dragging them into bed. I could rationalize those encounters, but I couldn't live with them. Sex isn't all that important, but it is when you love someone very much.

Perhaps I expected too much from my husbands, and they inevitably disappointed me. God knows I've got so many frailties myself, I ought to be able to understand and forgive them in others. But I don't. If I was capable and wanted to give, then why couldn't I expect the same thing in return? Maybe, in the final analysis, they saw me as something I wasn't and I tried to turn them into something they could never be. I loved them all but maybe I never understood any of them. I don't think they understood me.

I suppose one of the strangest things about my trio of failed marriages—and in passing I would like to gently point out that none of my three exes were asked to pay a penny in alimony—was the fact that the marriage bond seemed to be a shackle that manacled us together. Once divorced, we enjoyed each other and retained a deep friendship. And more than anyone else, that was true between Frank and me.

Frank and I have the kind of friendship—relationship—where you don't have to say, "I'm going to telephone you every day" or "I'm going to write you every month, or every six months." When you feel like talking, you talk, and when you feel like seeing each other, you do that. There are no ties, no strings. And there shouldn't be.

We might have been in different cities, different countries, but we were never apart. And every once in a while, Frank would call me in Madrid, London, Rome, New York, wherever I happened to be, and say, "Ava, let's try again." And I'd say, "Okay!" and drop everything, sometimes even a part in a picture. And it would be heaven, but it wouldn't last more than twenty-four hours. And I'd go running off again, literally running. We could never quite understand why it hadn't and couldn't work out.

Our phone bills were astronomical, and when I found the letters Frank wrote me the other day, the total could fill a suitcase. Every single day during our relationship, no matter where in the world I was, I'd get a telegram from Frank saying he loved me and missed me. He was a man who was desperate for companionship and love. Can you wonder that he always had mine!

TWENTY-TWO

O f all the pictures I've made, and honey, you better believe I have no idea exactly how much territory that covers, there's no doubt that *The Barefoot Contessa* is the one that most people identify me with. That damn advertising line, "The World's Most Beautiful Animal," will probably follow me around until the end of time.

The irony of all this is that not only didn't anyone initially think of me for the part, but also that Metro, my always cooperative studio, did its damnedest to try and keep me out of the picture. The only reason I finally got in is that in Joseph L. Mankiewicz the studio ran up against someone who was just as stubborn as it was.

When *The Barefoot Contessa* was first announced to the press by United Artists in the middle of 1953, Joe Mankiewicz was the hottest behind-the-camera talent in the business. Not only had he just finished turning Marlon Brando into Mark Anthony in *Julius Caesar,* but he'd also won Oscars for *both* writing and directing on *both* of his previous two pictures, *Letters to Three Wives* and *All About Eve. Eve* had taken home six Oscars that year, including best picture, out of an all-time-record fourteen nominations.

So whatever Joe wanted, Joe usually got, and finally, after thinking about everybody from Elizabeth Taylor to Joan Collins, he decided that I was the best choice to play the woman who began life as plain Maria Vargas and ended it as the Contessa Torlato-Favrini.

To get me, however, Joe had to deal with Metro, and the bad blood between them was considerable. I heard he'd gotten into a hellacious shouting match with Nick Schenck, the man who pulled the financial strings at Metro, a silver-haired gentleman who'd gotten so mad at Joe he actually uttered that famous line, "You'll never work in this business again."

Even Schenck wasn't powerful enough to make that threat stick, but he could make Mankiewicz's life a living hell when he tried to procure my services. He had the nerve to insist on, and to get, an exorbitant loanout fee of two hundred thousand dollars plus ten percent of the gross over one million dollars. My God, even Humphrey Bogart, my costar and one of the biggest names in Hollywood, was only getting one hundred thousand. Of course, when it came to my salary, Metro wasn't feeling so expansive. Even though the studio ended up making a million dollars on the deal, all I got out of it was sixty thousand dollars. God but those bastards could be stingy.

Contessa was to be Joe's first film as writer, director, and producer, and he made damn sure he had a solid story to work with. And though the presence of a Howard Hughes clone in the script made some people think the film was based on my life, it actually was much closer to the story of Rita Hayworth, who was discovered as Margarita Cansino dancing in Mexico and ended up married to Aly Khan.

The film opens in a hell of a way, at least from my point of view. It's my funeral, and one of the mourners, whose voice-over narrates the film, is Harry Dawes, a tough-talking film director played by Bogart. He tells how, in the company of a womanizing tycoon named Kirk Edwards and Kirk's fast-talking, sweaty, and amoral press agent (a dead ringer, in Edmond O'Brien's Oscar-winning performance, for Howard's main man Johnny Meyer), he first meets Maria Vargas dancing in a sleazy Madrid cabaret.

Though they're never anything more than good friends, Harry and Maria like each other immediately, and though she doesn't trust Kirk any further than she can throw him, she agrees to go to Hollywood for the inevitable screen test. Without saying goodbye to a soul, without carrying so much as a suitcase, she walks in her bare feet across the cobblestone street to the waiting taxi.

And then, as it only does in pictures, the incredible happens: under the name of Maria D'Amata, Maria becomes a big, big star. But though she spends a lot of time in the company of very rich, very arrogant men, first Kirk, then South American playboy Alberto Bravano, she doesn't sleep with them and she makes it clear that she belongs to no man. In fact, the only place she feels safe looking for love is back in the gutter where she came from.

Then one night, in one of those glamorous European casinos, she meets Count Vincenzo Torlato-Favrini. And what kind of a guy is he? "He is a count, but among counts he is a king," says one sad-faced onlooker, "just as among kings I am a clown." Maria thinks this is the real thing, and marries the count in the kind of ceremony I'd always dreamed of having myself.

Then comes the bad news. The count was in the wrong place at the wrong time during the war and has to tell his bride that "Almost the only undestroyed part of me is my heart." Maria is distraught, but thinks she knows a way out. She'll have an affair with the count's conveniently available chauffeur, present her husband with a much-wanted heir, and everyone will live happily ever after. Unfortunately this count is very much the jealous type. He kills both Maria and the chauffeur, and at the film's close he is led, handcuffed, off to jail.

Though I loved the script, felt I understood the girl and even thought my feet were pretty enough for the essential dance sequences, when I arrived in Rome early in 1954, I was nervous at being in such high-toned company. And I have to say that Mr. Bogart did not make my life any easier. He was always needling me, calling me the Grabtown Gypsy, and complaining that he needed a running start toward the set if he wasn't going to be trampled by my entourage.

Not to mention that my usual stage fright wasn't helped any when, on the very first day of shooting, he yelled at the director, "Hey, Mankiewicz, can you tell this dame to speak up? I can't hear a goddamn word she says." That did a lot for my confidence. Bogart hated Italy and lived on ham and eggs and steak whenever he could, but he certainly knew a lot more acting tricks than I did, and he didn't hesitate to use them. But I have to admit he probably forced me into a better performance than I could have managed without him.

Getting along with Joe Mankiewicz was also problematical at times. I respected him enormously, but though he was clearly the cerebral type, I don't think he ever really understood me or my insecurity about my work. One day, for instance, Jack Cardiff, our excellent cameraman, came up to me and said, "Ava, darling, I want to do a close-close-close close-up of your face, and I'd prefer to have you and not a stand-in for the preliminary work. It'll take a little time, and you've got to sit on the edge of that sofa. Do you mind?"

"No problem," I told him.

So I'm sitting there looking pensive, waiting for Jack Cardiff to finish fiddling with his lens, when Mankiewicz spots me as he's hurrying by and says, and not in the friendliest way either, "You're the sittin'est goddamn actress I've ever worked with." I was so surprised I couldn't even get my mouth open in time to say "Go fuck yourself" to his departing back. And the truth is I was never able to give him my complete trust after that.

Some of the scenes in *The Barefoot Contessa* were among my all-time personal favorites, especially the one where I had to perform a flamenco-style dance wearing a tight sweater and a cheap satin skirt, enticing my partner, luring him closer, swirling out of his grasp, taunting him with my body.

Not only was I getting personally more and more intoxicated by the romantic rhythms of flamenco, but this was the first time I'd ever danced in a film, so I practiced every night on those cold Roman floors for three full weeks. We shot the scene in an olive grove in Tivoli, outside Rome, with one hundred Gypsies beating time to a photograph record. When the phonograph broke, they kept right on beating, and that was the take we used.

When *Contessa* first came out, a lot of people thought it was either too talky or, like the good folks in Tupelo, Mississippi, who banned it from their town, too risqué for public consumption. These days, the film seems to be one of those late-night classics; if you show anything enough times, it does become popular. The French, however, immediately took to it with both feet, with people like François Truffaut calling me "Hollywood's most exquisitely beautiful actress." If *Mogambo* was the best I ever did as an actress, this was the apogee of my life as a so-called star.

Stardom. My name in a Cole Porter lyric, my footprints in concrete at Grauman's Chinese. Voted the girl they'd most want to measure for a new suit by the Custom Tailors Guild of America, the girl they'd most like to be stuck with at the top of the Empire State Building by the United Elevator Operators. Edmond

O'Brien's Oscar Muldoon didn't know how right he was when Joe's script has him say, "Whatever it is, whether you're born with it, or catch it from a public drinking cup, she's got it and the people with the money in their hands put her there." And as someone who's been there and back, what I'd really like to say about stardom is that it gave me everything I never wanted.

What you have to understand about me, honey, is that I'm a normal human being, just like any other. Sanity is more important to me than celebrity any day of the week, and I consider my personal life to be my own affair. If people like what I do on the screen, they can come to the box office and pay their money. I don't feel I have any responsibility beyond that.

Unfortunately, when your face and name are on posters all over the world, you're treated like public property. I've tried to tell myself it's ungrateful to complain, that you accept the money and you should accept what goes with it: the loss of privacy, the constant spotlight. But I never could get used to going out for an evening and having everyone in the place watching to see whether I took one drink or three before dinner. No one thinks I have feelings. They'd read the magazines and think they knew all about me.

It's no secret that I've had some terrible experiences with the press. You can't understand what it's like without living it. People ask the most amazingly personal questions and get furious if you don't answer. Then, when I did put my trust in some writers, discussed all sorts of things, subjects I shouldn't have touched on, everything I said was twisted or changed to infer things I didn't mean or say at all.

In fact, it was *The Barefoot Contessa* that led to two of the most infuriating encounters with the press I've ever had. I was doing a publicity tour all over South America for the film, which went fine until we got to Rio. United Artists had not put us into the hotel I'd asked for, but rather into some hellhole that reeked of stale tobacco and had more cigarette burns than the entire state of North Carolina. So I very calmly moved out and went directly to the one I preferred.

The newspapers the next morning, however, told an entirely different story. I had arrived drunk, disorderly, and barefoot (that much was true; my heel had broken off when I was mobbed at the airport). I had gone on a rampage and the hotel management, all too eager to provide the photographs to prove their point, had had no choice but to eject me.

What had really happened is that as a kind of revenge for what they perceived as my slight, the management had sent in, within an hour after we'd left, a real wrecking crew. They'd broken every mirror, strewn whiskey bottles everywhere, destroyed furniture, literally torn the place apart.

Never mind that if we'd been given axes and a week to try and smash the place up we would never have made near the mess they'd made, everyone believed the headlines. Not even the press conference I held or an apology from the Brazilian government could keep that lie from beating the truth all the way around the world.

Then no sooner did I get back to New York after that tour than I got a phone call from Sammy Davis, Jr. He had stood by Frank at his darkest moments, and he had also taken the time—which I thought was terribly sweet—to have little gold loop earrings made for my wedding. They had "A.S." on them, too, for Ava Sinatra.

So when Sammy called up and asked if I would do the Christmas cover of *Ebony,* I felt I had to agree. He came in with a whole troupe of photographers, and they made an awful mess covering one whole wall of our hotel with a sheet of red paper. I found a red dress somewhere, he put on a Santa Claus beard and a red suit, and we did the cover as well as some informal shots for the inside of the magazine—Sammy sitting on the arm of my chair with his hand around the back, stuff like that.

What I hear next is that somehow these pictures have gotten into the hands of a trash publication called *Confidential.* Naturally, it was Howard Hughes who broke the news to me in his most serious voice. As a means of self-protection, he had planted spies inside the publication, and he knew exactly what was coming out in every issue.

"Ava," he said, "they are going to do a devastating piece about you and Sammy Davis, Jr., not implying but stating as truth that you and he are lovers and have been for some time. They say that red wall identifies his flat in Harlem and that you often go there and spend hours with him."

So I went to Metro and the bigwigs called a meeting the size of the League of Nations. The lawyers talked for hours about suing this and suing that, but Howard Strickling, the head of publicity, once again knew exactly what to say.

"I have to maintain," he said, very quietly, "that perhaps I am better versed in these situations than most of us sitting around the table. And really, this is my responsibility. This is a rag that is published in a cellar somewhere [I made a mental note to get him to say "sewer" next time] and has a circulation of nothing. If we sue, it's going to be front-page news in newspapers and magazines around the world, which is exactly what they want. And if you win the case, on the back page of all the newspapers there will be a little scribble that Ava Gardner won her suit. In the meantime, the story is plastered all over the world. The best thing to do is ignore it completely." Which is what we did.

What is so maddening about these things is that they take an acorn, a little kernel of truth, and build an oak tree of lies. It hurts every time it happens. You never get used to it. Never. And it hurts to have to swallow it without answering. But it's best not to.

Maybe I just didn't have the temperament for stardom. I'll never forget seeing Bette Davis at the Hilton in Madrid. I went up to her and said, "Miss Davis, I'm Ava Gardner and I'm a great fan of yours." And do you know, she behaved exactly as I wanted her to behave. "Of course you are, my dear," she said. "Of course you are." And she swept on. Now that's a star.

TWENTY-THREE

The first time I met Luis Miguel Dominguin, it was the same old story all over again: I knew without a doubt that he was for me. Luis was tall and graceful with piercing, watchful dark eyes which he liked to move without turning his head. And he had a slightly bemused expression that seemed to say, "The American lady knows I am interested in her. I hope she is interested in me."

I damn sure was. And, frankly, who wouldn't be? Though four years younger than me, Luis Miguel was universally acclaimed as the best-paid, most-talked-about, most-sought-after bullfighter in the world. The son and brother of successful matadors, a great athlete and a faultless technician, he had the ability to make an exquisitely dangerous sport seem like child's play. To see pictures of him poised gracefully as the huge horns of the bull slid just inches past his heart, to see how with an arrogant arch of his body and a sweep of the cape he would take charge again, was breathtaking. Not to mention the fact that he was a cultivated gentleman who, as someone once said, spoke four languages in a field where some people could barely read and write. And he numbered among his friends people like Picasso and Papa Hemingway, who called him "a combination of Don Juan and Hamlet."

When I met Luis Miguel at a Madrid party right around the time Frank and I were breaking up, he was, having conquered all the bullrings in the world, enjoying the pleasures of semiretirement as well as recuperating from a near-fatal goring of a few months before. He was the absolute idol of Spain, a country whose unspoiled passion I was beginning to love more and more. He smiled, bowed slightly, and said, "No English." I smiled back and said, "No español," and that was pretty much the way we operated for most of our relationship. But, as Papa Hemingway liked to say, we communicated what counted.

If I was part of Luis Miguel's convalescence, he was part of mine after the goring Frank and I had given each other. Exhilarated by flamenco music, we laughed, we drank, we went places. I was his girlfriend, he was my guy; it was as simple as that. We were good friends as well as good lovers, and we didn't demand too much from each other. Luis Miguel was great fun and I loved having him around. Quite frankly, I was intrigued by the fact that he didn't seem to need me and he certainly wasn't looking for publicity like so many of the European men who came my way. I guess I loved the easygoing way we could just hang out together after all the fuss I'd aroused with Frank. We stayed in a small hotel in Madrid after I finished filming *Contessa*, he and I in one room and Bappie in another. I don't think we even discussed marriage; it never even came up. What was good at that moment was good. I guess that means I was growing up. About time, too.

The thing that always surprised me about Luis Miguel was his sense of humor. It was more than outrageous, it was downright wicked. Take, for instance, the way he'd act in one of his favorite Madrid bars, the Cervecería Alemana, a noisy place packed with the whole goddamn bullfighting world: matadors, cuadrillas, agents, hangers-on, groupies, the works. Even the Madrid gentry would go there when they felt like slumming, and that's when Luis Miguel would bait his trap.

Very carefully in his broken English he would explain to Bappie what she should say in Spanish when she shook hands with these dignified ladies and gentlemen. But what he was really instructing her in were the most diabolically obscene phrases he could think of. A gracious gentleman and his equally gracious wife would sweep up, Luis Miguel would introduce me and then Bappie, who would shake hands with the lady and say in her best Spanish, "Good evening, you big fat cunt."

The sound level in the bar was so high that only Luis Miguel's intimates were close enough to get the joke and collapse in laughter. The lady's eyebrows would rocket up, putting an end to all conversation. Bappie knew she'd dropped a bombshell, but Luis Miguel would try to comfort her, insisting, "Just a little mistake." We were awful in those days.

The great thing about Luis Miguel was that he could also take a joke on himself. I remember one day at his breeding farm when he was testing young bulls for their potential courage in the ring. I was given the job of kneeling down and holding one end of the bullfighter's cape, while Luis Miguel stood up holding the other. The calves would be let out one at a time and immediately charge at the cape. But Luis Miguel would sort of shuffle his feet to divert the charge and then move out of the way like a shadow. And as long as I kept absolutely still, I was in no danger.

Luis Miguel had a cameraman photographing the action, and when it was shown at the local cinema, he took me down to see it. He was the hero to end all heroes in his hometown, but when the audience saw the *brave* Ava Gardner on her knees as the bull rushed past—because in the bullfight only the bravest matadors get on their knees while facing a bull—they began to roar continual "Olés" for me, and loud shrieks of "Gilda" at Luis Miguel. That name was a mocking reference to Rita Hayworth, who'd just appeared in a very silly bullfighting movie, the implication being that Luis Miguel had chickened out. It was all a great joke and everyone enjoyed it, including Luis Miguel. Whenever the crowd yelled out "Gilda," he would stand up and raise his arm in salute.

Then, one night in April 1954, I was fast asleep in bed with Luis Miguel when suddenly I was awakened by terrible, excruciating pains in the pit of my stomach. As I began to shout in agony, he leapt out of bed and called a doctor, who guessed what it was: I had a kidney stone passing through my gut, which is one of the most totally painful experiences known to man. I was immediately rushed to a hospital, which turned out to be staffed entirely with nuns. Sweet, implacable ladies—their belief in God was absolute, but about painkillers they were not so sure. Aspirin was about as far as they would go.

My Spanish was awful, and Bappie's, you may remember, was even worse. We had no way of communicating with anybody, except through Luis Miguel, who somehow seemed to understand everything I needed. So the hospital authorities did what was normal in Spanish family situations: they put a camp bed in my room and Luis Miguel stayed there twenty-four hours a day. He talked to the doctors, held my hand when the pain got too terrible, and tried to coax some nourishment down my throat. And all this took place during the Festival of San Isidro, when, as *the* bullfighter of his era, Luis Miguel would have been cheered and saluted at the start of every day's events. But instead he was at the hospital day and night, looking after me.

One night they decided they had to X-ray me, but the pain was so awful I thought I was going to die and I frankly didn't care. Those little black penguin nuns who crept in and out all night to look at me were starting to get on my nerves. Jesus, I was a wreck. And Luis Miguel, bless him, carried me to the X-ray room, held me tight and calmed me down long enough for the technician to take one quick picture and then brought me back. Maybe I should have thought about marrying the guy after all.

Luis Miguel left the hospital only once during those two weeks, and when he did he came back with Papa Hemingway, who I'd never met until then. Though I obviously wasn't crazy about the circumstances, I was delighted to meet Papa and absolutely floored that he'd take the time to visit me in a hospital. I just adored the man; I idolized him, in fact, and we became friends from that moment on.

When the nuns finally turned me loose, I discovered that Metro had put me on suspension for refusing to play the singer Ruth Etting in *Love Me or Leave Me,* which I turned down because I was afraid it would be just another fairly standard biography. Besides, my philosophy, for better or worse, has always been, "If I'm in love or having an affair, I stop working." It didn't happen an awful lot, but it did mean that I didn't rake in the money I should have. So Luis Miguel put me on a plane to Hollywood, and who should be literally waiting for me when it arrived but Howard Hughes.

Howard Hughes knew all about the kidney stone. Howard Hughes knew all about everything. The goddamn CIA could have done worse than hire Howard to oversee its operations. If there was anything to be discovered, Howard could ferret it out. And, as Reenie used to say, the man knew how to throw a brick and hide his hand.

Howard had rented a large house on the banks of Lake Tahoe for me to recuperate in, and Reenie and I moved in in June. Living there also enabled me to establish a residence in Nevada, which facilitated my filing for a divorce: if loving Luis Miguel had shown me nothing else, it was that the marriage between Frank and me was truly over.

If I'd thought—and I did—that old Howard had by now gotten used to the hands-off, no-pressure rules I'd imposed, I was proved wrong once again. Mr. Hughes was plotting yet another old-fashioned pincer movement against my determination to neither marry him nor climb into his bed.

It started, as many of these things do, with what would be an innocent remark coming out of anyone's mouth but Howard's. We were out on the lake in his boat one evening and I couldn't help but notice that the color of the surface was an almost indescribably lovely shimmering pale shade of sapphire.

Well, Howard had noticed it, too. "Ava," he said, his voice dripping with choirboy innocence, "do you see this beautiful shade of sapphire?"

"Yes," I said. What else *could* I say?

"It's perfect. More than that, it matches your perfection. I think I'll try and find a sapphire to match it for you."

"Good luck," I said, trying not to pay attention. I wasn't trying to mock Howard. He was a brilliant man, brilliant in a dozen ways, with courage and self-confidence to burn. But he did things, shall we say, differently, and that was hard to get used to. Maybe it came from being one of the wealthiest men on the planet.

Well, at dinner that night, Howard presented me with the perfect sapphire. All that preamble on the lake was his idea of a little joke; he'd already brought the damn thing. And, set with two magnificent diamonds, one on either side, it was beautiful enough to take your breath away.

And, of course, it wouldn't have been Howard if he'd just sent someone to Cartier to order up one nice blue sapphire and send him the bill. Instead, he'd send his lieutenants scouring the world to discover the perfect stone. Kashmiri sapphires are the very best, their beauty legendary. And Howard had turned up the one man in all Europe would could identify a real Kashmiri sapphire.

The one Howard gave me would probably be worth a million bucks today, if I still had the damn thing.

That night, though, I flaunted the jewel a bit when Howard and I went gambling at the local casino. Howard loved to gamble, and he was lucky, too. Can you beat that? All that money and a lucky streak to boot. Plus knowing that if he did chance to lose too much, he could always buy up the casino and get his money back.

Howard brought me home after the gambling was over, waiting in the driveway for the dust to settle before he let me open the door. Howard had an antipathy to dust for health reasons that only Howard understood. When I looked at him, I noticed with some surprise that he had tears in his eyes. He'd won a lot at the tables, so I wondered what the hell he was up to now.

"Ava," he said, emotion in his voice, "I know you're not in love with me. But you've already been married three times, so I wonder if you could now consider me?"

Then he began to tell me how many millions and billions of dollars he was worth until I got lost in the extent of his holdings and properties and God-knows-what. Then he went into things that were more my style.

"I used to own a yacht, with a captain and crew and a great chef, and I'll buy another one. We'll travel in style wherever you want to go. If you want to keep working in movies, I'll buy you the best properties available, the greatest directors, the best leading men. You won't have to worry about studios and contracts and all that nonsense. You can have a wonderful life, and you can enjoy every second of it. And you might, eventually, learn to love me."

All that was delivered with all the sincerity that Howard could muster, but I have to say that my first thought was: Goddamnit, Howard's trying to buy me. He wants to make me one of his possessions, and that's something I never intend to let anyone do.

The dust had settled by now, and we could go in. I patted his hand and said, "Howard, let me think about it." And I did think about it, then and for all the years that followed. But I wasn't in love with Howard, and I knew that no matter how hard I tried, I never could be. But I have to confess it would be nice to be sitting here in London thinking: Now how will I get away from this cold winter while I still own TWA?

I suppose I didn't do much for Howard's blood pressure when I invited Luis Miguel to come visit me in July. But Howard wasn't really in Tahoe all that much; he was always off on some flying adventure or gigantic financial scheme or, for all I know, tucking in some of the babes he had stashed around. Some husband he would have made.

Howard returned soon after Luis Miguel arrived, and he was the soul of politeness. True, it would have been hard for him to play the part of the jealous lover, since lovers were the one thing we'd never been. But on the other hand, Howard wasn't the type to sit back and contemplate a situation like that for long, either. If there ever was a time that called for throwing a brick and hiding your hand, this was it.

It started one night when Luis Miguel and I returned from the casino and had a fight. Unlike the fights between Frank and me, they were very much the exception with Luis Miguel, but on this night I stormed up the stairs and slammed the door shut behind me. Now in the ordinary course of events I would have floated downstairs next morning and we'd have made up and been lovers again. But nothing was ever ordinary when Howard Hughes was involved.

I didn't get all the details until much later, but Howard, who had the habit I usually ignored of planting spies thinly disguised as household help around me, was immediately told of our little battle. Next thing you know, his number-one stooge and full-time Iago, Johnny Meyer, has just by chance dropped by to say hello.

Now you have to understand that whatever else Luis Miguel was, he was a very proud man, and my storming off like that annoyed the hell out of him. And Johnny Meyer was primed to sprinkle all the verbal poison he could, inflaming Luis Miguel's natural indignation. "Why do you let these women run you around?" he said. "Leave them alone for a while, teach them a lesson."

Egged on by Johnny and his own anger, Luis Miguel said that if it was up to him, he'd leave right that very minute, go back to Spain and the hell with everybody else. Well, surprise, surprise— it turned out that the ever-helpful friend in need Howard Hughes had a small plane fueled up and ready at the airport to ferry Luis Miguel direct to Los Angeles where he could make connections with a TWA flight that could conveniently get him back to Europe in a wink. So when I came down the next morning, there was no Luis Miguel. You better believe I thought it was odd, unlike him to let little storms permanently darken our horizon. But he was gone, and dear sweet Howard was right there and just itching to fly me and Reenie off to someplace exotic. So what the hell.

We finally ended up in Miami on that trip, all three of us staying in a most beautiful luxury villa with wide lawns and palm trees and a huge swimming pool. We settled down to enjoy the sunshine, but before long Reenie had a discussion with one of the house's handymen, someone I'd see around the place occasionally. You guessed it, he was one of Howard's men, but with an assignment unlike any I'd come across before.

"For God's sake," he'd told Reenie, "can't you get that woman of yours into bed with Mr. Hughes? I've been here day and night for ten days guarding this pearl-and-diamond necklace that once belonged to the Czarina of Russia. It's so fucking valuable I have to sit there with a loaded pistol and not let it out of my sight, even while I'm eating. If I leave it at all, I have to get a replacement. I can't see a broad, I can't go to a bar, I can't even have a drink. For Christ's sake, if you have any influence with her, get her into bed with him so he can reward her with the necklace and I can rejoin the human race."

We'd been in this villa for nearly two weeks, and we were getting bored. Even the loveliest place can feel like a prison if the circumstances are wrong, and this necklace business was the last straw.

"Honey," I said to Reenie, "it's time to make a move."

Reenie glanced at her watch. "It's four o'clock in the morning."

"Good," I said. "Then we won't have to say good-bye."

"Where are we going?" A not unreasonable question.

"I don't know. We'll find a taxi on the main road and I'll think of somewhere."

We packed our bags and crept down the stairs just as dawn was breaking. We tiptoed across the hall toward the door, and suddenly Howard appears, fully dressed, as if it's the most normal thing in the world to find his two female guests sneaking out at dawn. The son of a bitch must have had our goddamn room bugged.

"Good morning," he said pleasantly. "What's this all about?"

"I'm leaving, Howard," I said with as much firmness as I could muster. "I'm tired of this, I'm bored to death. And I'm going to Havana." That was the first destination that flashed into my head.

"You are?" he said, nice as you please. "I wish you wouldn't."

"I don't care what you wish," I said. "I've made up my mind and I'm going."

With that, I pulled off my lovely sapphire ring and threw it at him. I realize now that that was not the most charming exit move a well-brought-up Southern lady could have made, not to mention that it wasn't terribly sensible either. But in those days I did whatever went through my mind, and my decisions were often not all that sensible.

We didn't get to the airport until around nine in the morning, with flights to Havana supposed to leave hourly. But what did we hear every hour on the hour for the goddamn rest of the day: "The flight to Havana has been canceled. The flight to Havana has been canceled. The flight to Havana has been canceled." Not a single flight left all day long. Now that couldn't have been an accident; it had to be that goddamn son of a bitch Howard Hughes. That's the kind of power that man had.

Finally, at eight P.M. that evening, the loudspeaker announced that a flight to Havana was ready to depart. I guess Howard had removed his ban. "Stubborn bitch," he probably thought. "Let her go."

If you think all of that convinced Howard Hughes to get the hell out of my life, you haven't been paying attention. No sooner did we get back to California and into a house in Palm Springs than who should come flying out of the sun but my old friend Mr. Hughes. Of course, Howard being Howard, the sun was nowhere in sight when he flew in. And the Palm Springs airport, with its small landing strip and no landing lights at all, suited his style perfectly. He just made a phone call and twenty cars were lined up at intervals along both sides of the runway with headlights shining when he came in for a landing.

For once, Howard had called me beforehand. "Can you meet me when I land?" he asked. "I've got something very important to show you and to talk about." Since I'd already turned down a fortune in jewelry in San Francisco and thrown a priceless sapphire ring in his face and laughed at a Czarina's necklace in

Miami, I was naturally curious about what he could be up to now.

The plane droned in and landed perfectly. It was a small one this time, not the enormous four-engined monster he usually piloted. Howard came down the steps holding tightly to yet another one of his ridiculous cardboard boxes. He smiled as he approached me, and removed the lid. Pieces of paper flew in all directions, and he put the top back on. I noticed that the drivers of those twenty cars seemed to go slightly berserk, chasing these bits of paper as if they were thousand-dollar bills.

"What the hell are they, Howard?" I asked.

"Thousand-dollar bills."

"What the hell are you doing with them?"

"Giving them to you."

I began to say, "What the hell for?" before it struck me that this was truly one of the more ridiculous moments in my life, standing there next to a cardboard box full of thousand-dollar bills that had started to blow away like so much confetti.

"Howard," I said. "We'd better go somewhere and talk."

We went somewhere and talked. Howard said, "Darryl F. Zanuck and I want you to make a picture with us. You in the lead?"

Howard was still clutching his box. I said, "Howard, how much money is in that box?"

"A quarter of a million dollars in thousand-dollar bills." He took the lid of the box to show me the tightly packed interior.

I thought: Well, I suppose there aren't many people in the world who have ever seen a quarter of a million dollars all in one piece.

"Howard," I said, "what's the film all about?"

"We haven't quite decided yet. But Darryl has some great ideas."

"What about the script?"

"Well, that hasn't been done yet either."

"Howard, what's the quarter of a million dollars for?"

"It's for you. It's a bonus."

"Howard," I said, getting a bit testy, "if you want to make a film with me, you know what to do. You go to my agent and discuss it. You don't come here in the dark offering me a quarter-of-a-million-dollar bonus."

Now, Howard was a very serious man. You did not insult him if you could help it, or try and make a fool of him or laugh at him. I never wanted to do any of that, so I pulled back and said, "Anyway, it's nice to see you again, Howard. I've got to get back now. You take care." After all, once you've resisted all the jewelry in the world, what the hell difference does turning down a quarter of a million dollars make? I would do the same thing today . . . I think.

TWENTY-FOUR

B *howani Junction* was a film with a split personality as far as Metro was concerned. On the one hand, as befitted the studio's biggest production of 1956, they were happy to ballyhoo it as an epic, with ads shouting, "Two Years in Production! Thousands in the Cast!" But on the other hand, it had *me* in it, didn't it? Which meant lurid copy lines on the order of "Half-Caste Beauty and Her Three Loves" and "Ava . . . enticing . . . primitive . . . she must choose . . . one world to live in . . . one man to love!" Oh, brother.

Actually, though you'd never know it from all that, *Bhowani Junction* was one of my more serious films, one that allowed me to get more emotionally involved in a part than I usually did. Partly that's because George Cukor was the director. I'd known George socially for years and had an enormous amount of respect for his ability. After all, *Bhowani Junction* was his thirty-eighth film in twenty-two years in Hollywood, and all that work had gotten him a reputation as a superb director of actresses.

Bhowani, however, would be a different kind of test for him, and for me. Based on a bestselling novel by English writer John Masters, which Metro had snapped up for a very serious two hundred thousand dollars, *Bhowani* was set in India in 1947, with the country on the verge of independence from Britain. Riots and mass demonstrations were commonplace, and George would not only have to put me through my paces, he would have to orchestrate explosive crowd scenes with thousands of extras milling around.

With the fight for India's soul between the peaceful Congress party of Gandhi and the violent and provocative Communists as background, the character I played, Victoria Jones, returns home to the railway center of Bhowani Junction, a subaltern on leave from the Women's Auxiliary Corps. I look the model of a British maiden in my uniform, but I'm not. I'm an Anglo-Indian, a half-breed or cheechee, in the local slang, someone who feels at home in neither camp. I may call my English train-engineer father "pater," but no one treats me like the Queen of England. As a result, says Colonel Rodney Savage, the man in charge, I had so many chips on my shoulder you only had to cough politely to send them flying.

Bhowani Junction is really the story of how my love for three men mirrored India's struggle and helped me to find myself. First on my list was fellow Anglo-Indian Patrick Taylor (played by six-foot-four Bill Travers), the railways' local traffic superintendent. However, I can't get used to Patrick's anti-Indian feeling, and next I become involved with Ranjit Kasel, a Sikh who longs for a fully independent India. I was always amused that with eight hundred million Indians around, MGM went and employed a goddamn *Englishman*, Francis Matthews, in that role. But he did an excellent job, and, after all, they hadn't cast an Anglo-Indian in my part, had they?

At any rate, Ranjit and his firebrand mother help me after I'm forced to kill a British officer who tries to rape me, and I consider marrying him, but it doesn't feel right. Only with the hard-nosed Colonel Savage, of all people, a man I once called "a cruel bully," do I find true love. But even though he offers to take me back to England with him, I let him know that I belong to India, "not as a phony Indian, not as a phony white, but as myself."

Playing Colonel Savage was an old pal of mine, Stewart Granger, a British-born Hollywood star whose real name, changed for obvious reasons, was Jimmy Stewart. Jimmy was great fun: handsome, talkative, assertive, and a nice guy under it all. He was married to Jean Simmons who, by an odd coincidence, was simultaneously making *Guys and Dolls* with Frank. Jimmy and I rendezvoused in Copenhagen on the way to our location, and we decided to see what that city had to offer in terms of night life. We got on like great pals, and sometime during the small hours of the morning Jimmy volunteered that he

213

couldn't possibly be unfaithful to Jean. I smiled, patted his hand, and said, "Honey, you've been reading the wrong press clips."

If the world were a logical place, the location Jimmy and I were headed toward would have been India. But the Indians were a bit resentful of the pro-British slant of the original novel and were insisting that they had to see the script and approve it. Metro was equally startled by the number of dollars the Indian tax collectors was eager to levy, including one tax of twelve percent of the net world profit on the picture. So when neighboring Pakistan suggested Lahore as the location and offered to waive all taxes, provide crowds as well as the use of the Northwestern Railway and the officers and men of the 13th Battalion Frontier Force Rifles, MGM had no problem accepting.

Lahore is an ancient city, so old that no one really knows when it first came into existence. And, honey, I often felt that some of the facilities we had to use were as old as the damn city itself. Not only was the place hot, often up to one hundred and thirty degrees, not to mention the backbreaking humidity, but the only air-conditioning available was in the form of large and not particularly active ceiling fans.

Outside, it was teeming, a potpourri of flies, smells, carts, horses, and masses of humanity. Dogs howled all night long, I'm sure from hunger, keeping me awake. I used to take food down to them, but the crew would warn me, "Jesus, Ava, be careful. Rabies is rampant in this part of the world." The food was not trustworthy either, and ended up giving me a hellacious case of amoebic dysentery, an illness I wouldn't wish on one of those poor dogs. In person and on the screen, no one was going to mistake this place for Metro's back lot, and I guess that was the whole point.

Getting the material needed to make a movie into Lahore turned out to be no mean feat. Almost every form of transportation known to man was used to get the hundreds of tons of gear into the city. Among the stuff that had to be brought in was a twenty-ton generator, brought from London, and more than ten tripod studio cameras, some of which were mounted on automobiles, station wagons, and trucks. Someone with a lot of time on his hands estimated that two hundred and fourteen thousand man-hours were devoted to preparations for filming, and I wasn't about to argue.

During the four months Reenie and I were in the city, our hotel was a two-story job with outdoor verandas running around each level. We shared a small suite, though that is really too grand a word for our rough square of rooms. But I have to confess that we did have that ultimate luxury in that climate, a working refrigerator.

I had the most exciting evening of my entire stay in that damn hotel suite, but unfortunately it wasn't a romantic encounter. I had just finished a soothing soak in the bathtub and was standing up, reaching for a towel, when I felt a sudden whoosh over my head. People talk about "a bat out of hell," but this damn bat came out of *somewhere*, apparently determined to nest in nowhere but my hair.

Oh, God, was I petrified! Stark naked, I ran out the bathroom door and down the corridor of our suite, screaming at the top of my lungs. The bat must have been some goddamn relative of Count Dracula because it just kept after me. My only escape route was through the door leading to the outdoor veranda. Reenie, who'd been chasing the thing with a broom, saw that was where I was headed, and she dropped the broom on the floor and a large bath towel on me just as I reached the veranda. A hotel servant in the vicinity, attracted by my unladylike screams, chased the damn thing away with a loose tennis racket, apparently the local weapon of choice in such encounters. And a good thing, too. I might have run as far as the Lahore town hall in my bare feet if he hadn't.

In circumstances like that, even the simplest shots and stunts became difficult. One sequence, which had me falling off the back of Bill Travers' motorcycle and into Jimmy Granger's arms, took a bruising fourteen takes to get right. And just being on the city's streets could be an adventure of sorts. I remember waiting for my cue behind a dilapidated building one bakingly hot day when I realized, never mind how, that I was standing literally on the edge of an open sewer. The sun was pouring down, the heat was unbearable, the flies were everywhere, and the smell—honey, don't even ask about the smell. What the hell am I doing here, why the hell am I trying to be an actress? I thought to myself. God almighty, I felt so sick, I was sure if they didn't call for me in another ten seconds, I'd die. Finally, the cue came, and though I managed to get through the scene, I swear my face must have been green. And definitely not with envy.

Still, I don't want to give the impression that everything in Lahore was dreadful. We filmed in the legendary Shalimar gardens, which were supposed to give a hint of the beauties of paradise and the world to come, and the government also agreed to reopen an exquisite Sikh temple for the first time since the Muslims had taken over Pakistan. The government even allowed some one hundred Sikhs to cross the border and participate in the filmed ceremony in which Victoria and Ranjit were to be received into the Sikh faith. People told us it was probably the first time in history that the temple had been opened to non-Sikhs. To get in, everyone had to be shoeless, which was definitely not a problem as far as I was concerned.

Though he'd never been known for directing crowd scenes, you wouldn't have known it from watching George Cukor interact with the extras. George was a tiger, a determined perfectionist totally possessed by a single thought—the film. He was always yelling and screaming to get the damn thing *right*. He never carried the whole script with him, just the half dozen pages or whatever for that day's shooting, and he'd hit people with them if he got mad or just to emphasize his point. One time he got so angry with this enormous, unruly mob of extras that wasn't doing what he'd told them to that he simply waded into the throng with that rolled-up script, a little guy yelling and screaming his lungs out and hitting them as if he were leading a battalion of armed Sikhs instead of being all by his lonesome. They could have torn him to pieces, and I nervously turned to Jimmy Granger and said, "Jesus, they'll kill him." Jimmy told me not to worry. "Ava," he said, "they *like* George." And he was right.

I can understand why. I liked George enormously myself. He was attentive to detail, he really cared, and he knew how to pull the kind of performance he wanted out of me. One afternoon, for instance, he was having trouble getting me to be angry enough for one of the many quarrels I had with the men in my life. Before shooting started, I'd told George about the particularly irritating lunch I'd had with a prying journalist. "Ava," he said to me now, "why don't you get mad the way you did this afternoon with that columnist?"

"You son of a bitch," I said to him. "I'll never tell you anything that happens to me off the set again." But of course, that piece of direction was exactly the key I needed to successfully unlock that scene.

Bad as conditions were in Pakistan, however, it turned out that my worst scene, the one that was so awful and horrific that it gave me nightmares, was shot not there but in a studio back in England. In it, Lionel Jeffries plays Lt. Graham McDaniel, a British officer who's always eyed me and, in Colonel Savage's words, "operated as if his duties were at the bottom of a sewer." And on this particular night, he follows me home and attempts to rape me.

I can still remember every moment of that scene. McDaniel springs at me and knocks me down. We scramble and fight in the mud. He rips off my uniform, my blouse, he's got my hair painfully twisted in his hands. I felt I was losing the struggle, being defeated by his strength and determination. Oh, my God, Lionel was serious . . . this was rape. And while I understood *theoretically* that you can't act a rape scene without it being brutal, angry, and terrifying, experiencing it was something else again. I felt terrified, hopelessly vulnerable, spitting and scratching like a cat. Defeated. I was almost out of my mind at the awful violence, the awful reality.

And, of course, the worst thing I had to do in that scene was kill my attacker. I somehow get an arm free, and my hand touches a piece of iron railing from the nearby railway track. It's heavy and lethal, and I raise it high and hit McDaniel as hard as I can on the head. You hear this crash. And I've killed a man.

I left that scene without speaking and went immediately back to my trailer. Trembling and shaking, I swallowed an enormous whiskey. At that moment, I felt sick with fright, as if I'd been literally fighting for my life. I'd known Lionel for weeks now; he was a sweet man and I adored him, but I knew that if I didn't see him *quickly*, that scene was going to stick in my mind forever and I'd hate his guts.

George knocked and came in to see if I was all right. "George," I said, "for God's sake, please get Lionel over here—*now*! Because unless I see him and give him a big hug, I'll never speak to him as long as I live."

Of course Lionel hurried over, I gave him my hug, and things

217

were all right between us. No film scene had ever affected me so deeply before, had left me with such a nightmare sense of terror, and no scene would ever do so again. For which absence I am profoundly grateful.

I don't think anybody bothered to mention that rape scene when the reviews for *Bhowani Junction* came out. Though my performance got respectful attention—*Newsweek* called me "surprisingly effective"—most of the critics felt the film didn't quite hit the mark. "The piece goes off in so many directions, and with such an enormous racket" said *The New Yorker* rather snidely, "that one longs for a quiet room and a copy of 'Kim.'"

What those know-it-all critics didn't know was that George's film had been seriously damaged, oversimplified, and oversentimentalized, by recutting after preview audiences didn't respond to Victoria's life and loves quite the way the studio thought they should. For instance, a nicely flirtatious scene between Victoria and Colonel Savage, where I borrow his toothbrush after first dipping it in Scotch, was cut, and the whole movie was rearranged and an extensive voiceover by the Colonel added on to explain over and over again that the sad plight of the Anglo-Indians was responsible for my passionate behavior. As if any damn excuses were necessary in the first place.

Whatever the final shape of the film, it didn't affect my feelings for George Cukor, or his for me. In fact it was George who said the nicest thing that's ever been said about me. "Ava," he told an interviewer, "is a gentleman." A gentleman. I like that.

TWENTY-FIVE

I n December of 1955, just short of my thirty-third birthday, I did something I'd been threatening to do for a long time, something that no one really believed I'd ever manage. No, it wasn't leaving the picture business, but it was close. I left the United States for good and all and settled in Spain.

Why did I go? For one thing, for as long as I lived there, I'd never liked Hollywood. It wasn't my favorite place, to put it mildly; I found it provincial and superficial by turns. I just didn't fit in with the way things were done in the movie capital, and it was becoming more and more impossible to have any privacy there. I couldn't walk my dog, go to an airport or a restaurant, I couldn't even go to the ladies' room without somebody around watching me, reporting on me, spying on me. I felt imprisoned by the lifestyle of a movie star and I just couldn't live with that anymore.

And if I hadn't cared for Hollywood in its heyday, it certainly had less attractions for me now that things seemed to be falling apart. The film business was becoming increasingly fragmented: more productions were basing in Europe for tax reasons, my old buddy Howard Hughes had actually gone and sold RKO, and television, growing like Topsy, was robbing the movies of much of its audience.

And then there was Spain. I don't know whether it was the weather, the people, or the music, but I'd fallen head over heels in love with the place from the first moment I'd arrived years before. It was so unspoiled in those days, so dramatic, so historic—and so goddamn cheap to live in that it was almost unbelievable. Combined with the fact that living abroad exempted me from paying domestic income tax, the whole package definitely appealed to the frugal side of my nature.

But there was more than dollars and sense involved in my decision. I fell in love with classic Castilian—when you hear it spoken and can understand it, it's so pure and musical that it's a delight to the senses. And I felt emotionally close to Spain—who can really say why?—and the Spanish people responded in kind, accepting me without question. Which couldn't have been easy for them. After all, I represented everything they disapproved of. I was a woman, living alone, divorced, a non-Catholic, and an actress.

The Spanish really did more than accept me; they seemed to be positively delighted that I had chosen to make my life among them. I had barely arrived when I was offered a fortune to do a soap commercial. A fortune. I said, "Not unless you give me a Rolls-Royce, too." Finally they came back. "Okay," they said. "We'll give you a Rolls-Royce as well." Still, I said no. Wasn't that crazy?

I bought a house in La Moraleja, a suburb just minutes from the center of Madrid. It was a low, sprawling, ranch-style red-brick building, nicknamed La Bruja, the witch, because just such a creature, complete with broomstick, was doing duty as the weathervane. Set on two acres of green lawn with magnificent weeping willows and a fine view of the distant hills, it was built for comfort, not for show, which was fine with me. It was also unfurnished, and Reenie and I rushed around Madrid buying everything in sight, especially furniture. The only necessities I couldn't seem to get—Hershey bars, Kleenex, and Jack Daniel's whiskey—were replenished by visiting friends. I filled La Bruja with books and records and, for the first time since I'd left North Carolina, I felt I was *home*.

I took Spanish lessons and worked very hard at them because I was determined to fit in. To hell with being a tourist; I wanted to experience the Spanish lifestyle. My teacher was an elderly gentleman, tall and graying with a commanding manner. He would walk in the door and say with a wave of his hand, "No English today! Solamente español."

I would nod and say, "Sí." And then, being polite and hospitable, I would ask in my best Spanish, "¿Quieres una copita?" "Would you like a drink?" and he would beam and say, "Sí, sí, señorita. Una martini, por favor." Before we knew it, we'd downed a pitcher of Reenie's knockout concoctions and could have been speaking Hindustani for all that it mattered.

Despite diversions like Mr. Martini, my Spanish did improve. It turned out that my accent was very good—we worked hard on it, so it damn well better have been—and I had a good ear for colloquial phrases. But even though I ended up reading and writing very well, my spoken Spanish was never quite what it should have been because my innate shyness got in the way.

When it came to going out and seeing the country, however, I certainly wasn't about to let any shyness stop me. Reenie and I often drove off on trips all across Spain, for instance visiting the Gypsies in Granada and having them plop their babies on my lap to hold during flamenco dances. Another time we stopped for coffee at a tiny roadside café and when we asked for milk, the old Spaniard who ran the place immediately put his hands on his nanny goat. Thanks, we said, but no thanks.

One thing Spain didn't do for me was improve my driving, which, you may remember, was not exactly a model of safety. It had even caused daredevil Howard Hughes to say to me, with typical Howard logic, "Ava, you drive too fast. If I were you I'd always drive in the middle of the road. That way, if anything happens, you've got room on both sides." And now I was in a country that had some very original thoughts indeed about speeding. The police once pulled a friend of mine over and when she protested, "But there aren't any speed limits in this country," they calmly replied, "That doesn't matter. You were going faster than anybody else, so we're going to give you a ticket."

The worst time I ever had with a car was on a tranquil road outside Madrid with very little traffic in either direction. I was on my way to the airport in a big, powerful Mercedes, and even though I was only meeting an MGM producer, I was late and I just hate being late. The end result was that I hit this sharp curve in the road way too fast, soared up the side of a grassy embankment, and completely lost control. The car did two full rolls and another half one for good measure and finally came to rest with its wheels in the air and me sitting upside down in the driver's seat, wondering what the hell had happened.

The windshield and side windows were smashed, there was glass everywhere, but the Mercedes' solid steel framework hadn't buckled and that's what saved my life. Spanish workers harvesting in nearby fields came to my rescue, hauling me out of the car and brushing the glass splinters off my clothes. And who should come by to rescue me but Ben Cole, Lana Turner's manager, who was helping me settle into Spain and had just made a great deal to sell the Mercedes to a gentleman in Switzerland.

"Well," I said, "you better call back and tell him you can let him have it a bit cheaper because it's not in the mint condition he expected."

I didn't seem to have any serious injuries, at least none that a couple of decent-sized drinks wouldn't fix, but within a few days I realized that when the steering wheel had hit my thigh with a tremendous bang, it had raised a huge bruise that seemed to be turning into a sort of a dent.

So later, when I was in London on some business, I reported the bruise to my doctor. He examined it, made a noncommittal "Hmm," and suggested I get in touch with Sir Archibald McIndoe, a well-known British plastic surgeon who had spent most of the war years attending to the broken bones and terrible burns suffered by Royal Air Force fliers.

Archie, as I soon began to call him, turned out to be a comfortably built man with a round face, wise old eyes, and a kindly smile. He was a New Zealander, but without any trace of the accent, and within minutes we were friends.

"Ava," he said, "take a bucket and drop in a couple of tins of tomatoes. Leave the tomatoes in the tins, dear, because it's the weight you need. Then put your foot through the handle and just lift the bucket and return it to the ground. Lift and return, lift and return, over and over again as many times as you can. That muscle has been very badly bruised and indented, and that exercise will give it strength and help it to rebuild."

Archie was dead right. For a Harley Street specialist, I thought he made a lot of horse sense, and though I hoped I'd never need him again, I didn't forget his kindness.

One of the ironic things about my living in Spain was that now that I was established in Luis Miguel's country, my relationship with him had come to an end. We had started to break up slowly and regretfully after he'd let Howard Hughes's people talk him onto that plane in Lake Tahoe. We said it didn't make any difference between us, but it did. And the months I was in Pakistan making *Bhowani Junction* were not the best thing for a shaky relationship.

Also, Luis Miguel was anxious to settle down, get married, and raise a family, and I knew that I was not ready for that sort of domesticity. And since we were great friends as well as lovers, and since I'd never been as jealous of him as I was of Frank, I was genuinely happy for Luis Miguel when he told me that he was going to marry the Italian actress Lucia Bose.

The funny thing was, the next man in my life turned out to be an old flame of Lucia Bose's, the Italian actor Walter Chiari. Though not terribly well known outside his homeland, Walter had some forty films to his credit and was considered a kind of Italian Danny Kaye. I'd first met him in Rome during the making of *Barefoot Contessa*. He had been flirting with me almost from the first day we met, but you expect that from Italian males: if they're not chasing someone, their lives aren't worth living.

What can I say about Walter Chiari? Walter was *nice,* and everyone knows what a kiss of death that can sometimes be. Walter was amusing, good-looking, even-tempered, highly intelligent, and a delightful companion. He followed me all over Europe, all over the world in fact. Our association lasted a long time and we even lived together on many occasions. And, yes, Walter often asked me to marry him, but I couldn't and I didn't. The distance that separates liking from love is as wide as the Pacific as far as I'm concerned. And that was always the bottom line between me and Walter Chiari.

There was an odd footnote to our relationship, however. Walter and I (along with Jimmy Granger and David Niven) actually made a film together. It was my next project for MGM, *The Little Hut,* and the less said about that fiasco the better. The feeble plot had the four of us stranded on a desert island, thinking about sex but not, the production code being what it was, doing very much about it. I hated it, every minute of it, but what could I do? If I took another suspension they'd keep me at Metro for the rest of my life. I would have played Little Eva if they'd wanted, anything to get through my contract fast.

A much more lasting male relationship, in fact one of the most gratifying of my life, also began in Spain. Through Betty Sicre, a good chum, I'd met Robert Graves at a party in Madrid. At first, I have to admit, I wasn't at all clear about who he was and I mistook him for some sort of scientist. How was I to know that he was a writer and Greek scholar of enviable eminence, someone the London *Times* would call, "the greatest love poet in English since John Donne"?

Robert was big and broad, six foot two with a thick shock of white hair. His face seemed to have been carved out of solid rock, but it was softened by his warmth and an impish, self-mocking sense of humor. He loved women, loved to be in their presence, loved the sound of their laughter and their talk. And I have to admit that I truly loved him as well, even though he was close to his middle sixties when we met and there was never even the slightest suggestion that we should carry things further into a physical relationship. The best way I can describe the situation is that there was sort of a love-conspiracy between us, and that being together with him and his wonderful wife Beryl and the kids in their house high on a hillside on Majorca gave me a kind of pleasure and satisfaction nothing else in my life could approach.

When I first went to visit Robert on Majorca, I was determined to learn all I could about the work he did. "You know, Robert," I said, "I really don't understand poetry."

And he said, to the point as always, "My darling, you're not supposed to understand it, you're supposed to enjoy it." Poems are like people, he told me; there aren't that many authentic ones around.

Later, on my way to bed, I turned up a copy of Robert's *Collected Poems* and I asked him which one I ought to read first. He picked one that he said I might perhaps agree to take personally, though it had been written long before we met. I still remember some of the lines:

> She speaks always in her own voice
> Even to strangers. . . .
> She is wild and innocent, pledged to love
> Through all disaster. . . .

There was a smile on his face the next morning.

"I loved it," I said.

"It's you to the life," he said.

Through all the years we knew each other, Robert wrote several poems for me, something that makes me very proud. The first ever, which came with a little note reading "To Ava from Robert with love—1964" was called "Not to Sleep."

Not to sleep all the night long, for pure joy,
Counting no sheep and careless of chimes,
Welcoming the dawn confabulation
Of birds, her children, who discuss why
Fanciful details of the promised coming—
Will she be wearing red, or russet, or blue
Or pure white? whatever she wears, glorious.
Not to sleep all night long, for pure joy,
This is given to few but at last to me,
So that when I laugh or stretch or leap from bed
I shall glide downstairs, my feet brushing the carpet
In courtesy to civilized progression,
Though did I wish, I could soar through the open window
And perch on a branch above, acceptable ally
Of the birds, still alert, grumbling gently together.

What can you say about a man who would send something like that? Is it any wonder that I felt the way I did about him?

TWENTY-SIX

T hough I'd been involved in a couple of previous film versions of Papa Hemingway's works that had turned out fine, I never thought that filming *The Sun Also Rises* was the best of ideas. I didn't think it could be done without spoiling it, and I'm afraid I turned out to be right.

Originally published in 1926, with its title taken from a particularly down-in-the-mouth section of Ecclesiastes, *Sun* was notorious because its main character, Jake Barnes, was sexually impotent owing to a wound suffered in World War I. Even Papa's own mother had called it "one of the filthiest books of the year." Papa had given it to his first wife, Hadley, as part of her divorce settlement, and she'd sold it practically right then and there for ten thousand dollars. By the time Darryl F. Zanuck decided he wanted to turn it into a movie nearly three decades later, those same rights cost him a hundred and twenty-five thousand, none of which came home to Papa.

Initially, or so I've been told, Zanuck wanted Jennifer Jones for the leading part of Lady Brett Ashley, but she turned it down and Papa personally informed Zanuck he thought I would be swell. When Henry King, who'd directed me in *Snows of Kilimanjaro*, sent me the treatment, I felt an immediate kinship with Lady Brett, who Papa wrote was "as charming when she is drunk as when she is sober." I always felt close to Papa's women.

The rest of the cast took a while to assemble and was a pretty

mixed lot. Tyrone Power played Jake, Mel Ferrer his pal Robert
Cohn, Errol Flynn was my besotted fiancé Mike Campbell,
Juliette Greco (who promptly caught Zanuck's eye) played a
French lady of the night, and Robert Evans, a former clothing
manufacturer from New York who later became head of production at Paramount, played Pedro Romero, the matador who
loved me.

More of a problem than the cast was the first draft of
the script. When I read it, I nearly had a fit. I took Papa
the script and told him for his own pride he had to change
things. Now, when Papa got mad he would stand on something
and make speeches. Perched on a chair, he started to scream,
"They haven't even got the right fucking kind of planes in it!"
Finally, he calmed down and Peter Viertel, a young man he
liked very much, was brought in and did another, much superior draft.

Still, the movie was hardly the damn book. For one thing, it
focused more on what the publicity called "Hemingway's colorful world," the mad whirl of fiestas, bulls, bistros, and parades.
And for another, it seemed obsessed, at least as far as that publicity was concerned, with the supposedly racy nature of the proceedings. "Again," the ads blared, "Twentieth Century–Fox
breaks tradition, as it brings you Hemingway's boldest love story
that shocked the world. So daring—so delicate—it could not be
filmed until now." Or how about, "Only Hemingway, master of
unspoken secrets, could successfully tackle this daring theme, . . .
could weave this shattering novel of dissipation and passion in
pleasure-mad Europe." Right.

Actually, it was always the romantic aspects of the story that
appealed to me. Lady Brett was an American who'd married a
British lord and had been widowed by the First World War. She'd
met Jake Barnes and fallen madly in love with him, but because
of his wound felt there was no hope for them. So both she and
Jake joined what used to be called the Lost Generation, the group
of bohemian pleasure seekers who sought to flee their pain
through drinking and general dissipation across the face of Europe.

In the course of the film, almost every man she meets falls
madly for Lady Brett: the Scot Mike Campbell, the American
Robert Cohn, the Spanish bullfighter Pedro Romero, and of

course poor Jake. This causes all sorts of dreadful complications, especially since I stay with no one and am happy with no one. Robert Cohn finally can't take any more and beats up everyone in sight, which appears to knock a bit of sense into me as well. Though Papa hadn't wanted a happy ending for these characters, the whole point of the thing being that they couldn't find contentment, Hollywood wasn't satisfied with that. So the film ends with me and Jake sharing a cab. I say, "Oh, darling, there must be an answer for us somewhere," and the poor man agrees, "I'm sure there is."

Though the movie starts in Paris, most of it is in fact set in the Spanish city of Pamplona, site of the world-famous running of the bulls at the San Fermín fiesta. Henry King had shot all kinds of footage at the real fiesta, and though that was used in the final film, by the time the cast was assembled, Pamplona was covered with four feet of snow. So we all went instead to Morelia, Mexico, where Henry and Tyrone Power had filmed *Captain from Castile* in 1946, to fill in the blanks. Not only was the city old enough to look Spanish, complete with a statue of the great Spanish writer Cervantes, but the city fathers agreed to repaint the interior of their bullring so it matched Pamplona's exactly.

Of all the actors who worked with me on that film, I got along best with Errol Flynn. I adored him, but although I dated him a couple of times when I first arrived in Hollywood, we were never physically involved. Errol was probably the most beautiful man I ever saw, his perfect body equally at home in a swimsuit or astride a horse. And he was fun, gallant, and well mannered with a great sense of humor. When he walked into a room, it was as if a light had been turned on. As he grew older, he drank too much and was chased around by scandal and gossip. But Errol Flynn always had style, honey. Real style.

Despite that silly ad campaign, *Sun* might have gotten better reviews than it deserved when it came out. *Time* magazine, which had practically laughed at me in *Bhowani Junction,* said this was "the most realistic performance" of my entire career. Papa, predictably, was not pleased. He called it "Darryl Zanuck's splashy Cook's Tour of the lost generation," and added that as far as he was concerned it was "all pretty disappointing, and that's being gracious. You're meant to be in Spain and all you see walking around are Mexicans. Pretty silly."

No one in Hollywood was too concerned about Papa's complaints, though. As David O. Selznick once told John Huston, "If a character goes from Café A to Café B, instead of Café B to Café A, or if a boat heads north instead of south, Hemingway is upset." This time, though, I think his irritation was justified. What happened to him shouldn't happen to a dog.

TWENTY-SEVEN

T hough I damn well knew I'd been nothing but lucky when the health and beauty genes had been passed around, I'd never bothered much about my looks. They didn't seem to have that much connection with who I thought I was, with what I felt was important. Then something happened, something terrible, that drove home the grim truth that without my face, the future was going to be pretty bleak.

Not long after I'd arrived in Spain, Papa Hemingway had introduced me to a man named Angelo Peralta, who owned a beautiful ranch in Andalusia near Seville where he bred fighting bulls. And not just any bulls, but the especially fast and dangerous Miura bulls that have killed more matadors than any other breed. When the great Manolete died, it was because of the horns of a Miura bull.

After nearly two years in Spain, I'd become something of an aficionada of bullfighting, so when, in October of 1957, Angelo Peralta invited me and any friends I chose to visit him on his ranch and watch the testing of young bulls, I was quite happy to accept. Both Bappie and Walter Chiari were staying with me at La Bruja at that time, so we all went down together.

The ring used for this testing was nothing near the size of the large bullrings found in all the major cities. It was a smallish circular arena built of wood, with openings at various places to admit the fast, specially trained horses and expert riders used in the procedure. The young bulls, intent on killing anything that

230

moves, are let in one at a time. They charge the horse, and the rider attempts to simultaneously keep his animal out of harm's way and plant barbed darts called *banderillas* in the bull's back. A few rushes and crashes, with horns smashing into the wooden barriers, and the experts have decided on the bravery of this particular youngster and another one is let in.

Bappie, Walter, and I joined the large crowd that had gathered around the ring to watch the spectacle. We were enjoying the action and the sunshine and not being shy about drinking mind-bending concoctions called *solasombras,* a particularly lethal combination of absinthe and Spanish cognac. Though in those days I was admittedly caught up in the passion and pagentry of the bullfighting ritual, desensitizing myself with *solasombras* was really the only way I could face seeing those beautiful animals slaughtered in a bullring.

Suddenly I began to hear murmurs all around me, a sort of increasing chorus. "What about it, Ava? Get up on a horse and try your luck. It's great fun. Give it a try, Ava."

Worse than that, I began listening to them. Well, why not? I thought. I'll just hang onto the horse; it knows what to do. Just lean down and plant the dart in the bull's back.

Which was an awful mistake. First of all, in films or out of films, I'd never ridden a horse in my life. The closest I'd come was perching on the back of a few tired old mules as a little girl in North Carolina. Sure I was a good athlete, but that had nothing in common with riding a spirited horse at dizzying speed and facing a charging young bull determined to kill you both.

Someone in authority should have stepped in and stopped me. You don't fool with bulls of that breed and ferocity. If Luis Miguel had been there, he would have stopped me at once. But Walter Chiari just stood there smiling. And Bappie for some reason had left the arena.

I can't remember who helped me into the saddle. Somebody said comfortingly, "Now you just hang onto the reins with your left hand. Hold the *banderillas* in your right. The horse knows his stuff and as the bull goes past just stick them in his back. Anywhere will do." Thanks a lot.

Whoosh . . . I was off, hurtling around the ring as the horse went into overdrive. I made three flying circuits before the young bull was let in and, oh, boy, did the action ever start then. The bull flew at the horse but just missed, crashing into the circular barrier with a bang. The next few seconds are still somewhat confusing to me, but as best as I can figure, just as I leaned down to stick in my *banderilla,* the horse reared high to avoid being disemboweled by the next charge.

I went overboard, plunging into a welter of horses' hooves, but I don't think either the horse or the bull touched me. My cheek smashed into the earth. I felt the impact, but no pain, no fear, no panic. I guess the *solasombras* had done their job and left me properly stupefied. I remember being picked up and carried from the ring. I was not hysterical or even frightened.

To this day, I'm pretty certain it was the force with which I struck the ground that created the large, discolored lump high up on my cheek, a lump that the photographs show had started to form even as I was being lifted off the ground.

Oh, yes, there was a photographer with a high-speed camera planted at a good angle in the crowd so he could catch everything that happened. It wasn't until later that I discovered that little fact, or that *Paris Match,* the French version of *Life* magazine, paid seventy-five thousand dollars for that unique set of prints. The whole thing had been plainly stage-managed with the idea of getting me a little woozy, putting me aboard a very fast and high-spirited horse and into the ring with a very dangerous animal. That's not a gag, it's a crime. I can only hope to God that there was nothing prearranged about the fall as well.

But on that day, life had to go on. A great party and barbecue had been prepared, an event that had been announced through the Andalusian grapevine. Gypsies had come from miles around, providing their wonderful flamenco singing and dancing. Fueled by an endless supply of wine, I joined in and danced until the sun rose behind the mountains.

I do remember looking into the mirror on my first visit to the bathroom and seeing this lump, which seemed to be the size of my fist, sticking out of my cheekbone. I thought it looked pretty horrible for a woman who depended on her face for a living, but I didn't panic. I simply went back to the dance.

The next day, in Seville, the horror began to focus. I ran into two American agents who lived in Rome. We had lunch together and they said, "For God's sake, Ava, you've got to go back to the States or England right away and get that fixed." When I took another look at myself in the mirror and realized that the lump had not gone down, I knew they were right. I needed Archie McIndoe.

So I went to see Archie at his East Grinstead hospital for the Royal Air Force. The war was over, but the RAF was still flying and there were always horrible accidents. I knew that in comparison to what was going on with those badly burned pilots, my little injury was of almost no consequence. But Archie was a man of enormous compassion and understanding, and he had enough to spare for me.

He told me that my lump was a hematoma, a blood clot. He said that a new method of treatment by injection had just come out, but he wouldn't dare to use it on me because it was so new that no one knew what the complications might be, including the possibility of another hematoma on top of the old one, which would certainly mean permanent disfigurement.

I sat there and looked at the man who was probably the greatest plastic surgeon in the world, let out a breath, and waited for his advice.

"It will take time," he said, "but it *will* go away of its own accord. You'll need heat treatment and massage, and we can try ultrasound, but it *will* go away. My advice is, don't let anyone try to operate or use a needle. Be patient."

When Archie McIndoe tells you to be patient, you're patient. I began his method of treatment in London and continued it daily when I returned to La Bruja. Then, about six months later, Frank came over to Spain. He came to the house and looked at the lump, which was still as large as a walnut, and said, "Friends of mine tell me about this great plastic surgeon in New York. It won't hurt to get a second opinion. Because, honey, you ain't gonna make any films looking like that."

I agreed. And on my next visit to New York, I went to get this man's opinion. He was quite certain about how to handle things. "We have this new injection that we can use immediately," he said. "It's a pity I didn't see you right after it happened, I could have injected you then."

Naturally, Archie's warning leapt right into my head. "Wait a minute," I began. "The surgeon who first advised me was Sir Archibald McIndoe. I'm sure you've heard of him."

Of course he knew about Archie McIndoe, the doctor said,

barreling right along and barely paying any attention to me. But it was still a pity that I hadn't come to see him immediately. And before he began the treatment, he wanted to inform me of his fee. He was building a new hospital in Texas and my fee, which he would naturally consider a contribution to that establishment, would be one million dollars.

Now it was my turn to be heedless. I stood up and said, "Fuck you and your new hospital and your outrageous fees," and marched out the door. As you can imagine, that was the last I saw of any doctor except Archie where my hematoma was concerned. And, just for the record, I'd like to say that not a single penny was I ever asked to pay by Archie McIndoe. To this day, I don't know why he felt I was worth ten seconds of his time.

As Archie had prophesied, the lump slowly subsided, though I was always conscious that it existed and I began to fear that my film career might be over. I continued to visit Archie and I became more involved with those badly mutilated pilots. It was the best possible therapy for me, because compared with their injuries, my lump couldn't have been more insignificant.

What Archie did for those boys my words can never adequately describe. Oh, God, their burns were terrible. Many had hardly any faces left; some didn't have limbs. Their treatments were long and often agonizing; sometimes more than a hundred operations were needed to give them a fighting chance. But Archie counseled and talked and gave them strength. I met a lot of them and we danced and laughed together. They were so brave I could have wept. Archie told me my visits did them a lot of good, but I'm sure they helped me more than I ever helped them.

One day, Archie rang me in Madrid and said, "Ava, I want a favor from you."

"It's yours," I said.

"We've got our annual fete in a couple of weeks, a sort of garden party that raises funds for the hospital. I want you to come over here to East Grinstead and sell your autographs in one of our tents."

"God, I'll be terrified."

"No, you won't. Will you do it?"

"Of course."

My fears were for once natural because since the accident the press reports had described me as half-dead, crippled, disfigured

234

for life. A lot of friends had called me up or written to say how sorry they were and how they hoped I'd get better. Jesus!

Down at East Grinstead, Archie chuckled at my fears, but I was wary. "I suppose there'll be press and photographers there," I said.

"Sure there will," he said in a matter-of-fact voice. He crossed the room and took my chin gently in his hand. Turning my face to the light, he said quietly, "Ava, there's nothing unsightly on your face now. You can go in front of any camera in the world, I promise you."

I didn't believe him. I looked at my face every morning in the mirror and I could feel the lump. Vastly diminished, yes, but still there, like a shadow under the skin. Despite Archie's words, a lot of fears remained in my mind.

The morning of the fair, I noticed that Archie opened the champagne rather early. We toasted each other, and by the time I reached my place in the tent I'd consumed my fair share. The photographers were everywhere, taking my picture from every angle known to God and man. I was frightened out of my mind, but I was doing this for Archie, so I smiled and signed autographs and got through it somehow.

The next day, there were glamorous pictures of me in all the newspapers, and Archie told me what he had done.

"Ava," he said, "I turned the press on you deliberately. I rang every newspaper editor in London and said, 'You can come down to my fair and photograph Ava Gardner from as close as you wish and from any angle. And you can see for yourself if any plastic surgery has been done, if any knife has ever touched that magnificent face.'"

That statement almost moved me to tears. What more could Archie have done for me? Without letting on, he'd given me back my self-confidence. As he'd done with so many young airmen, he had given me back my life.

TWENTY-EIGHT

*T*he Naked Maja, a better title than a film, was not my most memorable effort: a rather tame biography of the great Spanish artist Francisco Goya. I played the Duchess of Alba, Goya's favorite model, and Tony Franciosa, a very nice man but a method actor to the teeth, played the painter. The lights would be set, the cast would be standing in front of the camera waiting for Tony to start the scene, and he'd be standing off to the side, carrying on as if he were choking to death and nearly vomiting before he would come on. Honey, that was one method I could live without.

Aside from Tony, however, *The Naked Maja* stays in my memory for two reasons. One is that it was the first time I worked with one of the greatest cameramen I've ever known, Giuseppe Rotunno, whose beautiful colors flooded the whole movie. More important, however, *The Naked Maja* was the last picture I had to do on my damn MGM contract. When it was over I was free at last—free to choose my own projects, free to command the kinds of fees I was worth. It was about time.

I didn't have to find my first script as a free agent; it found me. Producer-director Stanley Kramer had bought the rights to *On the Beach*, Nevil Shute's novel about the end of the world, and he wanted me to play the heroine of the piece, the heavy-drinking, disillusioned but still vulnerable Moira Davidson. I'd read the book and liked it, so I thought, Honey, maybe this time you can make yourself some real money.

236

I was still working on *The Naked Maja* in Rome when the thing came up, and Stanley agreed to fly across to discuss the project. I set up a dinner with a few friends and he, very sweetly, brought me a gift of half a dozen flamenco records. Of course, I had to play them, and, of course, I had to dance to them as well, so naturally the party went on into the wee hours.

The next morning I said to David Hanna, who was my manager at the time, "What's the matter with Stanley? I set aside all last evening to get to know him and discuss the picture, and he didn't even bring the subject up."

David smiled at that. "Ava," he said, "I just got the same message from Stanley. He asked me, 'How do you do business with her? I've only got forty-eight hours.'"

Once Stanley and I did get together, things went smoothly. Shooting was to begin in January 1959 and I ended up with a salary of four hundred thousand dollars, happy to finally have the money for my services go to me instead of the damn studio. And I was delighted that Stanley was able to secure the services of Giuseppe Rotunno as cinematographer, not to mention a cast that included my old pal Greg Peck, Fred Astaire in his first straight dramatic role as a disillusioned scientist, and a young newcomer named Anthony Perkins as an Australian naval officer.

Though I'd read the book, Stanley's script made me weep. You couldn't say it was marvelous—that was somehow the wrong word. It was compelling, tragic, moving, chilling . . . I don't know what expression you can use about the end of the world. Stanley liked to call it "the biggest story of our time," and who could disagree? It was a fictional scenario, but my God, everyone in the cast and crew knew it could happen. And that added a dimension of reality to the unreal world of filmmaking that none of us had experienced before.

The film was set in 1964, five years in the future. A nuclear war, precipitated by a small, unnamed country, has ended all human life in the Northern Hemisphere, and the southern half of the world is only give four more months to survive. The Australian city of Melbourne, at the most southern tip of that continent, will survive the longest, but even for the people there, it's just a matter of time.

Into Melbourne harbor comes a U.S. nuclear submarine which survived the war intact only because it was submerged when the bombs went off. Its captain, Dwight Lionel Towers, lost his wife Sharon and their two children. As played by Greg Peck, Towers is a model of decency, trying to put the best face on things and do his duty in a society in which people are preparing for the inevitable end by handing out poison pills to all and sundry.

Inevitably, Captain Towers falls in love with my character, the cynical, boozy but very human Moira Davidson. It's a tough relationship because he is still very much in love with his wife as well, and at times confuses her with me. And both of us can't flee from the knowledge of how finite our span on earth is. "If Sharon were alive," I tell a pal, "I'd do any mean trick to get him. There isn't time. No time to love."

One thing I definitely didn't love was being on location in Melbourne. Not that the Australian people weren't wonderful individually; they were—down-to-earth, gutsy, and awfully friendly. In groups, however, they seemed overwhelmed by the idea of being the location for a Hollywood movie, something that had never happened to the city before. There were crowds everywhere, and everything we did seemed to cause controversy. When we had to cordon off a city block on a Sunday morning, for instance—something that citizens usually take in stride—one of the country's leading churchmen lambasted Stanley for interfering with "one of the fundamental freedoms—freedom of worship" because a church happened to be on the block.

And, naturally, we hit a heat wave when we were there, with temperatures regularly going over one hundred degrees. And I don't have to be bashful about stating what every Aussie will agree to: that the drinking situation at that time was nearly as bad as it was back home during Prohibition. Joy left town every night at six P.M. sharp, as every pub on the continent closed. At restaurants, any wine you happened to be drinking with your meal was snatched from the table promptly at 9 P.M. and taken down and locked away with the rest of the forbidden fruit.

Fortunately, Greg Peck and his wife Veronique had not only rented a huge old Victorian house, they'd had the foresight to bring their own French chef with them. The Pecks' place became a second home for me, Fred, Stanley, and Anthony Perkins, who was shy about everything but attacking his plate.

And poor Stanley, used to the good things of Hollywood, found to his chagrin that he had to ship a great deal of equipment and props from America, including a pair of mobile generators and a mobile dressing room. The Australian navy helped him out with the temporary loan of an aircraft carrier, and the Royal Navy pitched in with one of their submarines, HMS *Andrew.*

As far as studio space went, Stanley also had to improvise. He got the use of the Royal Showgrounds, a massive establishment used most of the year for storing wool, of all things. His production office was in an auto showroom and his wardrobe department in a place that usually housed farm tools. None of the indoor facilities were properly soundproofed, and on days when things like Billy Graham revivals took place nearby, filming became awfully difficult.

Still, despite all these troubles, *On the Beach* contains some fine technical achievements, most of them due to the genius of Pepe Rotunno. One scene had Greg and me kissing in front of a campfire as the camera circles us from a distance and does a beautiful three-hundred-and-sixty-degree turn that the other technicians kept telling Pepe wasn't possible. By the time the camera was finished circling, it might have qualified for the longest kiss in screen history, but Jesus Christ, hanging in there for almost two minutes was very exhausting.

The film ends with Captain Tower bowing to his men's wishes and taking his ship back to the States so they can die near their loved ones. I was saying good-bye to him—forever. He was leaving—forever. As I run toward him on the dock, you can just see our two profiles come together as the sun sets between our lips. It was a shot that once again everyone said was impossible, because Pepe was shooting straight into the sun, but he made it work, and I personally think it's one of the greatest in cinema history. You know some shots will live in your memory forever, and that one always will in mine.

On the Beach premiered simultaneously in eighteen of the world's most important cities on December 17, 1959. The idea was to position it as a film you had to see if you never saw another one as long as you lived, and because of its subject matter, the film quickly moved off the movie page and onto the front page. The New York *Journal-American,* for instance, headlined "'On the Beach' Hits Like an Atom Bomb."

Everywhere the film opened, controversy went with it. The

New York *Daily News* ran an editorial calling it "a defeatist movie" and insisting that "the thinking it represents points the way toward eventual enslavement of the entire human race." Even as patrician an observer as Stewart Alsop was moved to comment that "it is simply not true that a nuclear war would mean 'everybody killed in the world and nothing left at all, like in *On the Beach*.'"

As for my performance, the critics couldn't seem to decide what was more surprising: how well I acted or how unglamorous I looked. *Newsweek* was typical, deciding that "Miss Gardner has never looked worse or been more effective." Frankly, I didn't care what the hell they thought. I was proud of being part of this film, proud of what it said.

A footnote to my Australia stay was that it marked the end of my long and generally pleasant relationship with Walter Chiari. He'd come across for a few weeks and did not amuse me when in one of the shows he gave at a local theater he did a takeoff on Frank Sinatra. I had suspected for a long time that Walter was more interested in the publicity he gained from our relationship than he was in our having a private life. This was made clear in spades when he felt he had to make a statement to the press about us before he left Australia.

"No one has to feel sorry because they think I've been hurt," he said. "I know when I'm hurt and I know how much hurt I'm willing to take. I suffer because I love Ava, and I love her because I understand her, because I know she is so good and defenseless, and because I know she suffers."

Hell, he might just as well have written me a personal letter with a copy sent to the press.

On a more positive note, my private life got a lift when the real Mr. Sinatra called and told me he was flying to Australia to see me. What's six thousand miles when you're still in love?

Ostensibly Frank was coming down to give two concerts in Melbourne and two in Sydney. The truth was, we wanted to talk, to look at each other, to be together. The press were, as usual, as thick as flies on the beach, but we had our ways and means of being private. And with only two nights, we didn't even have time to have a fight!

GREGORY PECK

I worked with Ava over the years in three totally different movies: *The Great Sinner, The
Snows of Kilimanjaro,* and *On the Beach.*
Certainly Ava grew in experience and maturity with every one of
them. I've always admired her as an actress and felt that she was
underrated because people were deceived by her beauty and did
not expect more from her. Also, she herself was not overly ambitious about becoming a great actress. Yet she did constantly
improve and at her best I think she could certainly be counted
among the better actresses on the screen.

The first thing everyone noticed about Ava was that excep-
tional beauty, but as a young fellow I was not as bowled over by
that as older fellows were. Yes, Ava was a beautiful girl, but I had
met other beautiful girls. Our relationship was and always has
been as pals. I suppose some fellas would say, "Oh, come on, this
is one of the most desirable and beautiful women in the world,
and you tell me you were just *pals*?" And the answer is yes, that's
the truth. You don't make a run at every beautiful girl you meet.
It's quite possible for a young man and a young woman in their
prime years to be great friends.

What I liked about Ava was that we had so much in common
it was like we were young people from the same hometown. We
both were products of middle-class, small American towns where
everybody knew everybody, and it was on that basis that we
struck up an immediate friendship. Ava was also outspoken, and
there was something refreshing about that because sometimes

she'd be outspoken when other people would be afraid to. That to me shows a strength of character and the kind of grass-roots, middle-American honesty she has. Sometimes I've thought that except for that out-of-the-world beauty—that sensational bone structure, those eyes, and that figure—she was typical of dozens of girls I knew in high school and college. But that beauty shaped and changed her, and she became an object of pursuit, adulation, and attention such as few girls ever know.

Ava was not as ambitious as I was. I think I worked more at the acting, did more homework, more preparation. I came from the theater and I had a great respect for fine acting. Ava was more diffident about her talent, and I always had a tendency to encourage her and even, God help me, to coach her a little bit. I wanted her to be good, to be her best. I must have told her hundreds of times that she had it in her to be a great actress, that all she needed was a little more courage to attack, to go at a scene with the intention of selling it, of *grasping* the audience's attention and holding it.

But as often as you would tell her, she was always a little reluctant about asserting herself. Also, her development as an actress wasn't easy because everyone—directors, producers, and to a certain extent the critics and the audience—was perfectly happy just to look at her. It was okay if she just said her lines and walked through without being awkward or amateurish or clumsy. They really didn't expect her to get beneath the skin of a part the same way that Bette Davis, for instance, always did. And Ava used to whisper in those days, which I think was due to the way they taught acting at MGM. They thought this whispering projected a kind of sex appeal and also covered for a lack of acting experience. Rita Hayworth did it, too; it's a kind of crutch.

The Great Sinner, which came out in 1949, was based very vaguely on Dostoyevsky's *The Gambler,* with me as the serious young man who can't resist the lure of the tables. Directed by Robert Siodmak, it had a big-time cast, including Walter Huston, Agnes Moorehead, Ethel Barrymore, and Melvyn Douglas, and here was young Ava, who'd only learned to whisper her lines in that young ladies' finishing school at MGM, holding the screen very well. And remember, those big-time people don't give anything away. They come on-screen and expect to dominate everything and everybody.

But it was very hard to dominate Ava because of her essential strength of character, her honesty, and this almost unreal beauty. And this was true even though she was not like some actresses who are in there scratching and scraping and fighting to dominate every scene. Ava is quite content to let somebody else dominate. But of course they never quite completely *do* because she's *there*. You're liable to find yourself looking at Ava when somebody else is acting their heart out and chewing up the curtains.

Ava and I had a mutually shared tendency on this picture to disregard the director, because Robert Siodmak was an absolute nervous wreck. He was a hyperthyroid type in the first place, jittery and nervous, and now he had the responsibility for this very "heavy" picture on his shoulders.

There was usually a nurse present on the set, and a couple of times a day, when Siodmak was talking to the cameraman or the actors, shouting and gesticulating, she'd just sidle up to him, roll up his sleeve, and jab a needle in his arm. I don't know if it was vitamins or a tranquillizer, something to keep him from going right through the roof. Whatever it was, he wouldn't pay any attention to it.

At other times, with hundreds of people in the casino scene and Melvyn Douglas eyeing me as I'm gambling away and Ava standing there watching me lose my shirt, Bob would really be overcome with the weight of the situation. He was always sitting on the seat attached to the camera crane, and he'd mutter, "Up, up, up" and off he'd go to hide eighteen feet above the crowds while he collected his thoughts. And Ava and I would grin at each other and say, "There he goes again!"

As for *The Snows of Kilimanjaro,* it was certainly successful at the box office. While success at the box office does not always mean artistic greatness, this was certainly a wholehearted attempt, a serious effort to make a fine Hemingway picture.

We had of course a very good director in Henry King. I made six pictures with him. I loved him and respected him, and I think Ava did, too. I believe that her work was much more subtle, and that she acquired much more confidence under his direction. She did things in *Kilimanjaro* that she could not have done three years earlier in *The Great Sinner.* And I think that is largely because Henry King was the kind of man she could trust. Ava felt good with Henry King. He was an old-time director who'd started in silent films, and he understood his trade and he understood actors.

He loved flying, he was a lifelong flier. A man's man. A tall handsome fellow. Probably in his early sixties at that time, with very clear pale blue eyes. A couple of actresses I knew who had worked with him said when he looked at you with those pale blue eyes your knees melted. I think that Henry definitely had an appeal for the ladies. He was a Virginia gentleman of the old school, and I think that Ava trusted him because there was that Southern flavor that she understood. And he understood her. I think he gave her confidence and suggestions that made it possible for her to come out and be a little more assertive. With Henry she was able to allow her emotions to have fuller play, to allow her emotions to dictate her playing, and to begin to get a sense of what acting is really like. I've always had a theory—I think probably most actors think that way—that the emotion below the surface is like an underground river that has to flow through the entire story. Sometimes it's a calm emotion. Sometimes it's violent. Sometimes it's a mixture of the two. But that dictates what the external actor is doing and saying, the facial expressions and what she or he looks like. It all has to come from that underground river of emotion. The words will come out right if the river is flowing below. And I think Ava began to be able to act like that by the time we did *Kilimanjaro.* I remember that in some of those scenes she was very moving and touching, and very, very sympathetic.

Stanley Kramer, who produced and directed *On the Beach,* is a filmmaker who, whether the subject is racial prejudice or the nuclear arms race, very much wants to say something about crucial matters of world importance. He seized on Nevil Shute's book and said, "I'm going to make a picture and perhaps I can have some effect on people's attitude, perhaps I can change their mind-set about the dangers of nuclear buildup." I think we all became somewhat imbued with Stanley's mission, we all wanted to help him do it, including Ava. I believe that she felt good about being in that picture.

It did turn into quite an adventure, however. Terribly hot. There was a spell where the temperature was over one hundred degrees. Ava and I, our characters having become lovers, were trying to play a lighthearted romantic scene on a beach. But the air was so thick with flies they almost blackened the skies. There would be thousands of flies crawling on Ava's forehead and in her hair, and the effects men would rush in with a smoke gun and blow smoke in our faces. That would get rid of the flies for a minute or two and allow us to say a few lines before they settled in again.

I have worked with a few actresses, who will remain nameless, who would just not work under those conditions. But Ava was never, never the kind of actress who would complain about her working conditions. She took it like a trouper and we just kept plugging away despite everything until we got the scene.

In Nevil Shute's novel, my character determined that since he was going to die, he would die faithful and true to the wife whom he loved. This in spite of being terribly attracted to Ava's character and it being obvious that they were meant to be lovers. But he resisted the temptation, and she understood that. So when they parted, when his submarine steamed out of Melbourne harbor and she stood on the point waving to him, it was a love that had not been consummated. That's what Nevil Shute wrote.

Stanley Kramer, however, decided that the audience just wouldn't accept that a man like me would be able to resist a beautiful, willing woman who was in love with him. "We have to give them some sex," he said. "This is a serious picture, it's about the death of the world, and we have to give them some romance and sex." I told Stanley he was wrong, that he was corrupting my character and Ava's character, that self-denial on a matter of principle was romantic. But he didn't agree. And Nevil Shute always hated that scene.

By the time we did *On the Beach,* Ava had a wonderful style. There were certain things she did that I think no one could equal. She was perfect for *On the Beach,* and I don't know of anyone who could match her performance in *The Snows of Kilimanjaro.* She had this natural poignancy and her feelings ran very deep. To my mind she developed into a fine actress. I've been telling her that for years, and she always waves it off.

TWENTY-NINE

*T*he *Night of the Iguana* started with a phone call. The year was 1963 and I was sitting around in Spain, getting up late, talking to my friends, dancing flamenco all night long. In short, I was enjoying life and minding my own business and I wanted to go on doing so. I did not want to be in a movie at all. And then the damn phone rang.

"Ava, darlin'," a voice said. No one could ever mistake that quiet, smoky, Irish-flavored way of talking. I hadn't heard it in eighteen years, since a certain party had chased me around a swimming pool, but I knew it could only belong to John Huston.

"We're here in Madrid," the voice said.

"Who's we?" I asked suspiciously. John on the phone could only mean work, and the three pictures I'd done since *On the Beach—The Angel Wore Red, 55 Days at Peking*, and *Seven Days in May*—didn't exactly make me bubble over with enthusiasm at the thought of getting back in front of the camera.

"Ray Stark and I. Nice guy. Producer. He's bought the rights to Tennessee Williams' fine new play, *The Night of the Iguana*. Great part in it for you."

And before I can tell him what to do with that great part, John slips in a line he knows I can't resist. "What about a drink tonight? Show us the town."

That's okay by me. I'm into this hospitality business. After three or four days of my usual regimen, I'd thoroughly exhausted the gentlemen from Hollywood. But they must have gotten to me, too, because I agreed to do the film and they agreed to pay me five hundred thousand dollars. And that was the start of my relationship with John, one of the greatest and most enduring friendships of my life, one that lasted until the day he died.

As written for the screen by John and Tony Veiller, *Iguana,* if not exactly identical to what had opened on Broadway in 1961, still was powerful stuff. Though most of the action takes place in Mexico, the film opens in suburban Virginia, where Episcopal minister T. Lawrence Shannon (Richard Burton, back from *Cleopatra* and *Becket*) has a nervous breakdown right in front of his congregation, screaming about having appetites that just had to be satisfied.

The good padre, it turns out, had been having an affair with one of his *younger* parishioners, conduct unbecoming enough to cause him to be turned out of his church for good and all. We next see him in Mexico as an alcoholic employee of Blake's Tours ("Tours of God's World Conducted by a Man of God"). He's showing the country to a group of vacationing teachers from a Baptist Female College, whose number includes a seductive little Texas wench named Charlotte Goodall (played by *Lolita*'s Sue Lyon) who casts a greedy eye on poor Shannon.

When Shannon and Charlotte are caught in an indiscreet position in Shannon's room, Charlotte's chaperone threatens to expose the poor man to his employers for the reprobate he is. In a frenzied and ultimately unsuccessful attempt to avoid this, Shannon takes the bus and the tourists to the only place he's ever felt comfortable in, a run-down establishment called Hotel Costa Verde. Which is where I come in. I play the good-hearted, hang-loose proprietor of the place, Maxine Faulk, the widow of Shannon's best friend and a pretty good buddy of his myself.

Though the mountaintop Costa Verde is supposedly closed for the season, I soon end up with another pair of guests. A penniless spinster artist named Hannah Jelkes (played by Deborah Kerr) shows up accompanied by her ninety-seven-year-old grandfather, "the world's oldest living and practicing poet."

Soon Hannah and Shannon are engaged in long-winded dialogues about the meaning of life, something that really gets

Maxine's goat. She suspects, not totally without cause, that the spinster and Shannon have something of a yen for each other. But at the film's close, little Charlotte has hooked up with the bus driver, Hannah walks off into the sunset alone and a chastened Shannon and Maxine are left together. They talk about going down to the beach for a swim, and when Shannon tells her he doesn't know if he can get back up the mountain, Maxine promises, "I'll get you back up, honey. I'll always get you back up."

Williams had set his play in Acapulco, but God forbid that John, whose motto clearly was, "Do things the hard way whenever possible," should even consider filming there. Instead he hit on the idea of Puerto Vallarta, a remote spot on the Pacific coast of Mexico that had been called the most unlikely resort this side of the Hindu Kush. There were no roads into the town, no telephones either, and both plumbing and electricity were decidedly erratic. When John told people, "It's not at all like getting up in the morning and driving to MGM," he was not kidding.

And if Puerto Vallarta wasn't inaccessible enough, the actual *Iguana* filming was done on an isolated peninsula called Mismaloya located some eight to ten miles further away. Reachable only by boat, and so small it wasn't even on the map, Mismaloya was nothing more than a tiny fishing hamlet where about a hundred Indians lived in thatched huts. Behind the village was a mountain plateau where, three hundred feet above the water, John had the hotel set constructed. I called it "Hollywood on the Rocks."

John had initially wanted everyone involved in the film to live on Mismaloya, but some of us understandably rebelled. Richard Burton and Elizabeth Taylor, who was in residence with him, rented a four-story villa in Puerto Vallarta and made the daily trip to the location in a yacht. I chose a speedboat, which I mostly waterskied behind, and though my place in Puerto Vallarta had one of the first air conditioners ever seen in those parts, believe me, honey, living there was no picnic.

Reenie and I lived in a funny little place with a high wall, but one not high enough to deter the Mexican beach boys, young kids who climbed over every night looking for a place to sleep. Because after you climbed the wall, everything in the place was totally open—there were no doors on any of the rooms.

Going to the bathroom, which was often a dire necessity, was also an adventure. You might find a cat or a dog or a rat as big as either one of them waiting for you. I remember one night we'd worked late, and I had my dinner brought to my bed on a plate. I nibbled at it, put the plate on the floor, fell into bed, and promptly went to sleep. By the morning, the rats had eaten it all. I'm surprised they hadn't eaten me as well.

Filming on *Iguana* began at the end of September 1963, and though my character didn't appear until about page forty of the script, John, who had determined to shoot in continuity, wanted everyone there for the start. Soon after we got there, John called together Richard and Elizabeth, Deborah Kerr, Sue Lyon, Ray Stark, and me and solemnly presented each of us with a small gold-plated derringer and five bullets, each engraved with the name of one of the other recipients. Naturally, the old fox hadn't put *his* name on any of the damn bullets. John didn't say anything, he just walked away looking bland. It was, Deborah Kerr later said, "almost like the start of an Agatha Christie mystery novel." I immediately locked mine in a suitcase—I can't stand guns.

Yet, despite the potential for a fracas presented by the combination of this high-powered cast and our godforsaken location, we all got along remarkably well. For one thing, Elizabeth and I were friends from the old Metro days. It's like we were two graduates from the same alma mater, pleased to find each other in the wilderness.

And though this was the first time I'd met Richard, I felt the same way about him. He was like someone I would've liked to have had for a brother, and his teasing manner made me feel at ease. He was also a ferocious drinker, at whose instigation John put bars both at the foot and at the top of our long, hundred-plus-stairs climb to the mountain plateau. But when we worked together, I went up on lines more often than he did. In one scene, when I was supposed to say, "In a pig's eye you are," what came out was, "In a pig's ass you are." Old habits die awfully hard.

All this equanimity, however, was really hard on the gentlemen of the press, who came down to the location in enormous numbers expecting who knows what kind of a ruckus. Even when nothing was going on, they sent back stories with headlines like "Liz, Richard, Ava, and Sue—Mighty Tense in the Jungle" and "Liz Keeps Her Eye on Burton and Ava Gardner." They were so hungry for anything to write about that when poor Sue Lyon got bitten by a scorpion, the story made the goddamn *New York Times*.

Even more preposterous was the fairy tale, which was sent all around the world, that I was going to marry the film's associate director, Emilio Fernandez. Emilio had once been a director himself, but he had a tendency, John used to say, to shoot people he didn't like. He'd winged his last producer, and that was that. The man was a character, but there as much chance of my marrying him as the man in the moon. But that didn't stop papers like the Los Angeles *Herald-Examiner* from running stories with headlines like "Ava's New Mexican Flame Is a Pistol-Packin' Firebrand." And people ask me why I get so furious with the press!

In fact, the only member of the cast who acted up at all— unless you count Sue Lyon's continual making out with her boyfriend as acting up—was the iguana. At a key point in the script, the damned fat lizard is supposed to make a rush for his freedom, no doubt symbolizing something profound about the human condition. Well, when the time came, that iguana had conditions of his own: he was so fat and happy after being treated like a pet for weeks that he absolutely refused to go anywhere. And who the hell can blame him? It took a few well-placed jolts of electricity to get the poor guy to scuttle off like he was supposed to.

There were two bad moments in the making of *The Night of the Iguana*. Though the cast didn't stay there, quite a few of the crew lived in Mismaloya (they called it Abismaloya) in a collection of apartment blocks that had been specially built for their use. Not terribly well built, however, as it turned out. Because late one night in mid-November, Tommy Shaw, John's veteran assistant director, and Terry Moore, the second a.d., walked out onto their balcony only to have it totally collapse underneath them. They both fell nearly twenty feet to the hard ground below. Terry was okay, but Tommy had broken his back; people said it was a miracle that he hadn't died. He had to be rushed to a hospital immediately, and the guys put him on a board and carried him shoulder high out to a boat, into Puerto Vallarta and onto an airplane. Fortunately, he survived to work on more of John's films.

One evening less than a week later, the news was worse. We were all crowded into one motorboat coming home, full of equal portions of song and tequila, when we noticed Ray Stark's ocean-going yacht, which he occasionally took back and forth to Los Angeles, closing in on us. He had picked up a terrible news flash on his radio: President John F. Kennedy had been assassinated. The boat's air of drunken cheerfulness turned immediately to sobriety, silence, and tears.

Despite all this tragedy, I was determined to do my best in *Iguana*. I even made myself look awful, had lines penciled in under my eyes, because it was that kind of part. My hair was pulled back into a tight ponytail and I didn't wear anything except a sloppy serape and toreador pants. And John let me go back to my North Carolina accent, which meant that I got to say things like "cotton-pickin'" and call folks "honey," which, you can imagine, wasn't exactly a strain.

Dear John. I have only one rule in acting—trust the director and give him heart and soul. And the director I trusted most of all was John Huston. Working with him gave me the only real joy I've ever had in movies.

Take, for instance, the scene I have when Maxine goes for a romantic swim with the two beach boys she keeps around the hotel for just such occasions. I was nervous about doing it, and John, bless him, understood. He stripped down to his shorts and got into the water with me for a rehearsal, showing me exactly how he wanted it to go, then directed the scene soaking wet. That is my kind of director.

And John helped with the conceptualizing of Maxine as well. In the original Broadway production, where the role was played by Bette Davis, Maxine had been a genuine man-eater, a woman who was lonely, hard-bitten, and cruel. Shannon ending up with *her* was much more of a curse than a blessing. John, however, felt the character, especially the way I played her, was warmer, more human, a better person than Tennessee's original ending allowed, and he had the scene rewritten to emphasize the point.

251

Tennessee was never happy with that, but anyone seeing the film knows that John's choice was the only one that fit.

All that aside, I've never been really happy with *The Night of the Iguana;* in fact, I got embarrassed about my performance the first time I saw it. The critics, however, must have been looking at a different picture. "Ava Gardner is absolutely splendid," said *The New Yorker.* "Ava Gardner all but runs away with the picture," said *Life.* "Miss Gardner gives the performance of her career," said the *Hollywood Reporter.*

Hell, I suppose if you stick around long enough they have to say something nice about you.

THIRTY

ilming *The Bible* wasn't John Huston's idea. Big as he thought, even he couldn't come up with a picture that included Adam and Eve, the Tower of Babel, Noah's Ark, Abraham and Sarah, not to mention the creation of the whole goddamn world. Only the Italian producer Dino De Laurentiis thought big enough for that, or had the nerve to rent a sign on Broadway, a huge thing that extended for an entire city block and grandly announced that "Dino De Laurentiis has reserved this space to announce the most important movie of all time."

Dino's ideas, however, didn't always pan out exactly as he'd planned them. He'd originally envisioned two six-hour films, costing a total of ninety million dollars, with four, maybe five directors assigned. What he ended up with was one normal-sized film with one larger-than-life director, John Huston. And once John came aboard, another of Dino's ideas, that opera star Maria Callas would play Sarah, also got the heave-ho. "You," John said as he handed me the script, "will be playing Sarah."

I looked at the script. It was written by Christopher Fry, a fine playwright, and though it looked great on the page, the dialogue was definitely on the arty side. For instance, Sarah had lines like, "Abram, behold now, the Lord hath restrained me from bearing. I pray thee, go in unto my maid according to that law which says, when the wife is barren, her maid servant may bear for her. It may be that I may obtain children by her." Quite a mouthful.

"John, honey," I said. "I can't speak lines like this. They're not my style. They're too contrived, too stagy."

John gave me one of his slow, cunning smiles and said softly, "Of course you can, darlin', of course you can." Maybe that hypnosis he tried on me twenty years before was finally taking effect, because I found myself agreeing with him.

John also told me that he had the actor who was going to play Abraham all picked out. It was someone I'd never met, George C. Scott. Now, if I had any female intuition at all, the mention of that name should have set off every internal alarm within earshot. Because the trouble that Abraham and Sarah were having on the biblical front was nothing compared to the storm between George and me that was about to break behind the scenes.

No sooner had I arrived at the Grand Hotel in Rome, where the filming was to begin in the summer of 1964, than my telephone rang. It was John, of course, saying, "Ava, darlin', come down and meet George." I liked him immediately. He was over six feet tall, broad-shouldered, and powerful, with a broken nose and a quick smile. And he couldn't have been nicer.

We chatted a bit, John made his usual jokes, and we parted outside his door, George heading down the corridor one way and me going the other toward the elevator. I was almost there when I heard him call my name.

"Ava," he said. "Why don't we have a drink and dinner tonight?"

"Sure," I said. "Good idea." We're going to be working together, he's a nice guy, so why not get acquainted? Famous last words.

To make a long story short, I fell for George and he fell for me, and in those early weeks of shooting, we saw a lot of each other off the set. George seemed highly intelligent and civilized, very gentle but with a slightly sardonic sense of humor, which suited me fine. He knew the film world backward and forward, and he was a magnificent, intense actor thrown into the bargain.

So what was the problem? The problem, honey, was booze. We both drank a fair amount, but when I drank I usually got mellow and happy. When George got drunk he could go berserk in a way that was quite terrifying. He began to be jealous of my friends—just mentioning Frank's name, for instance, infuriated him—and though he was still attached at the time, he began to talk about our getting married.

George's outbursts weren't limited to our time off the set. One day, for instance, we were shooting this very delicate scene where I say something like, "Go into the tent of my handmaiden," that sort of jazz. George, I knew, had been a bit pissed all day, and suddenly he went absolutely bonkers and began ripping his costume off. He literally flung the clothes on the floor and stormed off the set in his underwear. Why? God only knows.

I went over and sat down next to John and looked up at him for some direction. The son of a bitch hadn't moved, hadn't even taken the cigar out of his mouth. I waited awhile, but John didn't say a word. Finally, I couldn't stand the strain so I whispered, "John, what are we going to do? We've got no Abraham."

And John gave me his little smile and said, "It's just right for the scene, honey. If we can get him back, he'll be great."

And, by God, after a few more minutes George C. strode back in again. There were still a few problems, like finding a costume to replace the one he'd torn to shreds, but after that it all went quite smoothly.

All of this came to a climax in a small hotel in Avezzano, a town in the Abruzzi mountains where we did some exteriors. As usual, George and I had gone out to dinner, and returning to the hotel we'd gone back to his room for a nightcap. George had drunk quite a lot that night, and after another two or three I could see he was getting into one of his rages. He began to argue with me and I decided it was time to leave. Fat chance. Suddenly, out of the blue, a hand smashed across my face and punches fell on me from all angles. What do you do? Scream? Faint? Try reasoning? I tried reasoning. The result was more punches, more accusations. It felt like hours before I managed to get out.

Back in my room, the remnant of a party was going on, with Reenie dancing with Peter O'Toole, who was cast as an angel. One look at my face and the party stopped abruptly. Peter tried to comfort me, but he couldn't really help.

The next morning, I took my swollen and bruised face and black eye in to the makeup man. God, I was a mess. He took one look at me and screamed, "For Christ's sake, who did this to you?" I didn't tell him, but it wasn't too hard to figure out, and within a few minutes most of the crew and technicians knew, and they were simmering. You better believe the atmosphere on the set that day was more than slightly electric.

Early that morning, George had apologized profusely. He

didn't know why he had done it, why it had happened. It was disgraceful, he was ashamed of himself, it would never happen again. Only much later in life did I discover that this kind of abject, heartbroken apology is very much the rule from the sort of men who beat up women.

Still, I have a gut feeling that if I hadn't been working with John Huston and *his* crew on *his* picture, I would have taken off after that first battering from George and never seen him—or the film—again.

But I didn't. I shared scenes with George. I went out to dinner with George. I kept up appearances with George. George wanted to marry me. I had no intention of marrying George—ever.

John, of course, was very much aware of what was happening, and I think he took some precautions. When we moved on to locations in Sicily, I noticed three very tough-looking guys just hanging around the set. They had nothing to do with our film crew, they were just *there*. As we were in Sicily, I naturally thought, I never knew Mafiosi were so interested in the Bible, but I soon forgot about them.

Then one night George and I and Reenie had dinner at a restaurant on top of a hill in Taormina. We took our seats and, lo and behold, those three tough guys showed up and were seated at another table some distance from ours.

George C. had had a few drinks, and was having a few more, and the tension was increasing. I can't remember how far into the meal we'd gotten before I began waving to the waiter for the check and preparing to leave. Because George, in the condition he was in, couldn't have cared less about whether we had a fight in public or in private.

Outside, it was dark and warm, and the lights from the restaurant were spilling across our faces. George was starting to get threatening, and I was frightened. Then, suddenly, out of the darkness that trio of toughs appeared at our side. Very quietly. Very swiftly. Very solidly. One took George's right arm, one took his left, the third trailed a little way behind. No noise, no tugging, no pushing. And no fuss from George as he was led away to a waiting car and placed inside.

No harm came to George; he arrived on the set next morning full of the usual apologies. I glanced at John to see if I could get the slightest confirmation that *he* might be paying the local

Mafiosi a few bucks to make certain that his Sarah arrived in front of the camera with her face in one piece. If he was, and I think he was, he never gave it away.

When *The Bible* wrapped, I flew to London to see Robert Graves at Oxford and to hear him give a public lecture in his capacity as professor of poetry. I was staying at the Savoy Hotel, and who should show up—on business of his own, or so he said—but the man himself, George C. Would I have dinner, for old time's sake? He was still in love with me. Could we forget the past, or at least have dinner? I agreed. London seemed pretty safe, the Savoy even safer.

At dinner I could sense that familiar tension growing, the conversation suddenly beginning to slide from the easy, happy familiarities to terse questioning. The number of drinks increased. I got through that dinner as quickly as I could, found a taxi back to the Savoy, and with similar speed said good night in the lobby and shot up to the safety of my suite.

Suddenly there was a loud banging on the door. "Tell him I'm not here," I said to Reenie. "Say anything. Try and get rid of him."

I looked around for a place to hide. My bedroom? Reenie's bedroom? The bathroom? Shouldn't a lady's toilet be inviolate? I ran into it and locked the door. I heard Reenie's frantic voice, the crash as he burst through the door. "Where is she?" George screamed. "I know she's here."

What I didn't know until later was that he had a broken bottle against Reenie's throat.

"Which bedroom is she in? . . . I'll find her." The voice trailed away as he searched in the bedrooms. Then I heard Reenie's voice at the bathroom door. "Miss G.! Miss G.!"

I unlocked it and pulled her inside. Relocked it and thought: What the hell do we do? Two friends were staying across the corridor. If only we could get to them, they could ring down to the desk. Now George was back at the bathroom door, banging and yelling. And then we saw our only way of escape. Above the tub on the corridor side there was a transom window about four feet long and two feet high. Fortunately, it opened from the bottom. And there was a chair in the bathroom. Reenie and I were both pretty trim. I can't remember who went first, but I do remember we got through the opening with something approaching the speed of light. We took refuge with our friends across the corridor and rang down to the desk. The Savoy's security men were up almost as quickly as the few seconds we took getting through the transom window. They escorted Mr. George C. Scott back to his own room and left him there. The rage and the noise he made as he smashed his own apartment to pieces brought the security men back again in a hurry, and then the British police. George spent the night in a London cell and was charged and brought before the magistrate next morning. The usual fine for drunk and disorderly was ten shillings. No doubt he settled the damage to the Savoy's property separately.

I thought I had said good-bye to George C. Scott forever. But no. Back in Los Angeles visiting Bappie and my friends, I was staying at one of the bungalows near the pool at the luxurious Beverly Hills Hotel. I suppose it must have been around one A.M. when someone smashed his fist through the back door, breaking the screen and the glass, and entered the bungalow. In a flash, I knew who it was, and when he entered my room I was terrified out of my mind at the sight of this huge, completely drunk, almost insane man. He loved me, he said, he wanted to marry me. Why wouldn't I marry him? If he couldn't have me, he was going to kill me. And he sideswiped me across the face with such force it knocked me to the floor. Then came more blows, more anger, more threats.

I was stretched out on the floor, with George astride me. I can't remember if he had any more drinks, but I think he must have, because he smashed bottles to get a weapon to threaten me with. He was kneeling across me, waving the jagged edges of glass in front of my face with one hand and hitting me with the other. Telling me he loved me, and smashing a fist into my eye. "Marry me, do you hear what I'm saying?", followed by another blow. And all the time I was thinking: Oh, my God. If his mind twists a little bit more he'll thrust this broken bottle into my face or my throat. With an enormous effort I held back the terror and the screams that were rising inside me. This was the *real* meaning of being scared to death.

I knew my only hope was being sweet and understanding. "George, darling," I managed to squeeze out, in a voice as soft and appealing as I could make it. "You're in a terrible state. Let me call a doctor and have him come over."

No way. He wouldn't even listen. And he wouldn't leave. This went on for hours.

Suddenly, and by this time it was early in the morning, the phone began to ring. "If you try and answer that," he hissed, "I'll kill you."

"George," I said. "People know that I'm here. If I don't answer, they'll send someone to find out why."

That appeared to make sense to him. He let me get up, but he stood behind me and said, "Be careful. One wrong word and I'll kill you."

I answered the phone. It was Veronique, Greg Peck's wife and a dear friend. I knew with absolute certainty that if I said anything, George would carry out his threat. But how could I let her know what was happening? Could I "act" into the phone to give her some idea of my terror? Veronique did not get the message. I replaced the telephone in its cradle. And I went on talking in my calmest voice to George.

"Listen, honey, you're in bad shape. You have to have a doctor. Let me call Bill Smith—he's a great friend, a good doctor. You don't have to behave like this."

I kept on that theme. Oh, God, it was the most realistic piece of acting I've ever done in my life. Finally, I got through. George said, "Okay."

Slowly I picked up the phone. Thank God, Bill was up. I told him where I was. "Please hurry. It's very urgent."

Bill caught the urgency all right, and was around in a few minutes. Oh, Jesus, I have never been happier to see a man in my life. It was growing light outside, but my curtains were still drawn and inside it was dim and dark. I said, "Bill, my friend here is in a terrible state. Can you help him with a sedative?"

Bill, of course, didn't know what the hell was going on, but he quickly examined George and gave him a rapid shot. "That should do it," he said as he closed his bag and moved back toward the door. Oh, my God, I thought, if he leaves me . . . and I can't scream out even now.

But I went with him to the door, and as he turned back to say good-bye I put my face out so that he could see it, and I saw his face react with absolute disbelief and horror. Then he was gone.

Inside, the sedative was beginning to work. George was sitting there, blank, not saying anything. Bill had gone straight to the hotel phone and called Bappie. God knows how long it took her to get to the bungalow. I was still dazed, shocked into silence by this confrontation. Bappie came in, saw my face—I later found out I had a detached retina in one eye and a badly bruised right cheekbone. She rushed to the fireplace to get a huge poker. I restrained her, whispering urgently, "Bappie, stop, stop . . . he'll kill us both."

A minute later, without a word, George walked out the way he'd come in, through the smashed back door. I have never seen him since.

I was sorry for George then, and I'm sorry for George now. I understand he's completely under control these days, but, my God, the fear he could impart in those terrible rages.

These days the whole world knows about the type of man who abuses and batters women. But then it was hushed up, something you didn't talk about. Now, thank God, it is, because I can tell you that those few hours with George C. Scott were the most terrifying of my life. Even today, if I so much as see him on television, I start to shake all over again and have to turn the set off.

RODDY McDOWALL

va was like the most fantastic relative, because she didn't make you pay a price for knowing her. She was the great older sister who just *adores* you. And spoils you. Her loyalty was devastating. In fact, it could be embarrassing. Because if she was your friend, she would kill for you, and sometimes you didn't want her to. She believed in the good decent things, she really did. And to the best of her ability, she lived that way.

Ava was an extraordinary woman because she never copped a plea. She was completely who she was and what she was, and she never made an excuse about it. Because she was volatile and honest, if somebody hurt her or took advantage of her, she'd just cut them to ribbons. But if she was wrong, if she'd done an injustice, her agony was terrible, her remorse phenomenal, and she would do everything to repair the damage.

I first met Ava in 1942, at a war bond rally in Pershing Square in Los Angeles. She was twenty and I was thirteen and I got her autograph: what she signed was "Mrs. Mickey Rooney." She was simply and in every way one of the most beautiful girls that one had ever seen in one's life. Her body was absolutely extraordinary; the way all her facial features were placed was perfect; she was classically beautiful. And her spirit was quite adorable. It's very strange to see that sort of tenderness radiating out of somebody that exquisitely beautiful.

We didn't become tremendously close friends until she was in her early forties, by which time the slings and arrows had both taken their toll and strengthened her. By the time I knew her, she was this gouache of remarkable qualities that I found to be deeply appealing, heartbreakingly moving. She was a survivor, but she had no armor for insult. She wasn't hard—there wasn't a hard bone in that woman's body. And she was one of the very few people I've known who don't have a shred of malice. Yet she could be a holy terror and hysterically funny if she was on a tear, if she took umbrage at something. But she didn't harbor resentments, and she would constantly be about repairing what she felt might have been a hurt. She was a study in contradictions.

The highly irritating thing about Ava, of course, was that she had no regard for her intellectual capacity or her talent. She was a wonderful actress and she never believed it. If you told her that, or if you told her how beautiful she was, she'd get very uncomfortable and virtually begin to shake. She didn't know what to do with the information; it unnerved her.

Ava was always alive. Even in the depths of depression or anguish, she was terribly alive. And she could get heartbreakingly depressed. There were times when she couldn't see people, times when she was so miserable, when life was so black for her. It couldn't have been easy for anybody to have been witness to the depths of her unhappiness or self-loathing. She didn't like herself.

And so everyone felt wildly protective about Ava, and therein, of course, lies madness. The vulnerability was part of her great appeal. Everybody felt that yes, they could bring her some solace or help for whatever this bottomless well of unhappiness in her was. Well, of course, you can't. But Ava didn't take advantage of that; she wasn't looking for you to be a nurse. Some people eat you up with that, but Ava wasn't inclined that way. She was a loner. Like a bear, she would go off somewhere and hibernate.

Yet she was a very passionate woman about things that she liked doing. For instance, I live right across the street from Gene Autry and that really *thrilled* her.

"I've got to go over and see him," she said.

"You can't," I said. "It's ten o'clock at night."

"But he was my mother's favorite actor."

Well, it was hysterical. Who's going to believe that Ava Gardner was down there on Autry's not-so-mini estate, throwing pebbles at his windows and saying, "Mr. Autry, my name's Ava Gardner . . ." I don't think he was even there. Her responses to things were so childlike, it was so sweet. She was totally immediate. She had no pretensions, none whatever.

In 1969, we made a movie together, I directed her in *The Ballad of Tam Lin*. She hadn't made a film in a couple of years, it was a very large part, and she was very nervous. It was not a successful movie, by any manner of means, but her performance is remarkable and dead-on.

The film was based on a Scottish border ballad by Robert Burns that is about a bitch-goddess who walks the earth in perpetuity, refurbishing her godhead with the sacrifices of young people. She takes them and she destroys their lives; she's a magnet for them and she sucks them dry. And the ultimate triumph in the piece is that a young man is saved by the true love of a pure young girl.

In modern terms, the film was about this very rich, opulent, seductive, enchanting woman who at base was a killer of creativity and productivity. It's a piece that could only be played by a creature who, when coming on from the wings, carried with her glamour, maturity, and mystery. Vivien Leigh could've played her, but she was dead. Probably Jeanne Moreau could've done it. But Ava was unique because she was an imperial creature with a great peasant streak, which is a miraculous combination to find. Her ability to scrub the kitchen floor, you know, was always there. Hers was the most unpretentious elegance I ever knew.

Ava was one of the most perfect screen actresses I've ever encountered because she had a childlike concentration, which is wildly important. It's one of the major things that a film actor or actress should have, because immediacy is tremendously important to hold. I found that when you were working with her you should really never have more than three takes. Because she really *did* it.

Watching her act was a fascinating thing to me—I was often stunned. There was one time when she had to take a dagger, stick it into a desk, and say something like, "I will not die." And when she said it, her eyes in that moment just filled with blood. It was incredible. She didn't have acting craft, but she had this immediate instinct. So in a sense perhaps the toll was larger for her than somebody who had craft at their fingertips. Because she had to really completely do it in that moment.

There were a lot of young people age eighteen to twenty-five in the cast of *Tam Lin,* and though at first Ava was afraid to meet them, within an instant she became absolutely devoted to them. There was one moment in the film where twelve or thirteen of them were playing games on the floor and she had to walk right through, up this huge staircase, turn around on a platform, and just lace into them, cut them to ribbons, and throw them out.

Ava was dressed in an evening gown—she looked incredible—and everything went fine until she turned around on the staircase and this really awful performance came out. It was like the motor ran out the moment she turned around and looked at them. We rehearsed it two or three times and I said, "What's wrong, Ava Lavinia?"

"Honey, I can't do this," she said.

"Why?"

"Those are my babies. I can't tell them off. I love them."

I began laughing and I said, "Why don't you just pretend it's five o'clock in the morning in Madrid, and you want to get those musicians out of the room." She came in and boom! did it. She longed for good direction. Immediately she'd connect, and immediately she would produce.

Ava's beauty finally became double-edged. In the first place, when you look in the mirror, you're not seeing the image that other people see, so you don't appreciate the fact of your beauty. But if you are continually told that you are beautiful, even if you can't really understand that, nevertheless you are still custodian of it, you are the keeper of that beauty. So you've got a problem, because that's schizophrenic.

We had to do a lighting test of her for *Tam Lin* and she was very nervous, very skittish, so I told her I'd be there with her. We went onto this dark soundstage, with just a work light, and she sat on a stool. And I sat there beside her talking very, very quietly as Billy Williams, our cinematographer, began to light.

And as the light slowly came on, it was like a painting happening. It was the first time in years I'd seen her with all the war paint on, and I was devastated.

"Good God, you really are gorgeous," I said.

"No, honey, no, no, no," she said in this very soft voice she had.

"Yes, you are. You are really some beautiful thing."

"No, I used to be."

"What do you mean? You are."

"No, honey. When I was young, I was beautiful. When I would work all day and then stay out all night, and then come to work the next day and still look okay. And then stay out the next night, and come to work the next day. Now, *then* I was beautiful."

STEPHEN
BIRMINGHAM

W hen I was in Mexico in 1963 doing a location piece on *The Night of the Iguana* for *Cosmopolitan,* the unit publicist warned me about Ava. "Everybody will talk to you," he said. "John Huston will talk to you, Burton will talk to you, Deborah Kerr will talk to you. But you must not approach Miss Gardner. She does not like the press; in fact, she wanted a closed set, which she didn't get. But we have promised her that she will not be interviewed. So you must *not* approach her."

After I'd been there a couple of days, we were all at the bar at the location one afternoon and somebody said, "Ava, do you want a ride back to town on my boat?"

"No thanks," she said. "I'm going to water-ski back." And she looked around and said, "Anybody want to come with me?"

"I'll go," I said.

And she said, "Fine."

When I was on the skis, I could tell she was telling the boat boys to give me a hard time. They'd slow down and practically stop and I'd sink down into the water. She was terrible—she was trying to knock me off. She did not succeed. And many, many boozy hours later, dancing and listening to Frank Sinatra records at her house and getting pissed drunk, we were the best of friends.

I went home after I finished my work, and she began telephon-

ing. From Los Angeles, from Mexico, from the Main Chance
Farm in Arizona, saying she wanted to marry me. At the time I
was happily married, and I kept trying to explain that to Ava.
"Well, that doesn't matter," she'd say. "I want to marry you.
We'll worry about your wife later." I think she probably saw me
as a reasonably stable and maybe civilized person who could
bring a little of that stability into her life, something she had
never really been able to find.

The first impression you had of Ava was that she was so beautiful. She would do her hair with toothpicks from the olives in
martinis and it would look great. She could walk out of a hotel
without makeup, wearing flats, one of those kilt-type skirts with
a big safety pin in it and a simple peasant blouse and she looked
gorgeous. She had an ability to find the key light, the one that
made her look the best. She even told me once, "When I'm in a
room, I know how to find that light." My wife and I were in
Madrid with her once, and the sun hit her face just so, and we
both said simultaneously, "Ava, you are too beautiful." And she
said, "Oh, shit, I'm sick of hearing that."

Yet by the time I met her, I think that Ava was a very damaged
woman, badly bruised by the awful, macho people in the industry. She felt injured by MGM, she hated Mr. Mayer, she was
always very bitter. She just wasn't tough enough to deal with it.
Because it's a rotten business.

Frank Sinatra was different. They stayed very, very close.
Every time I'd be with her, he would call at least once. And she
would go up into her bedroom, close the door, and talk for half
an hour. The only time I saw them together, she was staying at
his suite at the Waldorf Towers. He was looking up an address in
the phone book and he couldn't read it without his glasses, which
he didn't have. And Ava, who had these funny little Ben Frank-
lin–type half-glasses, said, "Here, try mine." And he put them on
and he said, "Hey, they work for me! That's another reason why
you and I should get back together." Which I thought was kind
of cute.

When he left, I said, "Why don't you get back together?" And
she said, "We'd be at each other's throats in five minutes." It was
all about jealousy. Sinatra liked to be recognized, and if a pretty
girl came up and spoke to him, Ava would get furious. And Ava's
eyes liked to travel around the room; she'd fix on this one and

that one, and the next thing you'd know the person would be over at the table and Frank would get furious. So they were always jealous of each other, just like teenagers.

George C. Scott was another story. He beat Ava up on several occasions. I was staying in her house in Madrid while she was in Rome doing *The Bible* with him and when she came back, her arm was in a sling and God, she looked like hell. He'd broken a collar bone, yanked out a whole hunk of her hair, and she had double vision in both eyes.

"How can you stand this guy?" I said.

"Oh, I've fallen for him," she said. "I've fallen for him."

The next thing I knew, Scott showed up in Madrid and I was invited for drinks in her apartment. I walked in and George's face looked like raw hamburger, sort of oozing and awful. Ava pulled me aside into the kitchen and she said, "You see George's face?"

"My God, what happened?"

"Last night he got drunk, he had a fire going in the fireplace, and he threw himself face-first into the live coals. I had to pull him out."

Ava did come from an environment, kind of redneck, where men beat up women. If you weren't happy with what your wife or your girlfriend did, you let her have it, you slammed her across the face. So I think she thought that was part of the way men and women interact. Or at least it wasn't strange to her. Also, she had a tendency toward liking violence. She obviously liked bullfighters, and she liked the bullfight itself, its kind of physical excitement.

Ava really liked Spain; she kept saying it was her spiritual home. But after she'd been there for a dozen years or so, the Spanish government suddenly claimed that she owed them about a million dollars in taxes.

Morgan Maree was Ava's business manager, and either he or someone from his office came flying over with all sorts of receipts to help her with this crisis. They showed evidence of the American dollars that she'd spent over there. They said she'd been a big attraction for Madrid and for Spain, that the publicity she got when she'd show up at the bullfights was good for tourism. Their argument was that she had done a lot for Spain, and therefore Spain should treat her a little better.

Now in Spain, protocol says that at a meeting you don't get

down to business right away. First it's "How is your daughter? How is your niece? How is your ailing Aunt Louisa?" You talk family and then after about fifteen minutes of that, you get down to business.

A big meeting was set up between Ava, the person from Morgan Maree, and Señor Manuel Fraga Iribarne, who was Franco's Minister of Tourism and the Police, which I always thought was a marvelous combination. And Ava, who always called him Señor Bragas, which means underpants in Spanish, was getting very impatient with this backing and filling.

Finally, Iribarne said, "Ah, Señorita Gardner, yes, we are now here to discuss your indebtedness to the Spanish government of ten thousand dollars."

"What the fuck?" she shouted. "I thought it was a million!"

"You're quite right, Miss Gardner," Iribarne replied. "It is a million dollars."

She had been offered a way out and she blew it. After that explosion, she had to move to London. I don't think she could ever have gone back to Spain. They would have jumped her for the taxes.

One of Ava's problems was that she had been told all along that she didn't have to have any talent. On *Night of the Iguana*, I heard Ava ask John Huston about her character. "Now, is Maxine in love with Shannon, or what? What do you think she's feeling?" And though they talk about what a wonderful director John Huston was, all he said was, "Don't worry, sweetheart. Just stand there and look beautiful. That's all you have to do." I think she'd been told that so often that she didn't think she had any acting talent.

The minute Ava got to a party, she'd say, "Where's the bar? Where's the bar? Where's the booze?" And she'd have a drink right away. She always talked about her shyness, she blamed the drinking on the shyness, but I think she suffered from low self-esteem that came from having been told that she didn't have any talent. "Honey, you just stand there and be beautiful."

That's why, when the looks really went, in her last seven or eight years, Ava became very reclusive. She wouldn't go out. When I'd go to see her in London, I'd try to make her get dressed up and go out, but she wouldn't leave the apartment. I think she felt that without her looks she was a nothing. Except a mind. She always knew that she was smart, but I don't think she thought she had any real ability.

Also, in the forties and fifties when Ava was getting started, it was considered rather chic to get drunk; she grew up in a Hollywood that expected people to get drunk. She'd go for long periods and not have anything to drink at all, but when she would start drinking, she wouldn't stop until she went off to her room and closed the door. Once at her house in Madrid, she cooked this whole elaborate Thanksgiving dinner. She was almost childlike, setting the table, getting the turkey out, and the dressing and the sweet potatoes. But by the time we all sat down at the table she wasn't able to join us.

When Ava was drinking, it was exciting, I must say, because you never knew what was going to happen. She had the capacity of an ox, and the energy. She never seemed to get tired. Sometimes she would be almost incoherent, you wouldn't know what she was talking about, but she wasn't about to fold her tent. And she'd get very suspicious. She'd point to my watch, for example, and say, "That's a tape recorder, isn't it?"

"No, it isn't, honey, it really isn't."

"Take off that watch!"

So I'd have to put the watch way over on the other side of the room.

One night in New York we started out with mai tai's and dinner at Trader Vic's. Then we went to some little bar on West Forty-fourth Street that was a favorite of Frank's where everybody knew her and fussed over her. At this point it was well after midnight and she decided she was hungry again. She was a great steak eater, so we went to a steakhouse on Third Avenue called Christo's where the owner, who'd heard she was in town, had reserved a bottle of aged Añejo tequila just for her.

Of course we had more drinks there, and then she said, "Damn, I promised Betty Sicre" (who was a great friend of hers from Spain) "that I would get together with her son Ricardo, who's at Princeton. I haven't done it and I really feel awful. I really should try to see little Ricardo."

Having had several drinks myself, I said, "Hell, let's take a taxi and go down to Princeton."

"Wonderful idea," she said. "That's a great idea."

So we went out and got a taxi, Ava dressed as the movie star with a long dress and a mink coat. The driver was delighted to take us the sixty-five miles to Princeton. Ava opened the tequila in the back of the cab, and she and I passed the bottle back and forth during the trip.

We got to Princeton around seven o'clock in the morning and Ava wouldn't let go of the tequila bottle. Her friend had given it to her and therefore she was not going to leave it in the taxi. I kept saying, "Can't we put it in the back of the cab?" and the answer was always, "No, I have to carry it with me."

We got on the campus and I said, "Where does little Ricardo live? What's his dormitory?" Well, she had no idea. "We'll just go up and down the streets here and we'll ask people." So, as the kids were headed toward their first classes of the morning, here was Ava Gardner in a long gown jumping out of this cab and saying, "Do you know my friend Ricardo Sicre?" Nobody did.

Soon the word spread across Princeton that Ava Gardner, clutching a bottle of tequila, was in a New York taxi with some unknown person cruising up and down the campus. And a little band of kids began following the cab, running after us and shouting, "Ava, Ava."

We stopped in front of a dormitory and she jumped out—she had these very quick little steps when she ran and it was awfully hard to keep up with her—and ran into the entrance hall saying, "Ricardo! Ricardo! Where are you?" No sign of Ricardo.

"Well," she said, "we'll just have to go to the top."

"What do you mean?"

"Who's the president of this university, anyway?"

"His name happens to be Robert F. Goheen, I happen to know that."

So she said to the driver, "Take us to the president's house."

At this point, it's about a quarter past eight in the morning. We pull up at the president's house, which as I recall was a stately white Georgian mansion. And Ava, clutching the bottle of tequila, starts to jump out of the cab.

"Ava, let's think about this now, let's think about this very, very carefully," I said. "You're very fond of your friend Ricardo and you're very fond of his parents. You, on the other hand, *are* Ava Gardner, and you have had, uh, a little bit to drink tonight. I'm not arguing with you about the bottle of tequila that has to be under your arm, but you are not really dressed for calling on the president of Princeton University, who's probably in there now in his bathrobe having breakfast with his wife. I have a terrible feeling that if you barge into the president's house at this point in the morning, you may have little Ricardo bounced right out of this college."

"Yeah, I guess you're right," she said.

So we get back in the cab and head to New York. We stopped at a Howard Johnson's on the Turnpike and had some breakfast. We got back into the cab and were almost to the Lincoln Tunnel when Ava said, "Jesus Christ! It's Yale!"

THIRTY-ONE

Much as I appreciated having a real home at La Bruja, living there made me feel too cut off from the center of things. It was Madrid I really loved. The damn place had *life*! The narrow streets were full of old bars with tapas on the counters and hams hanging from the rafters, places that rang with the sounds of guitars, castanets, and flamenco dancing. If you knew your way around, the nights went on forever.

So I sold La Bruja and rented a beautiful apartment at 11, Avenida Doctor Arce in Madrid. I've never been entirely sure who the hell Doctor Arce was, but one thing I found out immediately: my next-door neighbor was none other than Juan Perón, the ex-dictator of Argentina.

Now, aside from the fact that I did not much care for the dame he was living with, Perón had one very disturbing trait. Every so often he would march out onto his balcony, which adjoined mine, and make long, loud, arm-waving speeches to the empty street below. Nobody took any notice; I don't suppose they even heard him against the sound of the traffic. But the speeches disturbed me, and damn it, I felt they let down the tone of the neighborhood.

After years in the country, my Spanish was now fully functional, and, as you can imagine, I was especially good with the bad words. I knew that the pejorative Spanish word for homosexual was *maricón,* which rhymes nicely with Perón. So, whenever Señor Perón stepped grandly onto his balcony and began to harangue his nonexistent supporters, Reenie and I and whatever other servants were around formed our personal opposition party by chanting in unison, "Perón es un mari*cón*. Perón es un mari-*cón*." After all, if you're involved in politics, you've got to expect a certain amount of opposition. If the son of a bitch wanted to make a comeback as the dictator of Argentina, let him rehearse in a studio like any other performer.

But if I thought this was the end of Señor Perón, it was because I had no idea of how powerful he was. One morning I was invited to come to a nearby American base for a flyby, with these wonderful young men doing formation flying, which looked almost suicidal to me. When they finally landed, each plane's nose was poised right over a cold bottle of beer.

I signed autographs for these guys, smiled, and did the usual things. There was supposed to be a beer party afterward, but for some reason, regulations or superstition, I was never sure which, they couldn't invite me to it. The boys were very nice, and so upset that they had to include me out that I suggested they collect their wives and girlfriends and head on over to my place for a party of our own.

They gathered in my lounge, about a dozen handsome young kids in uniform with wings on their tunics and pretty women on their arms. Gleefully, they showed me the present they'd brought: an orange flying suit with the special shoulder insignia of a one-star general in the U.S. Air Force. They didn't say if they'd received the proper authorization for this stunt, but the suit fitted perfectly, and as far as I was concerned I was the first female one-star general in the Air Force's whole damn history.

As I opened the door to let in one more guest, I noticed the Perón broad sailing past with her nose in the air and her pair of yippy lap dogs yipping their way down the stairs. So I said to my two dogs, both very aristocratic corgis, "Go get those two little mutts!" As if on cue, they dashed down the stairs, making lots of noise, but I don't think they ever attacked or hurt the Perón dogs.

The next thing I knew—it couldn't have been more than ten minutes later—the doorbell rang and my secretary came back to tell me, "Ava, there's a bunch of Guardia Civil out there looking very serious." So I strolled out, feeling very formidable in my orange flying suit, smiled and said, "Can I help you?"

There were four Guardia Civil in their black capes and intimidating three-cornered hats, as well as an officer, and it was the officer who said, "We are here to arrest the owner of this apartment, all the servants, and all the guests." And, we learned later, there was a line of police cars waiting outside for just that purpose.

"How interesting," I said. "Why don't you come inside and have a drink."

They came inside, but brother, they didn't look like they were in a drinking mood. The sight of all these American fliers, however, changed the atmosphere, even though you wouldn't have known it by looking at the Guardia's stern faces. The officer was polite and courteous. A quick nod, a few muttered phrases, and they were filing out through the door again. But we were that close to having landed in jail. And that's how close Perón was to Francisco Franco, the man who pushed all the buttons in Spain.

The case was officially closed, I suppose, but it continued to rankle me. I mean, Jesus Christ, here's Franco welcoming this little tinpot dictator, setting him up in an apartment, and allowing him to orate any time he damn well pleased from the balcony next to mine, and when my poor little dogs open their mouths it's a goddamn international incident.

Other things about Spain began to bother me as well. For starters, nothing works there. It doesn't matter who you are or how much money you've got, you can't find a telephone that functions properly. And I doubt if even the Duchess of Alba has a toilet that works. Not to mention that I hadn't made a single close friend there in all those years.

So, when some time later the tax authorities arrived on my doorstep demanding something like a million dollars in back taxes, I was not exactly in the most receptive frame of mine, especially since as far as I knew I'd been paying my damn taxes every year. They were insistent, however, and since the idea of getting embroiled in lawsuits with the local authorities gave me the shudders, I packed up and moved to London in 1968 and never looked back.

Since that first visit on my way to *Pandora and the Flying Dutchman*, I've always loved London. So it rains sometimes. It rains everywhere sometimes. And I happen to like the rain. More important, the British leave you alone. They take three or four photographs when you arrive and then they forget you exist. It's a very civilized town. If I choose to walk down the street or go across the park with my dog, nobody bothers me. When people do recognize me, they smile and nod their heads, which is a hell of a lot different from the treatment I've been used to.

And whenever I needed the loot, I took a deep breath and agreed to some film work. Naturally, I turned down more roles than I accepted, including the one that was such a wonderful success for Anne Bancroft in *The Graduate*. And to be honest, the ones I accepted were often for all the wrong reasons.

When the chance for a cameo as Lily Langtry in John Huston's *The Life and Times of Judge Roy Bean* came up in 1971, for instance, I was planning to go waterskiing in Acapulco around that time anyway, so I figured I might as well let them pay for the trip and a few other things besides.

And when I was offered *Earthquake* a few years later, I was sitting in London feeling very fed up because the weather was dreadful and energy shortages meant I had no hot water or heat. Suddenly the idea of making a film again in Hollywood sounded like fun. I was just ready for a change of scenery.

I got a bigger change of scenery than I bargained for in 1975, when I agreed to fly to the Soviet Union and take a small role in George Cukor's *The Blue Bird*. I was told the assignment would last three weeks. It turned out to be three months of unending Russian monotony.

Before I got over there, I was under the impression that all Russians were hard workers. Jesus! They never appeared on time, took no pride in their work, nothing. It was the saddest country I've ever been in. One day Reenie and I were sitting in what was supposed to be a dressing room, and I said, "I'm going to sit here in this window and smile at every Russian that passes. And I won't give up until I make one Russian smile back at me." I even waved at them and said hello. Did I get even a single smile back? Not on your life. When we all finally arrived back in London, I swear to you I saw several members of our crew fall to their knees and kiss the ground. You've never seen so many people happy to be back home.

THIRTY-TWO

Unless you count television, which I don't, it's been a good half dozen years since I made a motion picture. And honey, if you think I miss the business, you had better think again.

I live my life now according to my own standards. In all my life I've never stuck to a schedule of any kind, and I'm not about to start now. I am really an uncomplicated person. I like to live simply and out of the public eye. I enjoy my privacy enormously. I'm not the playgirl I used to be. And though I do miss the cuddles a man in my life would mean, other than that I prefer to be alone.

I do, however, have a lot of friends in London, what the English call "chums." Really good friends, so I'm far from lonely. We have dinner at our homes or, if we go out, it's to places where we won't be disturbed. Thank God, I'm not a public figure here. If I have to, as I once did, slip into a robe and, with my hair looking a mess, steal down the street to a friend's house to bathe because he had hot water and I didn't, people pretend not to notice me on the street. God bless the English. I even once received a letter addressed simply to "Ava Gardner, Hyde Park, London." And some character at the Post Office had scrawled across the envelope, "Which bench?"

Actually, my apartment in Ennismore Gardens in Knightsbridge suits me so well I hate to leave it, even for a park bench. It takes up the entire second floor of a converted Victorian building, with one huge room living/dining room running from

277

front to back and corridors branching off to the kitchen and bedrooms that are happily pressed into service when Bappie, who now lives in Los Angeles, or Reenie, who moved to Sacramento, comes for a visit.

The place is decorated in Oriental style, with huge screens, tall vases, and massive chests, but I made sure to place comfortable armchairs on either side of the fireplace where I can sit around in jeans and a shirt, reading, listening to music, or doing crossword puzzles. And though I'm not very big on mementos, there are photographs of my favorite people all over the place.

The best thing about the apartment, however, is its floor-to-ceiling French doors that open out onto the lovely gardens. They each have a balcony, and Morgan, my current Welsh corgi, uses one of them as his office, barking salutations to everyone who passes by on the street below.

Morgan, who is named after Jess Morgan, my friend and financial adviser, is really one of the joys of my life. I make sure he never runs out of his favorite treat (raw carrots, of all things), I've scribbled him cards when I've been out of town, and I've always enjoyed taking him on long daily walks. We'd often trek into Hyde Park, where like a good fellow he'd fetch his ball for as long as I had the energy to keep tossing it out there.

When Morgan and I are at home, I'm likely as not to wander over to the television and see what's on. Every once in a while one of my old films will turn up and I'll think, God, I was pretty, wasn't I? The beauty thing was fun—it's always nice to be told you're beautiful—but honestly, I think I look much more interesting now. I don't hanker after lost youth or any of that rubbish. And I'll never be one of those women who look in mirrors and weep.

There is something I resent about age, however, and that's that you can't do the things you used to be able to. Believe me, honey, my days of staying up all night and then taking a shower and plunging on are long behind me. But still, I really resent it when people tell me I ought to cut down on this or that. Tell me to stop drinking and I'll drink. Tell me to stop smoking and I'll smoke. I once called John Huston, who'd been an outrageous smoker and ended up living attached to a cylinder of oxygen, and asked him when *he* finally gave up smoking. "When I had to, darling," he said in that molasses voice of his. "When I had to."

A few years ago, something happened to me that I never anticipated. I had a stroke, which affected my walking and made my damn left arm just about useless. Having always been an active person, if I'd fully realized that I was even partially paralyzed, I would have jumped out of the window—if I could have made it that far.

Instead, I went on. I had no choice: that's one lesson I learned very early in life. You have to persevere. And I learned to compensate, to take joy in sights and sounds and situations I once took for granted. One thing I've always known is that the process of growing up, growing old, and growing toward death has never seemed frightening. And, you know, if I had my life to live over again, I'd live it exactly the same way. Maybe a few changes here and there, but nothing special. Because the truth is, honey, I've enjoyed my life. I've had a hell of a good time.

FRANKA

About fifteen years ago I was asked to design the clothes for *Permission to Kill,* one of Ava's films. You meet people, either the chemistry works or it doesn't; and from that day we became very great friends. There was something very human, very vulnerable about her. I felt like protecting her, and then she protected me. She never went to fashion shows before, ever. But she never missed any of mine. She would just say, "Honey, I'll be there." It was real support.

I would go out in the evening and she would say, "Oh, honey, what are you wearing?" And the jewelry would come round and I would wear it and the next day it would go back again. Or once I was ill, I had a very bad cold, and she phoned me. It was almost midnight, it was very ugly winter weather, and she said, "Honey, do you have anything?" And there she was in a taxi, with the medicine, with the *hot soup,* at midnight.

And this was the lady who gave me my wedding reception, who gave me away. She was all dressed up in white, with a white fox, wonderful, because she said, "I've been married three times and I've never been in white, honey." The ceremony was very early in the morning, nine o'clock, and she ordered a cab for herself and Charles Gray, a friend who lived down the street. For some reason, the cab didn't come. There were workmen on the square, and she just went into their lorry and asked them, "Can I go?" She arrived in that, with a workman driving them, and she said, "Honey, even MGM could not have done it." When she relaxed with people, she was terrific.

Ava moved to London because she quite liked the privacy of it, and the culture. In London you can choose the life you want, and you are left alone to it. You don't feel that you *have* to do things that you don't want to do. You're quite accepted if you don't.

I deal with lots of ladies, all those who are in front of the camera. They can deal with people they are working with, and the moment someone else comes from the outside they just freeze. It's not just Ava; you'll find most of film stars are *very* private people. It's a very tough journey when you really have to continuously be *it*. And know that you are looked *at*. One is not prepared always. When day after day, day after day, every little scene that you do is reported, you just get fed up. Although being a public person you understand that it has to be done, that doesn't mean that people take it very easily. Ava would say, "Honey, it's a bitch." Because sometimes it just gets too much.

But whether you feel like it or not, the public wants you. Ava said that what it had become was sheer ugliness. She said when they were in Hollywood, they were not allowed to smoke in public, they were not allowed to do this and that. It was all about beauty. And now they will photograph you only when they see you in an awful pose, position, situation. The world has changed. People *like* ugliness. They don't like perfection, they don't like stars.

Ava really loved life. She wasn't negative about things; she was the most completely passionate person. About everything. She just loved beautiful things. Even clothes—she'd just *enjoy* them. Everything was like she'd never had a dress before. A *wonderful* quality. She hated, as we called them, the long faces, negativeness in anything. She was positive. She would never say, "No, you mustn't do that." It was "Just do it. You deserve it. Come on, you must have it."

And she *never* ever said anything against or about anybody. Never, never, never. Whenever she married, she loved the man she married. And when it didn't work, it didn't work. It's as simple as that. And she had the kind of respect that she would never allow *anyone* to say anything. I remember when she gave an interview to someone who was divorcing and talking so badly about her husband. She said, "Honey, I can't understand that you could possibly talk like that. You must have loved him sometime and you grew apart."

She liked in men a thing that is very difficult to find, a complete person where you could feel good about everything. Protected and loved, being able to share and to talk, not just the physical side. And if you have one, it's very difficult to find the other. When she was with a man, he had to be looked up to, respected. She couldn't respect someone who was just hanging around her. She couldn't. It would destroy her and she would destroy him.

Today, you have these actresses who go to school and they can't wait to get success. They can cope with it because they feel secure. Ava, because it started so early in her life, she wasn't quite ready for it. Very often she would sort of say, "Oh, well, you know, honey, I'm just a movie queen." But she was a much warmer person than these other actresses. She gave more to life, and wanted more out of it.

I see her as this beautiful little girl who left Mama and Papa, who was happy in her childhood, and had a sort of vision and dream of something completely different. And suddenly she was discovered and sent to this MGM. She called it not a factory, but much worse. Like a prison camp—every name that is not nice. They were absolutely tortured, treated like God knows what. And that, she said, destroyed her. "We were exploited like animals," she said. "Just exploited."

So that wonderful beautiful girl, who was brought up with freedom, with love, with everything, suddenly was like a flower with a chain put around her. You are allowed to grow just that way. You can't open your arms, you can't do what you want naturally to do. So you suppress yourself your whole life. And because of it, you simply try to run away. That maybe is where alcohol came in, because through struggling and running and not being able to be yourself, you need to get the simple courage to get into another room.

You look to life for that something that was there in your childhood. And you cannot find it. This fame makes you like an animal, really, like a hunted animal. You're just beautiful, you're not allowed to be yourself. I think it was very, very difficult for Ava to live that life. She was a free woman, she couldn't be locked in.

MEARENE JORDAN

M y older sister was working for Miss G. around the time she was married to Artie Shaw. When my sister found she had to go back to Chicago, she said, "Reenie, why don't you work for Ava? She's such a sweet little girl and she needs somebody that she can trust. She's going through some terrible times."

I began working for Miss G. in 1947 or 1948 and we were just pals from day one. We could get mad at one another, but we never stopped speaking. All these years, whether we were together or not, that was the one thing we had. I guess that's why we remained friends.

She was fun, and very sharing. If I ever made her anything, from a cup of coffee to a martini, she'd say, "Well, where's yours?" She wasn't what we thought of as the stereotypical Southerner. We'd go to clubs during the time before integration, and if they threw me out, she'd leave, too. So to keep her, they'd tolerate me.

We were both Capricorns, and Capricorns just work with the present. Sometimes I'd wake her up and she'd say, "Oh, shit, what's today gonna bring?" She was like that. She never said tomorrow or yesterday. It was "Do I want to face this day?" Then sometimes she'd cover her head back up.

Her work was, as she would say, a paycheck. She knew this was the only work she could do where she could make a decent living, and she'd say, "If you can get me there, Reenie, I'll work." And sometimes getting her to the set was a major difficulty. She did not like working. Period.

"I'm not going today," she'd say. "Call 'em up. Tell 'em anything."

"You've got to be kidding, lady. You *know* you got to go. Why do you do this?"

"I'm *not* going. Tell 'em *anything*."

"Okay, if you don't go, I'm going to sing." And then she'd get up, because she knew I was a lousy singer. We played games like that. Once she got there, she would act as if there was no place she'd rather be. I could have socked her. . . . But my God, sometimes to get her there.

If a producer or somebody offered her a script, if she didn't want to do it she didn't care how much money was involved, she just wouldn't do it. Wouldn't discuss it, wouldn't even look at it. In Spain they had a hamburger place called Pam-Pam and she would say, "I might end up working in Pam-Pam, but I'm not going to do anything I don't want to do." It didn't bother her one bit.

She was a very demanding person at times. She wanted complete loyalty; that's why she didn't like a lot of people around her. If six of us went into a restaurant and two over here were talking quietly, saying, "Tomorrow, if it's not raining, we'll go fishing," if she didn't hear what we were saying, she would think we were maybe saying something concerning her that we didn't want her to hear. She was very self-conscious that way.

And she loved to curse. It would just tickle her to put a whole string of words together. "Not one word you've said makes sense, you know that, don't you?" I'd say to her. "Why do you have to say all of them? Why don't you just say one?"

She could change when she drank. It was like night and day then. It was a thing we used to say: "Watch the third martini." She would get more suspicious of the people around her. But she had no dealings with drugs. She'd say, "Anything you can't get out of a bottle of gin, you don't need." We had a code for it, we called it the three G's: Good Gordon's Gin. She'd say, "Reenie, do we have any of those three G's?"

We just had codes for everything, especially people, so we could talk all day and nobody would know who we were talking about. Barbara Stanwyck, we'd call her Short Lips. Hugh O'Brian we referred to as Tight-Ass. Robert Taylor was Mr. Clark; Fred MacMurray, Mr. Gordon. One actor we called

Snowflakes. We had a director we called Cornflakes. We called Deborah Kerr Miss Continuation because her voice never changed from one film to the other. I won't tell you the name we had for Elizabeth Taylor because she was a very sweet girl and we loved her very much.

Miss G. was an extremely funny person. She should have been a comedian. She could get fun out of the darnedest things, and would nearly kill herself laughing. And she loved getting back at people. When she and Eileen, her secretary, were in Africa for *Mogambo*, they wanted to go to this club that was right across the street from the hotel. But the club didn't want any actresses, especially without an escort, so they kept saying they were filled up.

Finally, she said, "Eileen, why don't you call and tell them that you are Clark Gable's secretary and that Mr. Gable is coming in out of the bush and he would like a table for about twenty-four people?" Then she and Eileen sat by the hotel window and they watched the waiters hustling to set the tables up. Of course, Clark Gable had no idea; he didn't know anything about it. She laughed about it for years. She'd say, "That's a just reward."

But I don't think she ever realized she was a star. People kept telling her she was, but to her, she just worked in the movies. She would say, "I take my paycheck, wash up, and go home." She lived for years without any of the regular things that movie stars have. If she didn't have a car, she'd get out and walk five blocks and take a taxi to where she was going. There was often nothing to remind her that she was a movie star.

She did become more movie-starrish in Spain. But she got tired of that, got tired of the distance that that put between people, and she finally got back to her old self. Sometimes we got in situations where I was really frightened for her, as well as for myself. We'd be out too late, trying to go home instead of staying on, and the Guardia Civil would stop us. And she had a flip tongue sometimes, she'd tell them, "You tell Franco . . ." and all that. Oh, my God, there was nothing timid about her. She had a tongue for you if you messed with her; it could get icy. Yes, indeed, she could back you off of her.

Spain is where she got into her flamenco phase. I think she liked it so much because it annoyed everybody else, I really do. She knew it drove everybody else up the wall. And once she left

Spain, she couldn't have cared less about that mess, she turned off it that quick.

Wherever we went, she could always find Gypsies. While we were in Australia for *On the Beach,* she found this little Gypsy fella, he had two girls with him, and they'd come back to the house and do the doggonedest flamenco. I wasn't too fond of it, but it didn't bother me. I could roll with the punches because she and I were the same age. But Bappie, being older, she hated it, and Ava would make me go down and wake her up because we were having a flamenco. She would be cussin', "Goddamnit, goddamnit, I'm so sick of this fucking flamenco." And I would say, "Come on up and give us some claps."

We always had wine for the Gypsies—that's all they drank, the cheaper the better. On this particular night, the music was going and the gals were flamencoing, and the little guy was going around and around. He grabbed Ava and she was going around doing the paso doble with him. She got all excited and snatched his hat off to put it on her head, and his hair was all in that hat. The poor little guy felt the air on his head and knew he had been uncovered. He was just a little short old man, he must've been seventy years old.

When Ava looked down and saw all this hair, I thought she was going to faint. She threw the hat down and tore out of there and hid. The little man retrieved his hat, plopped it back on his head and flew down the stairs with the two girls. They never collected their money that night. And her sister continued to cuss. "Goddamnit, serves her goddamn right. Goddamn Gypsies." Boy, we laughed hard for years at that.

I've met all of Ava's husbands. She loved all of them, and she was on a friendly basis with them afterward. One thing was, she didn't take any money from them. Men always love you when you don't get their pocketbooks.

Mickey Rooney was a funny little guy—she got a big kick out of him. She saw him last year and she said, "Reenie, he's still the biggest liar in the world. Poor Mickey, he cannot tell the truth, he never could. But he's cute."

Artie Shaw was not fun. He was nice, but certainly nothing fun about him. Now one thing Ava *never* referred to was nationality. But this particular time, after she saw him in New York, she said, "Reenie, when I think of how crazy I was about that man. When

I saw him the other day, he was just a little ol' half-baldheaded Jew. I don't know why I loved him, but he had me goin' so."

Howard Hughes was so rich he didn't have to dislike or like anybody. He could throw a brick and hide his hand. He wasn't a man, he was a giant in how he could rule people. He would go to universities and get the best brains in there and hire them. These poor guys thought they were going to be engineers or something, and maybe a year later, he might call one of them up and tell him to bring him a loaf of whole wheat bread or a can of figs. They thought they were going to be working on airplanes, but he had them for when and if he needed them. Ava liked him, she admired him, but I don't think she loved him. It was sort of, "I don't mind."

Frank Sinatra, that was her big love. He was and is a lovely man, and they did love one another so much. They really did. It was too bad they just couldn't make it. There were not many peaceful moments between them—they didn't have that kind of temperament.

Little things, anything, could set them off. If he looked across the room in a restaurant, she would swear, "Reenie, I saw him, he was winking at a girl." Probably wasn't a girl in sight, but she'd say, "I saw him give her the look." And the fight would be on.

Or they'd be in her house down at the beach in Pacific Palisades. He'd get mad and he'd call his man, Hank Sanicola, and say, "Come get my clothes." So we'd put the clothes on a broom handle, he'd be on one end, I'd be on the other, and by the time we got the clothes in the car, he'd call downstairs and say, "Tell Hank to bring my clothes back." They'd made up. And Hank would get so mad. "Goddamnit," he'd say, "I wish they'd make up their minds."

After he calmed down from the fact that he was famous and all after *From Here to Eternity,* he always wanted her with him. But, as he became famous, he took on this entourage of people. And Ava couldn't deal with that, as she got older; she just couldn't deal with a lot of people. He was always calling her up; even when he was marrying Barbara, he called her several times and asked if she would come back. She loved him; she just didn't love some of the people that he had to have with him. The timing was bad for them. That was the whole thing. Timing.

Now George C. Scott, he was a very dangerous man. He would drink that vodka, oh, my God, he would tear up a place. We were staying at the Savoy in London, and they went to see *Othello*. I knew that was a mistake, because when he got full of his liquor, he would relive these horrible things. So they came back and naturally, he thought he was Othello. He was pounding on her and finally she got away from him and ran into her bedroom.

I was in the adjoining room, and I heard her calling to me. But he was sitting on the couch in the living room right by the little hall to her room and dared me to pass. At first I ignored him, I said, "She's calling me, I have to go, that's what I'm getting paid for." And he took a glass and broke it and got right in my face, waving this broken glass and saying, "You gonna go by? You goin' by? Come on by, come on by." And I realized, my God, he was serious, so I backed off.

I had cased the place and I remembered that there was a little window over the bathroom that went into the main hallway. So I left the room and got a bus boy and he got some orange crates. I eased up to the window, pried it open, and slid down to the tub. She had the door closed, and I opened it and just popped my finger a little bit to get her attention. I got her up over the tub and out the window and then I followed. You think that's scary? You should have been there.

One thing about Miss G., though, she was not a sad person at all. Even last May, when she was quite crippled. She couldn't use her left arm at all, she would just have to carry it around. Or she would be sitting on it and couldn't get up. "Come here and get this fucker out from under me," she'd say. "I can't do a goddamn thing with it. One of these days I'm going to take a knife and chop the fucker off." She'd want to see your expression when she said it, and then she'd fall out laughing later. She could even find fun in an arm that wouldn't move.

We'd go to the park with her dog, and it took us forever to walk there, bumping against one another, because I don't walk too good myself at times. We walked a little too far one day, just talking about old times and laughing, and coming back she said, "I'm kinda tired."

"Well, I am, too," I said. "You think we can make it to that bench over there?"

"I don't think I can make it, Reenie. Let's sit down and rest a bit."

Without thinking, we both plunked down on the ground. Of course, after we rested, we couldn't get up. Here we are, two cripples, trying to get up. We had to roll over and crawl to the nearest tree. The dog is having a fit, "Yap-yap-yap-yap-yap," and Ava is saying, "If the fucker would shut up, everybody wouldn't see us."

We finally got close enough to the tree for me to pull myself up. After I got my balance I went back and got her. By then we were laughing so hard water was running down our legs. She said, "Reenie, did you ever think we would come to this?" And I said, "No, never, never, never."

AFTERWORD

On January 25, 1990, Ava Gardner died of pneumonia after a long illness in her beloved Ennismore Gardens flat. She was just a month past her sixty-seventh birthday. Her long-time housekeeper Carmen Vargas, and Morgan, her Welsh Corgi, were with her when she died.

Ava worked for more than two years on her autobiography, contacting old friends, organizing photographs, and filling some ninety tapes. The Ava Gardner Living Trust would like to thank Alan Burgess and Kenneth Turan for putting her reminiscences into book form.

Burial took place in Smithfield, North Carolina, on January 29. As she expressly stipulated, Ava was buried in the Gardner family plot, laid to rest among the people she knew and loved best.

JESS S. MORGAN
Trustee
Ava Gardner Living Trust

FILMOGRAPHY

The facts in the following listing were compiled by James R. Parish for *The Hollywood Beauties* (Arlington House). His research is hereby gratefully acknowledged.

1942

WE WERE DANCING

Norma Shearer, Melvyn Douglas, Gail Patrick, Lee Bowman, Marjorie Main, Reginald Owen, Alan Mowbray, Florence Bates, Sig Ruman, Dennis Hoey, Heather Thatcher, Connie Gilchrist, Ava Gardner (Girl)

MGM
Producers: Robert Z. Leonard, Orville Dull
Director: · Robert Z. Leonard
Screenwriters: Claudine West, Hans Rameau, George Froeschel
Based in part on the play *Tonight at 8:30* by Noël Coward

1942

JOE SMITH—AMERICAN

Robert Young, Marsha Hunt, Harvey Stephens, Darryl Hickman, Noel Madison, Jonathan Hale, Joseph Anthony, Ava Gardner (Ringsider)

MGM
Producer: Jack Chertok
Director: Richard Thorpe
Screenwriter: Allen Rivkin

1942

SUNDAY PUNCH

William Lundigan, Jean Rogers, Dan Dailey, Jr., Guy Kibbee, J. Carroll Naish, Connie Gilchrist, Sam Levene, Leo Gorcey, Rags Ragland, Ava Gardner (Ringsider)

MGM
Producer: Irving Starr
Director: David Miller
Screenwriters: Allen Rivkin, Fay and Michael Kanin

1942

THIS TIME FOR KEEPS

Ann Rutherford, Robert Sterling, Virginia Weidler, Guy Kibbee, Irene Rich, Henry O'Neill, Connie Gilchrist, Ava Gardner (Girl in Car)

MGM
Producer: Samuel Marx
Director: Charles Riesner
Screenwriters   Muriel Roy Bolton, Rian James, Harry Ruskin

1942

KID GLOVE KILLER

Van Heflin, Marsha Hunt, Lee Bowman, Samuel S. Hinds, Cliff Clark, Eddie Quillan, Ava Gardner (Carhop)

MGM
Producer: Jack Chertok
Director: Fred Zinnemann
Screenwriters: Allen Rivkin, John C. Higgins

1943

PILOT NO. 5

Franchot Tone, Marsha Hunt, Gene Kelly, Van Johnson, Alan Baxter, Dick Simmons, Steven Geray, Ava Gardner (Girl)

MGM
Producer: B. P. Fineman
Director: George Sidney
Screenwriter: David Hertz

1943

HITLER'S MADMAN

John Carradine, Patricia Morison, Alan Curtis, Ralph Morgan, Howard Freeman, Ludwig Stossel, Edgar Kennedy, Ava Gardner (Katy Chotnik)

MGM
Producer: Seymour Nebenzal
Director: Douglas Sirk
Screenwriters: Peretz Hirschbein, Melvin Levy, Doris Malloy

1943

GHOSTS ON THE LOOSE

Leo Gorcey, Huntz Hall, Bobby Jordan, Bela Lugosi, Ava Gardner (Betty), Ric Vallin, Minerva Urecal

Monogram

Producers:	Sam Katzman, Jack Dietz
Director:	William Beaudine
Screenwriter:	Kenneth Higgins

1943

YOUNG IDEAS

Susan Peters, Herbert Marshall, Mary Astor, Elliott Reid, Richard Carlson, Allyn Joslyn, Ava Gardner (Girl)

MGM

Producer:	Robert Sisk
Director:	Jules Dassin
Screenwriters:	Ian McLellan Hunter, Bill Noble

1943

THE LOST ANGEL

Margaret O'Brien, James Craig, Marsha Hunt, Philip Merivale, Keenan Wynn, Henry O'Neill, Donald Meek, Ava Gardner (Hat Check Girl)

MGM

Producer:	Robert Sisk
Director:	Roy Rowland
Screenwriter:	Isobel Lennart

1943

SWING FEVER

Kay Kyser, Marilyn Maxwell, William Gargan, Lena Horne, Ava Gardner (Girl)

MGM

Producer:	Irving Starr
Director:	Tim Whelan
Screenwriters:	Nat Perrin, Warren Wilson

1944

THREE MEN IN WHITE
Lionel Barrymore, Van Johnson, Marilyn Maxwell, Keye Luke, Ava Gardner (Jean Brown), Alma Kruger, Rags Ragland

MGM
Director: Willis Goldbeck
Screenwriters: Martin Berkeley, Harry Ruskin

1944

MAISIE GOES TO RENO
Ann Sothern, John Hodiak, Tom Drake, Ava Gardner (Gloria Fullerton), Donald Meek

MGM
Producer: George Haight
Director: Harry Beaumont
Screenwriter: Mary C. McCall, Jr.

1945

SHE WENT TO THE RACES
James Craig, Frances Gifford, Ava Gardner (Hilda Spotts), Edmund Gwenn, Sig Ruman, Reginald Owen

MGM
Producer: Frederick Stephani
Director: Willis Goldbeck
Screenwriter: Lawrence Hazard

1946

WHISTLE STOP
George Raft, Ava Gardner (Mary), Victor McLaglen, Tom Conway, Jorja Curtright, Florence Bates, Charles Drake

United Artists
Producer: Seymour Nebenzal
Director: Leonide Moguy
Screenwriter: Philip Yordan

1946

THE KILLERS

Burt Lancaster, Ava Gardner (Kitty Collins), Edmond O'Brien, Albert Dekker, Sam Levene, John Miljan, Virginia Christine, Vince Barnett, Charles D. Brown, Donald MacBride, Phil Brown, Charles McGraw, William Conrad

Universal
Producer: Mark Hellinger
Director: Robert Siodmak
Screenwriters: Anthony Veiller, John Huston (uncredited)
Based on the story by Ernest Hemingway

1947

THE HUCKSTERS

Clark Gable, Deborah Kerr, Sydney Greenstreet, Adolphe Menjou, Ava Gardner (Jean Ogilvie), Keenan Wynn, Edward Arnold, Aubrey Mather

MGM
Producer: Arthur Hornblow, Jr.
Director: Jack Conway
Screenwriter: Luther Davis
Based on the novel by Frederic Wakeman

1947

SINGAPORE

Fred MacMurray, Ava Gardner (Linda), Roland Culver, Richard Haydn, Thomas Gomez, Spring Byington

Universal
Producer: Jerry Bresler
Director: John Brahm
Screenwriters: Seton I. Miller, Robert Thoeren

1948

ONE TOUCH OF VENUS

Ava Gardner (Venus, Goddess of Love/Venus Jones), Robert Walker, Dick Haymes, Eve Arden, Olga San Juan, Tom Conway

Universal
Producer: Lester Cowan

Director: William A. Seiter
Screenwriters: Harry Kurnitz, Frank Tashlin
Based on the musical play by Kurt Weill, S. J. Perelman, Ogden Nash

1949

THE BRIBE

Robert Taylor, Ava Gardner (Elizabeth Hintten), Charles Laughton, Vincent Price, John Hodiak

MGM
Producer: Pandro S. Berman
Director: Robert Z. Leonard
Screenwriter: Marguerite Roberts
Based on the short story by Frederick Nebel

1949

THE GREAT SINNER

Gregory Peck, Ava Gardner (Pauline Ostrovski), Melvyn Douglas, Walter Huston, Ethel Barrymore, Frank Morgan, Agnes Moorehead

MGM
Producer: Gottfried Reinhardt
Director: Robert Siodmak
Screenwriters: Ladislas Fodor, Christopher Isherwood
Based on the novel *The Gambler* by Fyodor Dostoyevsky

1949

EAST SIDE, WEST SIDE

Barbara Stanwyck, James Mason, Van Heflin, Ava Gardner (Isabel Lorrison), Cyd Charisse, Nancy Davis, Gale Sondergaard, William Conrad, William Frawley

MGM
Producer: Voldemar Vetluguin
Director: Mervyn LeRoy
Screenwriter: Isobel Lennart
Based on the novel by Marcia Davenport

1951

MY FORBIDDEN PAST

Ava Gardner (Barbara Beaurevel), Robert Mitchum, Melvyn Douglas, Lucille Watson, Janis Carter

RKO

Producers: Robert Sparks, Polan Banks
Director: Robert Stevenson
Screenwriter: Marion Parsonnet
Based on the novel *Carriage Entrance* by Polan Banks

1951

PANDORA AND THE FLYING DUTCHMAN

James Mason, Ava Gardner (Pandora Reynolds), Nigel Patrick, Sheila Sim, Harold Warrender, Mario Cabre, Marius Goring, John Laurie, Pamela Kellino

MGM

Producers: Albert Lewin, Joseph Kaufman
Director: Albert Lewin
Screenwriter: Albert Lewin

1951

SHOW BOAT

Kathryn Grayson, Ava Gardner (Julie Laverne), Howard Keel, Joe E. Brown, Marge Champion, Gower Champion, Robert Sterling, Agnes Moorehead, William Warfield

MGM

Producer: Arthur Freed
Director: George Sidney
Screenwriters: John Lee Mahin (uncredited), George Wells, Jack McGowan
Based on the musical by Jerome Kern and Oscar Hammerstein II

1952

LONE STAR

Clark Gable, Ava Gardner (Martha Ronda), Broderick Crawford, Lionel Barrymore, Beulah Bondi, Ed Begley, William Farnum, Lowell Gilmore, Moroni Olsen, Russell Simpson, William Conrad, James Burke

MGM
Producer: Z. Wayne Griffin
Director: Vincent Sherman
Screenwriter: Borden Chase

1952

THE SNOWS OF KILIMANJARO

Gregory Peck, Susan Hayward, Ava Gardner (Cynthia), Hildegarde Neff, Leo G. Carroll, Torin Thatcher, Marcel Dalio

Twentieth Century–Fox
Producer: Darryl F. Zanuck
Director: Henry King
Screenwriter: Casey Robinson
Based on the short story by Ernest Hemingway

1953

RIDE, VAQUERO!

Robert Taylor, Ava Gardner (Cordelia Cameron), Howard Keel, Anthony Quinn, Charlita

MGM
Producer: Stephen Ames
Director: John Farrow
Screenwriter: Frank Fenton

1953

THE BAND WAGON

Fred Astaire, Cyd Charisse, Oscar Levant, Nanette Fabray, Jack Buchanan, Ava Gardner (The Movie Star)

MGM
Producer: Arthur Freed
Director: Vincente Minnelli
Screenwriters: Betty Comden, Adolph Green

1953

MOGAMBO

Clark Gable, Ava Gardner (Eloise Y. Kelly), Grace Kelly, Donald Sinden, Philip Stainton, Laurence Naismith

MGM
Producer: Sam Zimbalist
Director: John Ford
Screenwriter: John Lee Mahin
Based on the play by Wilson Collison

1954

KNIGHTS OF THE ROUND TABLE

Robert Taylor, Ava Gardner (Guinevere), Mel Ferrer, Anne Crawford, Stanley Baker, Felix Aylmer, Robert Urquhart, Niall MacGinnis

MGM
Producer: Pandro S. Berman
Director: Richard Thorpe
Screenwriters: Talbot Jennings, Jan Lustig, Noel Langley
Based on *Le Morte d'Arthur* by Sir Thomas Malory

1954

THE BAREFOOT CONTESSA

Humphrey Bogart, Ava Gardner (Maria Vargas), Edmond O'Brien, Marius Goring, Valentina Cortesa, Rossano Brazzi, Elizabeth Sellers, Warren Stevens

United Artists
Director: Joseph L. Mankiewicz
Screenwriter: Joseph L. Mankiewicz

1956

BHOWANI JUNCTION

Ava Gardner (Victoria Jones), Stewart Granger, Bill Travers, Abraham Sofaer, Francis Matthews, Marne Maitland, Peter Illing, Edward Chapman, Freda Jackson

MGM
Producer: Pandro S. Berman
Director: George Cukor
Screenwriters: Sonya Levien, Ivan Moffat
Based on the novel by John Masters

1957

THE LITTLE HUT

Ava Gardner (Lady Susan Ashlow), Stewart Granger, David Niven, Walter Chiari, Finlay Currie, Jean Cadell

MGM
Producers: F. Hugh Herbert, Mark Robson
Director: Mark Robson
Screenwriter: F. Hugh Herbert
Based on the play by Andre Roussin

1957

THE SUN ALSO RISES

Tyrone Power, Ava Gardner (Lady Brett Ashley), Mel Ferrer, Errol Flynn, Eddie Albert, Gregory Ratoff, Juliette Greco, Marcel Dalio, Henry Daniell, Robert J. Evans

Twentieth Century–Fox
Producer: Darryl F. Zanuck
Director: Henry King
Screenwriter: Peter Viertel
Based on the novel by Ernest Hemingway

1959

THE NAKED MAJA

Ava Gardner (Duchess of Alba), Anthony Franciosa, Amadeo Nazzari, Gino Cervi, Lea Padovani, Massimo Serato, Carlo Rizzo

United Artists
Producer: Goffredo Lombardo
Directors: Henry Koster, Mario Russo
Screenwriters: Norman Corwin, Giorgio Prosperi

1959

ON THE BEACH

Gregory Peck, Ava Gardner (Moira Davidson), Fred Astaire, Anthony Perkins, Donna Anderson, John Tate, Guy Doleman

United Artists
Producer: Stanley Kramer
Director: Stanley Kramer
Screenwriter: John Paxton
Based on the novel by Nevil Shute

1960

THE ANGEL WORE RED

Ava Gardner (Soledad), Dirk Bogarde, Joseph Cotten, Vittorio DeSica, Aldo Fabrizi

MGM
Producer: Goffredo Lombardo
Director: Nunnally Johnson
Screenwriter: Nunnally Johnson
Based on the novel *The Fair Bride* by Bruce Marshall

1963

55 DAYS AT PEKING

Charlton Heston, Ava Gardner (Baroness Natalie Ivanoff), David Niven, Flora Robson, John Ireland, Harry Andrews, Leo Genn, Paul Lukas, Elizabeth Sellars, Jacques Sernas

Allied Artists
Producer: Samuel Bronston
Director: Nicholas Ray
Screenwriters: Philip Yordan, Bernard Gordon

1964

SEVEN DAYS IN MAY

Burt Lancaster, Kirk Douglas, Fredric March, Ava Gardner (Eleanor Holbrook), Edmond O'Brien, Martin Balsam, George Macready

Paramount
Producer: Edward Lewis
Director: John Frankenheimer
Screenwriter: Rod Serling
Based on the novel by Fletcher Knebel and Charles W. Bailey II

1964

THE NIGHT OF THE IGUANA
Richard Burton, Ava Gardner (Maxine Faulk), Deborah Kerr, Sue Lyon, James Ward, Grayson Hall, Cyril Delevanti

MGM
Producer: Ray Stark
Director: John Huston
Screenwriters: Anthony Veiller, John Huston
Based on the play by Tennessee Williams

1966

THE BIBLE (. . . IN THE BEGINNING)
Michael Parks, Ulla Bergryd, Richard Harris, John Huston, Stephen Boyd, George C. Scott, Ava Gardner (Sarah), Peter O'Toole, Franco Nero

Twentieth Century–Fox
Producer: Dino De Laurentiis
Director: John Huston
Screenwriter: Christopher Fry
Adapted from episodes from the Old Testament

1969

MAYERLING
Omar Sharif, Catherine Deneuve, James Mason, Ava Gardner (Empress Elizabeth), James Robertson Justice, Genevieve Page, Ivan Desny, Maurice Teynac

MGM
Producer: Robert Dorfmann
Director: Terence Young
Screenwriter: Terence Young

1972

THE BALLAD OF TAM LIN
Ava Gardner (Michaela), Ian McShane, Stephanie Beacham, Cyril Cusack, Richard Wattis, David Whitman, Madeline Smith

American International
Producers: Alan Ladd, Jr., Stanley Mann
Director: Roddy McDowall
Screenwriter: William Spier

1972

THE LIFE AND TIMES OF JUDGE ROY BEAN

Paul Newman, Jacqueline Bisset, Ava Gardner (Lily Langtry), Tab Hunter, John Huston, Stacy Keach, Roddy McDowall, Anthony Perkins

National General
Producer: John Foreman
Director: John Huston
Screenwriter: John Milius

1974

EARTHQUAKE

Charlton Heston, Ava Gardner (Remy Graff), George Kennedy, Lorne Greene, Genevieve Bujold

Universal
Producer: Jennings Lang
Director: · Mark Robson
Screenwriters: George Fox, Mario Puzo

1974

PERMISSION TO KILL

Dirk Bogarde, Ava Gardner (Katina Peterson), Bekim Fehmiu, Timothy Dalton, Frederic Forrest

Avco Embassy
Producer: Paul Mills
Director: Cyril Frankel
Screenwriter: Robin Estridge

1976

THE BLUE BIRD

Elizabeth Taylor, Jane Fonda, Ava Gardner (Luxury), Cicely Tyson, Robert Morley, Harry Andrews, Will Geer

Twentieth Century–Fox
Producer: Paul Maslansky
Director: George Cukor
Screenwriters: Hugh Whitemore, Alfred Hayes, Alexel Kapler
Based on the novel by Maurice Maeterlinck

1977

THE CASSANDRA CROSSING

Sophia Loren, Richard Harris, Ava Gardner (Nicole), Burt Lancaster, Martin Sheen, Ingrid Thulin, Lee Strasberg, John Phllip Law, Ann Turkel, O.J. Simpson, Lionel Stander, Alida Valli ·

Avco Embassy
Producers: Sir Lew Grade, Carlo Ponti
Director: George Pan Cosmatos
Screenwriters: Tom Mankiewicz, Katy Cosmatos

1977

THE SENTINEL

Chris Sarandon, Cristina Raines, Martin Balsam, John Carradine, Jose Ferrer, Ava Gardner (Miss Logan), Arthur Kennedy, Burgess Meredith, Sylvia Miles, Deborah Raffin, Eli Wallach, Jerry Orbach

Universal
Producers: Michael Winner, Jeffrey Konvitz
Director: Michael Winner
Screenwriters: Michael Winner, Jeffrey Konvitz

1979

CITY ON FIRE

Henry Fonda, Susan Clark, Ava Gardner, Barry Newman, Shelley Winters, Leslie Nielsen, Richard Donat

Sandy Howard–Bellevue Pathé
Producer: Claude Heroux
Director: Alvin Rakoff

1980

THE KIDNAPPING OF THE PRESIDENT

William Shatner, Hal Holbrook, Ava Gardner, Van Johnson

Safel Pictures
Producers: George Mendeluk, John Ryan
Director: George Mendeluk
Screenwriter: Richard Murphy
Based on a novel by Charles Templeton

1981

PRIEST OF LOVE
Ian McKellan, Janet Suzman, Sir John Gielgud, Ava Gardner

Filmways Pictures Inc.–Enterprise Pictures Ltd.
Producer: Stanley J. Seeger
Director: Christopher Miles
Screenwriter: Alan Plater

TELEVISION

<u>1985</u>

KNOT'S LANDING
CBS

<u>1985</u>

A.D.
NBC

<u>1985</u>

THE LONG HOT SUMMER
NBC

<u>1986</u>

MAGGIE
CBS

INDEX